SHADOWS IN THE SUN: THE EXPERIENCES OF SIBLING BEREAVEMENT IN CHILDHOOD

SERIES IN DEATH, DYING, AND BEREAVEMENT
ROBERT A. NEIMEYER, CONSULTING EDITOR

Davies—*Shadows in the Sun: The Experiences of Sibling Bereavement in Childhood*

FORMERLY

SERIES IN DEATH EDUCATION, AGING, AND HEALTH CARE
HANNELORE WASS, CONSULTING EDITOR

Bard—*Medical Ethics in Practice*
Benoliel—*Death Education for the Health Professional*
Bertman—*Facing Death: Images, Insights, and Interventions*
Brammer—*How to Cope with Life Transitions: The Challenge of Personal Change*
Cleiren—*Bereavement and Adaptation: A Comparative Study of the Aftermath of Death*
Corless, Pittman-Lindeman—*AIDS: Principles, Practices, and Politics, Abridged Edition*
Corless, Pittman-Lindeman—*AIDS: Principles, Practices, and Politics, Reference Edition*
Curran—*Adolescent Suicidal Behavior*
Davidson—*The Hospice: Development and Administration, Second Edition*
Davidson, Linnolla—*Risk Factors in Youth Suicide*
Degner, Beaton—*Life-Death Decisions in Health Care*
Doka—*AIDS, Fear, and Society: Challenging the Dreaded Disease*
Doty—*Communication and Assertion Skills for Older Persons*
Epting, Neimeyer—*Personal Meanings of Death: Applications of Personal Construct Theory to Clinical Practice*
Haber—*Health Care for an Aging Society: Cost-Conscious Community Care and Self-Care Approaches*
Hughes—*Bereavement and Support: Healing in a Group Environment*
Irish, Lundquist, Nelsen—*Ethnic Variations in Dying, Death, and Grief: Diversity in Universality*
Klass, Silverman, and Nickman—*Continuing Bonds: New Understanding of Grief*
Lair—*Counseling the Terminally Ill: Sharing the Journey*
Leenaars, Maltsberger, Neimeyer—*Treatment of Suicidal People*
Leenaars, Wenckstern—*Suicide Prevention in Schools*
Leng—*Psychological Care in Old Age*
Leviton—*Horrendous Death, Health, and Well-Being*
Leviton—*Horrendous Death and Health: Toward Action*
Lindeman, Corby, Downing, Sanborn—*Alzheimer's Day Care: A Basic Guide*
Lund—*Older Bereaved Spouses: Research with Practical Applications*
Neimeyer—*Death Anxiety Handbook: Research, Instrumentation, and Application*
Nord—*Multiple AIDS-Related Loss: A Handbook for Understanding and Surviving a Perpetual Fall*
Papadatou, Papadatos—*Children and Death*
Prunkl, Berry—*Death Week: Exploring the Dying Process*
Ricker, Myers—*Retirement Counseling: A Practical Guide for Action*
Samarel—*Caring for Life and Death*
Sherron, Lumsden—*Introduction to Educational Gerontology. Third Edition*
Stillion—*Death and Sexes: An Examination of Differential Longevity, Attitudes, Behaviors, and Coping Skills*
Stillion, McDowell, May—*Suicide Across the Life Span—Premature Exits*
Vachon—*Occupational Stress in the Care of the Critically Ill, the Dying, and the Bereaved*
Wass, Corr—*Childhood and Death*
Wass, Corr—*Helping Children Cope with Death: Guidelines and Resource. Second Edition*
Wass, Corr, Pacholski, Forfar—*Death Education II: An Annotated Resource Guide*
Wass, Neimeyer—*Dying: Facing the Facts, Third Edition*
Weenolsen—*Transcendence of Loss over the Life Span*
Werth—*Rational Suicide? Implications for Mental Health Professionals*

SHADOWS IN THE SUN

The Experiences of Sibling Bereavement in Childhood

Betty Davies, R.N., Ph.D.

USA	Publishing Office:	BRUNNER/MAZEL *A member of the Taylor & Francis Group* 325 Chestnut Street Philadelphia, PA 19106 Tel: (215) 625-8900 Fax: (215) 625-2940
	Distribution Center:	BRUNNER/MAZEL *A member of the Taylor & Francis Group* 47 Runway Road, Suite "G" Levittown, PA 19057-4700 Tel: (215) 269-0400 Fax: (215) 269-0363
UK		BRUNNER/MAZEL *A member of the Taylor & Francis Group* 1 Gunpowder Square London EC4A 3DE Tel: 171 583 0490 Fax: 171 583 0581

SHADOWS IN THE SUN: The Experiences of Sibling Bereavement in Childhood

1 2 3 4 5 6 7 8 9 0

Edited by Edward A. Cilurso and Jean Anderson. Printed by Edwards Brothers, Ann Arbor, MI, 1998.

A CIP catalog record for this book is available from the British Library.
♾ The paper in this publication meets the requirements of the ANSI Standard Z39.48-1984 (Permanence of Paper)

Library of Congress Cataloging-in-Publication Data

Available upon request from the publisher

ISBN 0-87630-912-0 (case)
ISBN 0-87630-911-2 (paper)

CONTENTS

FOREWORD

Shadows in the Sun: The Experience of Sibling Bereavement in Childhood is an impressive combination of insightful caring, informed scholarship, rigorous research, and practical utility. Professor Betty Davies is uniquely qualified to introduce us to sibling bereavement in childhood and to guide us to an intelligent appreciation of its nature, characteristics, and significance. In my judgment, no other contemporary author could have produced this rich and rewarding manuscript. You are about to embark on an enlightening journey as you begin reading this excellent book.

Shadows in the Sun has a clear introduction and organizational plan. By way of background, the book tells us about the importance of the relationship between siblings in childhood, the very slow development of the systematic study of sibling bereavement, and what we now know about children's understandings of death. In its central, substantive chapters, we learn about common responses of children who experience the death of a brother or sister, three critical variables in childhood sibling bereavement (the circumstances of the death, the characteristics of the particular bereaved child, and the social environment of the surviving child), the key issue of family functioning, and the long-term impact of what it means to experience the death of a sibling during childhood. The final chapter of the book offers what the author calls a "paradigm model of sibling bereavement," designed to integrate all that has gone before in a comprehensive understanding of childhood sibling bereavement and to provide guidance for professional caregivers, parents, and other adults who seek to help children who have experienced the death of a brother or sister. This final chapter also explains the meaning of the illuminating metaphor in the book's title: *Shadows in the Sun*.

All of this is quite clear in the text. We need not pursue it further here. Instead, we might try to gather some sense of the importance of this book by considering the issues that it addresses in terms of selected examples from literature about death that was written specifically for young readers.

This is not an arbitrary or a foolish approach. Literature designed to meet their needs can be very influential in the lives of children. Typically, young readers have little tolerance for books that are not interesting, instructive, or enjoyable. And children's literature about death can be enjoyable when it tells appealing stories about the growth and triumph of the human spirit in the face of confrontations with loss and grief. In fact, stories are one important way in which children learn to cope with dying, death, and bereavement.

There is, actually, a long oral tradition of tales and stories for children that touch on issues related to death in one form or another (Lamers, 1995). In many of these stories, death does appear, but the real focus is on action and adventure, not bereavement and grief. One of the best-known stories of this type is "Little Red Riding Hood" (Dundes, 1989). Almost everyone is familiar with this tale of a little girl who sets off through the woods to visit her grandmother. As we are aware, eventually Little Red Riding Hood and her grandmother are threatened by the menacing figure of the Big Bad Wolf. However, modern readers often take comfort in the fact that Little Red Riding Hood and her grandmother are both saved at the last moment—either by the helpful intervention of a passing woodsman who uses his big ax to cut them out of the wolf's stomach just after they have been gobbled up or by a handy hunter who uses a more advanced form of technology to kill the wolf with a rifle shot before he can swallow up his intended victims. In these versions, death is an unfulfilled threat warded off by a last-minute rescue (and, in the woodsman version, an instant resurrection).

There are many interpretations of the meaning of this story (Zipes, 1983). But few contemporary readers realize that the original 17th-century version of this story by Charles Perrault emphasizes that Little Red Riding Hood had disobeyed her parents' instructions. She had been told to stay out of the dangerous woods but did not do so. Even less well known is the fact that at the end of the original story, "the wicked wolf fell upon Little Red Riding Hood, and ate her up, too." There is no last-minute rescue; both grandmother and Little Red meet a harsh end. Although death appears to contemporary readers as a severe and shocking outcome, it has not always been seen as an unlikely punishment for misconduct in stories of this type. In fact, such stories were often told or read to children precisely in order to encourage them to behave in morally and socially acceptable ways.

Charlotte's Web (1952) is another example of an adventure story for younger readers in which death appears primarily as a threat to be surmounted. In this classic tale by E. B. White, a pig named Wilbur faces the threat of being slaughtered. This is, of course, the fate of many pigs on a farm, but Wilbur is special because he is the runt of the litter and the pet of a little girl named Fern. To his good fortune, Wilbur is also the friend of a spider name Charlotte A. Cavatica. As Wilbur fattens and grows, Fern pleads to protect him from the butcher's knife. Her pleas go for naught and Wilbur seems doomed until Charlotte intervenes. She produces a series of dazzling webs containing slogans like "SOME PIG," "TERRIFIC," and "RADIANT" that draw adult attention, turn Wilbur into a celebrity ("ZUCKERMAN'S FAMOUS PIG"), and save him from a cruel fate.

Thus far death has played a familiar role in the story of *Charlotte's Web.* But the author included an important subplot: near the end of the book Charlotte produces a clutch of 514 offspring in an egg sack (her "magnum opus"). Not long after, Charlotte dies and is mourned by her animal friends. A bit later, Wilbur saves the egg sack, takes it home, and soon the young spiders emerge into their new world. His contemporary critics are said to have chastised White for adding to his story this more realistic element of death, mourning, and ongoing life. But he had a firm grip on his materials and has been subsequently shown to have known his readers much better than his critics did. White demonstrated that a book that included the death of one of its main characters and the grief responses of others could be read and loved by generations of young readers.

Many adults have suggested, or at least have appeared to want to believe, that children are not really aware of death in their young lives. This erroneous conviction seems to take many forms. For example, (1) some adults appear to believe that young children *do not encounter death* in their pristine world of innocence; (2) others contend that young children *are not able to understand death* even if it should come into their lives; and (3) still others assert that preadolescent children are *unable to grieve* when death and loss intrude into life, and *do not have the capacity to mourn.* These are all mistaken convictions about childhood bereavement, as is evident in *Shadows in the Sun* and in four additional examples from literature for young readers.

The Dead Bird (1958) is a picture book for beginning readers. In this simple story, Margaret Wise Brown describes a group of children who come across the body of a dead bird as they play outdoors. At first, the children are simply curious about their discovery. They touch the limp and lifeless body of the bird. A little later, they decide to bury the bird and place a marker over its grave. Imitating adult ritual, the children hold a brief funeral service at the site and they return each day in commemoration. Or, at least, they continued to return (as the text tells us) "until they forgot." In brief, death is encountered, examined, and memorialized as one among many unexpected and intriguing events in the lives of these children.

My Turtle Died Today (1964) tells the story of a young boy seeking help for his sick turtle. The boy's father suggests (not very wisely) giving the turtle some food, his teacher (more aware of her limitations in this area) admits that she does not know what to do, while the pet shop owner (more knowledgeably and more directly) says that the turtle will die. The turtle does die and is buried. But that is not the end of the story. The boy and his friends strive to understand what all of this means. In the end, they conclude—much like *Charlotte's Web*—that life can go on in a different form through the newborn kittens of their cat, Patty. Along the way, they pose questions for which they do not always have satisfactory answers: Can you get a new pet in the way that one child now has a new mother? Do you have to live—for a long time—before you die? The efforts of the boy and his friends to make sense out of their death-related encounters are obvious. Their difficulties in resolving all of their queries in fully satisfactory ways suggest that their understandings of death are limited, not that they are without any insight or grasp on what is happening around them.

Two further books for young readers explore childhood grief directly. In *The Mother Tree* (1971), when their mother dies 11-year-old Tempe and her 4-year-old sister, Laura, turn for comfort to a temporary spiritual refuge in the large, backyard tree of the book's title. In so doing, they examine and share good memories of their mother that endure within them. Similarly, in *Meggie's Magic,* the death of 8-year-old Meggie from an unidentified illness leaves her mother, father, and sister (the unnamed narrator of the story) feeling sad and lonely. But one day when Meggie's sister goes to a special place that they had shared, she finds it still filled with the magical qualities of the games they used to play. And she realizes that Meggie's magic still remains inside each surviving member of her family. Each of these books is a poignant tale of loss and grief in childhood, and a tender reminder of the many ways in which children strive to cope with their experiences.

Even these few examples from the growing body of death-related literature for young readers remind us of the many types of death that may be encountered during childhood and the many dimensions of childhood bereavement that need to be understood and appreciated. The history of the development of children's literature in this subject area suggests that authors and publishers tended to begin with tales of the deaths of pets and other animals. Perhaps they thought these were "safer" deaths for children to contemplate, but of course that depends on the individual child in question. A little later, stories about the deaths of human beings began to appear, but they were mostly confined to grandparents and other older adults. It took a third stage of development to bring us books for children that depict the dying and death of parents, friends, and siblings.

Of course, all of these examples have been taken from books for young readers. I believe such books can be read with profit by interested adults. But still, no matter how carefully, tenderly, or insightfully theses tales are presented, they are by their very nature not sufficient for the education of professionals and other adults who seek to understand and help bereaved children. For that, we have been very much in need of a book like *Shadows in the Sun*.

Betty Davies has been studying issues related to children who have experienced the death of a brother or sister since the early 1980s. Her work has always been thorough, careful, and nuanced, as is evident in this book. She is aware that children do encounter death in their young lives, all too often the death of a sibling. Being young is no infallible shield protecting children from all of the harsh realities of life. Davies knows that children who experience the death of a sibling will hurt or grieve. And she also recognizes that such children will be aware that something very important has happened in their lives. Quite naturally, they will try to understand how their worlds have been forever altered. Furthermore, as Davies points out, such children will wonder where or how they belong in the changed family, and they may come to feel that as survivors they can never be good enough for their parents, their dead sibling, or themselves.

Many adults would like to believe that children simply "get over" the death of a sibling. Just as Davies recognizes the complexity of childhood sibling bereavement, she also appreciates that the impact of the death of a brother or sister during childhood will last a lifetime. In teaching us that often-unrecognized moral, along with so many other important lessons, the author of *Shadows in the Sun* has done a great service to all who care about children and about the shadows brought into their lives by death.

Charles A. Corr
Southern Illinois University
at Edwardsville

References

Brown, M. W. (1958). *The dead bird*. Reading, MA: Addison-Wesley.
Dean, A. (1991). *Meggie's magic*. New York: Viking Penguin.
Dundes, A. (1989). *Little Red Riding Hood: A casebook*. Madison: University of Wisconsin Press.
Lamers, E. P. (1995). Children, death, and fairy tales. *Omega, 31*, 151–167.
Stull, E. G. (1964). *My turtle died today*. New York: Holt, Rinehart & Winston.
White, E. B. (1952). *Charlotte's web*. New York: Harper.
Whitehead, R. (1971). *The mother tree*. New York: Seabury Press.
Zipes, J. (1983). *The trials and tribulations of Little Red Riding Hood: Versions of the tale in sociocultural context*. South Hadley, MA: Bergin & Garvey.

PREFACE

I was the head nurse of a pediatric unit in a general hospital in southern Arizona. The hospital was located beside the major freeway. As a result, children were frequently admitted with injuries sustained in motor vehicle accidents. Following one of those accidents late one hot summer afternoon, Juan came to our unit, along with his younger brother and his baby sister. The two younger children had broken bones and internal injuries. Juan had only a broken arm, but he had no place to go, so he too was admitted to the hospital. Juan's father was admitted to the critical care unit, in serious condition. Juan's older brother and his mother had been killed in the accident. Eight-year old Juan knew something terrible had happened, but he didn't know what, and he was afraid to ask. His brown skin was pale. His little chest expanded and trembled with one deep breath after another. His lower lip quivered constantly. Tears pooled in his large brown eyes. He was exhausted from the physical and emotional trauma of the day, and he soon drifted off into a fitful sleep. Juan's family's local parish priest from across the border in Mexico was contacted and would arrive early the next morning. We thought it best for this man, a familiar and friendly face, to tell Juan about the deaths. We also expected that a priest would know how to tell Juan such bad news.

Father Gonzales was an old man, bent over with the weight of many years and countless sad stories. The agony of having to tell Juan about his mother and brother showed through a veil of bravado. He refused my offer of assistance, and I silently accompanied him to Juan's bedside. Juan's legs hung loosely over the side of the bed, his uncasted little arm resting on the overbed table for support as he tried to sip his first drops of liquid. From the other side of the bedtable, Father Gonzales peered down at the tiny boy in hospital pajamas. Matter of factly, he preached the words he had obviously carefully rehearsed, "Juan, your father is in the critical care unit. He is very sick. We hope that he will be all right, but we don't know that. He may not make it. Your mother and Jose are dead from the accident. Your other brother and the baby will need someone to look after them now . . . and you are the only one. You will have to be a man now and care for the others."

In the few moments it took to say those words, a total transformation came over the little boy. He swallowed and swallowed again, as if trying to ingest whole the directive that had just come to him from Father Gonzales—someone with much authority in Juan's young life. His brown eyes grew into big round satellites, alert and ready to receive additional messages pertaining to the safety of what was now "his" responsibility. His skinny little shoulders, previously hunched over from discomfort and dread, now were pulled back straight, ready to take on all the responsibility that had just been bestowed on them. Only seconds had changed Juan from a child in need of the mother no longer there, to a soldier ready to swallow his fear for the sake of the duty he had now been assigned. My heart ached for the part of the child that died in the echo of those spoken words.

I often wondered what came of Juan, of that little boy who grew up in a matter of seconds. I wondered what came of other children given similar messages after a death in the family. In particular, I wondered how it was for them to have a brother or a sister die. I was a pediatric nurse, committed to caring for ill children and promoting the health of all children. If I was really interested in optimizing the well-being of children, then siblings, the forgotten children, were worthy of more attention after the death of another child in the family. Thus began the program of research that is reported in the pages that follow.

For my dissertation research, I explored the responses of siblings to the death of a brother or sister from cancer, up to three years after the death. I learned a great deal about the grief of bereaved siblings—about the behavior changes they experienced and about the competencies they developed in response to their loss. I learned that children's responses cannot be studied in isolation from contextual variables—characteristics about the death itself, about the child, and about the child's environment, particularly the family environment. And, I learned that the effect is long-lasting.

I continued to explore the nature of long-lasting effects of sibling bereavement during my postdoctoral study with Dr. Ida Martinson at the University of California San Francisco. There, I focused on siblings up to nine years following the death of their brother or sister, and learned about the critical role that self-concept plays in sibling bereavement and more about the significance of the family environment. I learned that siblings do not "get over" the loss of their brother or sister. Rather, to varying degrees, they learn to live with the loss. To further explore the long-term impact of sibling death on surviving siblings, I then interviewed adults who, in their childhood, had lost a sibling. Individuals, ranging in age from their late teens to their eighties, verified that the effect endures always.

Over the years, I continued to explore the factors that might influence sibling response, such as cause of death (sudden or resulting from long-term illness) and age and gender. Finally, using the procedures of grounded theory analysis, I synthesized the findings from all my work to develop a comprehensive conceptualization of sibling bereavement.

The purpose of this book is to share the knowledge of sibling bereavement accumulated from my program of research that extends over the past 15 years. This research, taken as a whole, includes siblings of all ages, whose brothers or sisters died from a variety of causes. It includes exploration of immediate and long-term effects and examines the influence of contextual variables on sibling bereavement. The book brings together, synthesizes, integrates, refines, and expands on work already completed and published in several scattered sources. It is not, however, simply an anthology of work already done but rather an integration of that work into a new and expanded whole for the ultimate aims of contributing to an improved understanding of the challenges that face bereaved siblings and of offering guidelines to those who care for these children.

The knowledge shared in this book, however, comes not solely from my research program. It is supplemented by my own clinical experiences in working with bereaved children and their families over the years. While working with and listening to the stories of other bereaved children and their families and adults who in their childhood lost a sibling, I have been able to share my research findings as a way of helping them with their grief. These experiences have enabled me to verify and more clearly delineate many of the research findings.

The first three chapters of the book provide background material that lays the background into which my research findings fit. Chapter 1 begins with a discussion of the significance and the uniqueness of the sibling relationship in childhood. It ends with reference to prominent figures whose life's work was greatly influenced by their experience of sibling loss. In Chapter 2, I chronicle the slow evolution of the systematic study of sibling bereavement. I include in the appendix a summary of articles from the professional literature that refer specifically to sibling bereavement in their titles. I share this information to assist those who want to build on the work already completed in this field. As background for helping siblings grieve, I review in Chapter 3 the subject of children's understanding of death and how their understanding influences their responses at the time of the death.

The next six chapters focus on various aspects of my research findings. In Chapter 4, I discuss the most common responses of children to the death of a sibling and incorporate direct quotes from siblings who participated in my various research projects. Throughout the chapter, I offer suggestions for how adults might assist children who are responding in various ways. I conclude the chapter with a discussion of how to identify children whose grief is disabling.

Siblings' responses to the death of a brother or sister do not occur in isolation but in the context of three types of variables: situational (having to do with the circumstances of the death), individual (pertaining to characteristics of each individual child), and environmental (contributing to the social atmosphere of the child's environment). In Chapters 5, 6, and 7, I focus on each of these types of variables in turn. The most significant factor influencing siblings' grief is the family. In Chapter 8 I discuss level of family functioning, how children are made to feel special, and how meanings are shared in families. My work has emphasized that the impact of sibling bereavement is lifelong for many children. In Chapter 9, I focus on the long-term effects of experiencing a sibling's death in childhood. In Chapter 10, the final section of the book, I attempt to explain how the content in the preceding chapters fits together into a meaningful whole by presenting a paradigm model of sibling bereavement, a comprehensive model of the conceptual relationships among the variables and siblings' responses. I also discuss the implications of the model for those who care for bereaved children. I conclude this last chapter with a description of the meaning of "shadows in the sun."

This book is intended primarily for professionals who work with children. Nurses, physicians, child life workers, psychologists, social workers, chaplains—all those who work in the health care field—have a critical role to play in setting families on a more positive bereavement course following a child's death. Teachers are another very influential group in the day-to-day activities of children. They can provide significant support during times of bereavement in their students' lives. Funeral directors assist the bereaved in the every day course of their work. They, too, can be instrumental in providing optimal experiences for grieving siblings. I hope that the content of this book will be of value to these groups of professionals in helping them make a difference in the lives of grieving children.

In addition, I hope that it will be helpful for parents who are struggling to help their grieving children. Parents are often overwhelmed when a child dies; they have limited emotional resources for helping their surviving children. However, most parents are concerned about their grieving children and desire information to help them understand and cope with their children's responses.

Finally, I hope that this book will be of interest to those who, in their childhood, experienced the death of a brother or sister. In talking with numerous siblings, I have learned that a common response is for siblings to feel alone in their grief. Their responses are ignored or forgotten, only to resurface again and again as the years go by. To see the relief in those who learn that they are not alone, that they are "normal" despite their recurring dreams and thoughts, reaffirms that this book may be of value to at least older bereaved siblings.

ACKNOWLEDGMENTS

"Gratitude is a memory of the heart."
Massieu

I wish to express my appreciation to those individuals who, throughout the course of this program of research and the writing of this book, have provided me with many "memories of the heart."

As I was preparing to write this acknowledgment section for this book, a young man in our nursing program came to my office. He was working on an assignment for his nursing research course, and he wanted to discuss some articles I had written pertaining to palliative care that he had been assigned to read. In the course of our conversation, I mentioned that another long-standing research interest was sibling bereavement. Immediately, his body language spoke loudly—he sat up straighter, he moved forward in the chair, his gaze concentrated. A moment passed, and he whispered, "My brother died." Our conversation then followed a different route than it had been travelling as I listened to his poignant story about his experience of sibling bereavement. Once again, the sadness, the sorrow, the loneliness, the confusion, the mystery, the longing, the growth, and the potential for meaning were exemplified by Desmond's story. Once again, I was reminded of how bereaved siblings have stories to tell, if only given the opportunity.

Desmond is only one of many bereaved siblings over the past 15 years who have shared their stories, their anguish, their achievements—some in the context of a research study, some in clinical contexts, and others, like Desmond, in the context of everyday life. It is to those individuals and their families that I offer my greatest gratitude. I consider myself privileged to have worked, talked, cried, and laughed with these special individuals who have taught me so much about life as they struggle with the impact of death.

This book has been a long time in coming. I owe many thanks to many people for their role in shepherding this book through the editing, reviewing, and publishing process. Hannelore Wass, after hearing me present some of my research findings at one of Jack Morgan's conferences many summers ago, invited me to write a book about my research findings for Taylor & Francis. Each time I saw her, she again fanned the little flame that she had lit. Her patient encouragement remained constant. Then, in Memphis in 1993, she introduced me to Ron Wilder. Over an early breakfast meeting, I committed to write the book. Ron subsequently left Taylor & Francis, but his efforts complemented Hannelore's in getting me started on this project. When I finally had material for Hannelore to read as editor of the series on loss, her comments and suggestions were constructive and, as always, encouraging. Bernadette Capelle, acquisitions editor at Taylor & Francis, inspired me with her own story of personal determination and adopted and guided the project to completion. This book, without doubt, benefitted from Charles Corr's careful reading and thoughtful comments on the completed manuscript. I am indebted to Chuck for his friendship, colleagueship, and willingness to provide ongoing support for my professional endeavors.

During the years that I conducted this research, I have been fortunate to have enjoyed the sustained support, encouragement, and friendship of several mentors and guides. I am indeed grateful to the late Dorothy Crowley, Sandra Eyres, Ida Martinson, Jeanne Benoliel, Jannetta MacPhail, and Anne Mills who, each in his or her own way, has made a deep impression on me and my work. I have also had the good fortune to collaborate with many outstanding individuals in various aspects of this research: John Spinetta, Ida Martinson, Sandee McClowry, Darlene McCown, Ruth Kalischuk, John Collins, Bill Worden, and Sharon Connaughty.

Four individuals helped with several practical aspects of completing this book. Julie Harper continually searched the literature for new references and read each chapter to ensure that all citations were included in the reference list. Barbara Sutherland typed and retyped the reference list and tables. Joy Franklin put the finishing touches on parts of the final manuscript in ways that I could never manage. Gary Bowman drew the figures. Their able assistance and persistent good humor made my task so much easier.

Over the years, I have negotiated with various agencies, hospitals, clinics, and associations to obtain access to families to participate in my research projects. In addition, I have had numerous opportunities to share my research findings with parents, siblings, and professional caregivers through conferences, workshops, and other presentations. To all the individuals in those many organizations who have facilitated this process, I also extend my gratitude.

Funding for my research projects was provided by grants, fellowships, and awards from the National Health and Research Development Program (Ottawa); the American Cancer Society, California Division; the Alberta Foundation for Nursing Research; Social Sciences and Humanities Research Council of Canada; the Vancouver Foundation; the British Columbia's Children's Hospital Telethon Fund; and the British Columbia Research Institute for Children's and Women's Health (formerly the British Columbia Research Institute for Child and Family Health and the Research Division of the British Columbia's Children's Hospital). Without their financial support, neither this book nor the projects on which the book are based would have been possible.

The writing of this book has taken me four years, during which time I have sacrificed time with my husband, Tom Attig, my mother and sister, my nephews, and my friends and colleagues so that I could concentrate on the book. It would have been easier if I had had nothing else to do during those years, but as is most often the case, other research projects, teaching, and professorial and general life responsibilities often took priority. Through it all, my family, friends, and several colleagues, particularly those in my International Work Group on Death, Dying, and Bereavement network, supported and encouraged me. For that, I am truly grateful. I am especially indebted to Tom for his perpetual and sincere encouragement, for taking the time to read each chapter as I completed it, for offering practical advice, for celebrating each phase of completion, for sharing his own work with me as we engage in mutually shared interests. His presence in my life proves that miracles do happen.

For me, writing this book has not only been the fulfillment of the dream to share my research findings for the benefit of others; it has also been an enlightening personal journey. Although for many reasons it did not come to be, my original vision for this book was to combine my research findings with my personal story—a story that started two generations ago with my maternal grandmother who was exposed early to the deaths of two brothers and then later both parents. The story continued with my mother who, as a child of 10, lost her much beloved older sister in a drowning accident and later her brother who was shot down over Germany in World War II. Although my own story does not include the death of a brother or sister, I have lived in the long shadows cast by those earlier deaths. I have learned firsthand, although not always with full awareness, how the shadows caused by a child's death extend far into the future. I have learned how important the family environment is and how children can be helped during grief to minimize the potentially deleterious impact of the loss. I have also learned that one's work and one's self are part of some inseparable whole. Through my grandmother's and my mother's examples, I have also learned how to incorporate the pain of loss into one's ongoing life, how to see sunshine despite the shadows.

This book, therefore, is dedicated to the memory of my Aunt Betty for her contribution to making me the person I am and to her sibling, my mother, who has, throughout my life, made me feel as though I am someone special in her eyes. It is also dedicated to the cause of helping adults realize what a contribution it is to the well-being of grieving siblings when they are made to feel special for simply being in this world.

The Sibling Bond

Echoes of each other's being.
Whose eyes are those that look like mine?
Whose smile reminds me of my own?
Whose thoughts come through with just a glance?
Who knows me as no others do?
Who in the whole wide world is most like me
yet not like me at all?

My sibling.

From *What Makes Us Siblings?* (Faber & Mazlish, 1989, p. 114)

Sibling. What does this word convey to you? The dictionary tells us that a sibling is "One of two or more individuals having one or both parents in common, a brother or sister" (*The American Heritage Electronic Dictionary*, 1992). This definition, however, does not begin to capture the many meanings associated with the word. If you think back over your own childhood and recall your experiences with your own brothers and sisters, you know the many meanings that can be associated with these words: awe at seeing that new baby sister for the first time; helping to hold her bottle; singing to her when she cried; feeling left out when mom held the baby in her arms; playing outside in the mud together; taking turns throwing the stick for your dog to fetch; feeling relief at seeing your big brother approach you when the other boys were beginning to look threatening; laughing uncontrollably at a private joke; crying when she borrowed your favorite sweater and lost it; wanting to throttle him for messing up the model airplane you had just finished; figuring out the math question for her homework; washing the dishes together; consoling her after the first lost love; shopping with him for dad's birthday present; planning a party for mom together; celebrating his new driver's license; watching as he smashed the lawnmower with your uncle's car; running together through the surf on spring break; feeling proud as she walked across the graduation platform. So many memories. So many thoughts and feelings—happiness, surprise, frustration, anger, sadness. Brothers and sisters have the capacity to love and to annoy, to comfort and to tease, to seethe with anger and to cry with compassion.

The memories and feelings that accompany thoughts of one's siblings in childhood are not based in the sibling status alone; they derive from the *relationship* between siblings. Cicirelli's definition of the sibling relationship comes closer to describing the breadth and depth of meaning that is aroused by thinking about siblings: "Sibling relationships are the total of the interactions (physical, verbal, and nonverbal communication) of two or more individuals who share knowledge, perceptions, attitudes, beliefs, and feelings regarding each other, from the time that one sibling becomes aware of the other" (Cicirelli, 1995, p. 4).

The sibling relationship, then, starts very early, beginning early in the life of the second child. Several investigators have in fact suggested that sibling relationships, and adjustment to a new baby, may begin early in the mother's pregnancy (Gottlieb & Mendelson, 1990; Murphy, 1993). Most of the research into the nature of sibling relationships focuses on the study of developmental changes in the relationships of young siblings (Dunn & Kendrick, 1982b), and on the study of relationships in middle childhood. Sibling relationships are not static; they change as children move through different developmental periods. Nor are they played out in a social vacuum, but they are embedded within the context of relationships with other family members and peers. Moreover, the sibling bond is ongoing—it does not end with childhood. Sandmaier (1994) talks about the value of redeveloping connections with siblings in adult life. Cicirelli (1980, 1982, 1988) states that relationships between siblings assume considerable importance in old age, with feelings of closeness and affection increasing with age, and the amount of help siblings desire and offer to one another increasing as people get older. Kahn (1983) regarded the trust and interdependence between siblings in later years to be one of the most important of human relationships. Thus, to experience the death of a sibling in childhood means not only losing a companion during childhood and youth but losing the potential of a lifelong companion who can offer something that no one else can offer.

☐ Unique Features of the Sibling Relationship

Sibling relationships have attributes in common with all interpersonal relationships, but they also have certain unique characteristics that determine the impact of sibling relationships (Cicirelli, 1995). First, sibling relationships last a long time, often a lifetime. In fact, it has been said that siblings are likely to spend at least 80–100% of their lifespans with each other, as compared with sharing only between 40–60% of their lifespans with their parents (Bank & Kahn, 1982). Second, the sibling relationship is ascribed rather than earned. It is obtained by birth or legal action (e.g., adoption), and once ascribed, it never ends. Even parents' divorce, while ending the marriage relationship, does not end the relationship between the siblings. When a child dies, the remaining children still think of that child as one of their siblings.

Sibling relationships are also more or less egalitarian, though power or status differences may exist because of age, size, intelligence, influence with parents, and so on. But there is usually equivalence in siblings' feelings of acceptance of one another, which allows them to relate as equals, and to expect to be treated by others as equals. When siblings are not treated as equals by the adults in their lives, particularly their parents, they suffer greatly. Differential treatment, as we shall see in a later chapter, makes for differential bereavement responses as well.

Finally, though siblings share many experiences, they also have many unshared experiences. The former contribute to their sameness; the latter contribute to their differences. Siblings cannot be assumed to be the same just because they are siblings. Their experiences as individuals within their families and social contexts make them different, with varying responses to shared events in their lives. Consequently, when a child dies, the surviving children each respond in their own unique ways.

When I began my exploration of the topic in the early 1980s, very little literature was available about sibling bereavement. In fact, there was very little written about siblings at all despite their unique relationship with one another. Why was this? It seems puzzling given that, historically, siblingship played a key role in determining and maintaining societal structure. The law during Biblical times, and later in Europe, upheld inheritance customs in which individuals of a given sibling status, commonly the firstborn son, received an allocation of property at the parents' death. Clear kinship divisions were critical in structuring 18th-century English society—as portrayed, for example, in the subtleties of sibling status and relationships in the literary works of Jane Austin. In fact, as Doherty comments, "Until recently, the insights of literary artists into the sibling relationship have surpassed those of behavioral scientists" (1988, p. 399). To support his claim, Doherty indicates that a prominent theme in drama from Plautus' Latin plays to

Shakespeare's *The Comedy of Errors* was the misidentification of twins who had been tragically separated in early childhood. Each carried the image of the other throughout life, feeling complete only when reunited in adulthood. Despite the historical and literary significance of siblings, however, siblings are a relatively recent topic for systematic investigation.

☐ The Systematic Study of Siblings

According to some, Darwin's cousin Francis Galton conducted the earliest studies of siblings in his British laboratory over 100 years ago. Galton's studies, however, did not have to do with siblings specifically but rather with genetic inheritance, where he examined variation in stature among brothers and fingerprints among paired siblings, for example (Forrest, 1974).

The study of ordinal position was perhaps the first major thrust of sibling research in the 20th century. Such studies were mostly of the survey type, in which large samples of varying ordinal position were assessed for differences in intelligence, rates of delinquency, and so forth (Jones, 1933; Murphy, Murphy, & Newcomb, 1937). During the 1960s, there was a resurgence of ordinal position studies, many of which were experimental in design. Sutton-Smith and Rosenberg, in their book published in 1970, provide a thorough review of sibling research that had been completed to that date. They were also the first to advocate that sibling studies should take into account a greater variety of factors than ordinal position and gender. They suggested that sibling research needed to extend beyond the individual to the study of the influence of developmental, family, and cultural variables on the sibling relationship (Sutton-Smith & Rosenberg, 1970).

Until this time, siblings had, at best, been seen as playing only insignificant supporting roles in the drama of individual child development. When considered at all, sibling relationships were often perceived in negative ways—relationships characterized by rivalry, hostility, and jealousy. Such characterizations of the sibling relationship have been reinforced throughout history. Commonly known Bible stories, for example, exemplify such rivalry. The story of Cain and Abel illustrates the point—Cain and Abel, the twin sons of Adam and Eve, are among the best known Biblical figures. When God asked for an offering, Abel, a shepherd, picked out the best of his flock. Because his sacrifice of the best he had was preferred by God to what Cain had presented, Cain flew into a jealous rage and killed Abel, thus committing the first murder in the Bible.

The story of Joseph, popularized by the musical, *Joseph and the Amazing Technicolor Dream Coat,* is also well known. The second youngest son of Jacob, Joseph was his father's favorite. Moreover, Joseph brashly told his brothers of his dreams in which he was made prominent over them. The brothers jealously planned to murder him but decided at the last minute to sell him as a slave to a caravan going to Egypt and reported to Jacob that Joseph had been killed by a marauding animal. In Egypt, Joseph eventually became the prime minister, second in command to the Pharaoh largely because of his correct interpretation of the Pharaoh's dreams. Joseph correctly forecast seven years of famine. Under Joseph's energetic leadership, ample crop surpluses were raised and stored. When the famine years struck, Egypt sold grain to the hungry. One of the most remembered scenes in Joseph's story occurred when his brothers came to buy food. Although they did not recognize Joseph, he knew them. Joseph forgave them and magnanimously moved his father and brothers to Egypt. Again, the sibling relationship is characterized by jealousy, rivalry, and cruelty. However, the story also illustrates that the sibling status remains always, and that forgiveness can also characterize the relationship between siblings.

Much of the earliest research also emphasized the negative aspects of the sibling relationship (Murphy, 1993). Murphy points out that sibling relationships have often been viewed from a Freudian perspective that emphasizes the concepts of sibling rivalry and displacement of the older child (Bank & Kahn, 1980; Neubauer, 1982). In the study of sibling response to the newborn, for example, the Freudian framework led researchers to focus on the negative aspects of sibling relationships and to use instruments that only measure regressive or negative behaviors, failing to recognize the wide variation in sibling response that occurs after the arrival of a new baby (Fortier, Carson, Will, & Shubkagel, 1991; Kayiatos, Adams, & Gilman, 1984; Legg, Sherick, & Wadland, 1974). The rich and varied sibling interactions reported by others (Abramovitch, Corter, Pepler, & Stanhope, 1986; Stewart, 1990) indicate that the Freudian perspective of rivalry and displacement does not characterize the newly forming sibling relationship which features many positive responses as well.

Unfortunately, clinicians also tended to disregard the significance of the sibling relationship. Minuchin (1974) noted the lack of research on sibling interaction in the family therapy literature. Family therapists, at best, viewed sibling relationships as the products of interaction between each individual child and the parents rather than among the children themselves (Bank & Kahn, 1975). The neglect of the "sibling underworld," as Bank and Kahn called it, was also notable in the clinical study of family behavior. Sibling relationships, although never entirely ignored by contemporary psychology, have only in the 1980s received widespread and systematic study by researchers and therapists.

Since the early 1980s several books have entered the field, serving as useful resources for the study of sibling relationships. Bank and Kahn (1982) described the multifaceted nature of the sibling bond. In the same year, Lamb and Sutton-Smith (1982) published a compilation of findings from a variety of research projects, ranging from birth order studies (Sutton-Smith, 1982) to studies of sibling interactions among young children (Abramovitch, Pepler, & Corter, 1982; Bryant, 1982; Nadelman & Begun, 1982), to an investigation of sibling relationships in nonhuman primates (Suomi, 1982). Dunn and Kendrick (1982a) published a comprehensive account of their study of mothers, fathers, and firstborn children when a new baby entered the family. Research into the nature and development of sibling relationships has more recently been summarized by Boer and Dunn (1992). The contributions to their volume are based on presentations held at the first international symposium pertaining to sibling research held in the Netherlands in 1990.

Lifespan and clinical issues are discussed in a book which is the first to specifically address sibling therapy—it addresses the complexity of the sibling relationship and its role in family therapy (Kahn & Lewis, 1988). Zukow (1989) brings together one of the first compilations of research pertaining to sibling relationships across cultures. The significance of sibling relationships beyond childhood has been emphasized by Cicirelli (1993, 1995) and Sandmaier (1994). Books about the uniqueness of sister relationships (McConville, 1985) and brother relationships (Waskow & Waskow, 1993; Wideman, 1984) have also appeared in recent years. A photographic essay celebrating "life's most enduring relationship" has added a poetic commentary to the significance of relationships between brothers and sisters (Faber & Mazlish, 1989).

Yet, in all of these, there is little mention of what happens when a sibling dies in childhood. In the books cited above, only Bank and Kahn (1982) devote much attention to the topic. Yet, if we look at the research that validates the various dimensions of the sibling relationship, it seems only common sense to realize that the death of a sibling may have profound effects on the surviving siblings.

Dimensions of the Sibling Relationship

Children see themselves as teachers, friends, comforters, competitors, and teasers, although it is more often the younger siblings who see their older brothers and sisters as teachers and comforters. Siblings describe what they like about their brother or sister with phrases such as "helps me with my homework," "makes me laugh," "talks to me about things no one else knows about," or "sticks up for me." Some express deep indebtedness to their sibling: "I wouldn't be like I am if it weren't for her"; "She has always been so good to me—when a lot of other big sisters were really mean to their little sisters." For some siblings, such sentiments coexist with negative feelings, expressed in quarrelling, persistent tattling, and antagonism. But even when negative feelings are expressed, there is most often also a sense of caring for one another, demonstrated in acts of friendship. The younger child in one family said, "She is nice to me. When the other kids made fun of me, she told them to leave me alone and gave me her bracelet to wear." In one study, almost three-quarters of all children said it was better to have a sibling than to be an only child (Brody & Stoneman, 1987). The various dimensions of the sibling relationship have been the focus of much recent sibling development research.

Siblings as Attachment Figures

Studies in the early 1980s (Dunn & Kendrick, 1982b; Samuels, 1980; Stewart, 1983) suggest that siblings can serve as attachment figures to their younger siblings. Stewart's (1983) work on sibling caretaking showed that some infants used their older siblings as attachment figures. In these families, when a stranger entered the laboratory playroom, the infants would appear uneasy and move closer to their older sibling. They would then position themselves so that the older child acted as a barrier to the stranger. From this protected position, the infants would start to engage the stranger in interaction. Samuels (1980) also found evidence of infants' attachment to their older siblings. Consistent with the notion that the presence of an attachment figure should facilitate exploration, she found that toddlers were more likely to explore an unfamiliar backyard when their older sibling was present than when the older sibling was absent. Attachment can also be signalled by missing the attachment figures when they are not available. Fifty percent of the mothers in an English sample (Dunn & Kendrick, 1982a) reported that their 14-month-olds missed their older siblings when they were absent.

Siblings as Antagonists

Most young siblings fight. In one study of home observations of toddlers with their preschool-aged siblings, fully 29% of the children's initiation/response exchanges were hostile (Abramovitch, Corter, & Lando, 1979). The older children typically initiated these conflicts, and the younger children usually submitted to the older children's aggression. In those rare instances in which the younger siblings initiated the aggression, the older children would then counterattack. Dunn and Kendrick (1982a, 1982b) also noted the incidence of aggression and fights between siblings. At the same time, there is a striking range of individual differences in the frequency of aggressive encounters.

Siblings as Playmates

In addition to fights and quarrels, young siblings also play with one another in ways ranging from imitative play to pretend play. For example, in one study of young siblings, 93% of the older siblings imitated their newborn siblings (Abramovitch et al., 1979). Dunn and Kendrick (1982a) concluded that those siblings who imitated one another more also had more affectionate and friendly relationships with one another. They also noted that older children who frequently played games with their younger siblings were more likely to help care for their younger siblings. Both children were also relatively more likely to imitate the other. In a later study, Dunn (1985) noted that not all young children engage in fantasy play together, but those children who share their fantasy play also have warmer and friendlier relationships with one another.

Siblings as Protectors

Siblings can be an important source of support in times of stress. For example, Jenkins (1992) have shown that children growing up in homes where parents experience marital disharmony have fewer problems if they have a good sibling relationship. They appear to benefit from offering and receiving comfort from their siblings. Confiding with a sibling was much more commonly reported as a coping mechanism than was confiding with a friend. An interesting line of clinical research that highlights the importance of sibling support is a study of siblings as therapists for children with eating disorders (Vandereycken & Van Vreckem, 1992).

Siblings as Socializers

The idea that child–child interaction plays a special part in the development of children's social and moral understanding is one that has had wide currency (Piaget, 1932; Sullivan, 1953). If such an argument is plausible, then it seems likely that siblings, who are so familiar with one another and who spend, at least in early childhood, much time interacting with one another, may well be a potent source of influence in these domains. Recent work suggests there are indeed associations between the kinds of experiences children have had with their siblings and various aspects of their sociocognitive development, at least during early childhood. For example, aspects of prosocial and cooperative behavior, pretend play, and conflict management in the preschool period have all been reported to be associated with sibling behavior (Dunn & Dale, 1984; Dunn & Munn, 1986). Studies of preschool and toddler siblings (Abramovitch et al., 1979; Lamb, 1978) show that the older siblings would offer toys to the younger ones; sharing and providing help, comfort, and physical affection were offered usually by the older to the younger siblings. In one study, however, 35% of such prosocial interactions were initiated by the younger siblings (Abramovitch et al., 1979). Furthermore, performance on sociocognitive assessments in middle childhood (Beardsall, 1986) has also been linked to experiences with siblings. Studies of young siblings have reported that children benefit from observing and imitating their older siblings (Wishart, 1986).

The childhood years are usually when siblings have the greatest impact on one another. During these years, siblings share much of their daily life—physically, socially, and emotionally. They spend much of every day together—at home, going to and from school, after school, evenings, and weekends. They may share the same room, sometimes even the same bed, the same clothes, toys, and books. They often share friends, depending on their ages, and social activities as well. They probably spend more time together than with their parents. Childhood and adolescence lay the groundwork for all future relationships. During these years, children learn how to love, how to problem solve, how to negotiate, start and end fights, and save face. They learn also how to care for, teach, and comfort others. It is a vitally important time. The relationship between siblings is distinctive in its emotional power. Common sense indicates that the relationship is of developmental importance. The losses following a sibling's death, then, encompass many dimensions for the surviving siblings.

Siblings in Special Situations

During the past 20 years, numerous researchers have examined the effects on well children of having a sibling who is chronically ill or disabled, either physically or cognitively. Several complete reviews of this literature are available (Faux, 1993; Stoneman & Berman, 1993). Faux provides a chronological approach to help understand the changes in research questions, methods, and findings that have occurred over the years. She indicates that earlier studies focused primarily on the assumed negative effects on siblings or their potential risks for maladjustment. Later studies have improved methodologically and are investigating sibling relationships within the broader context of their families, communities, and society. Such research shows that experiences with illness or disability have not only negative effects but positive outcomes as well.

Closely related to this area of study are investigations of effects on well siblings of an ill sibling's hospitalization (Craft, Wyatt, & Sandell, 1985; Knafl, 1982; Knafl & Dixon, 1983; Simon, 1993). Findings concur that the nonhospitalized children perceive a sibling's hospitalization as a stressful event. The issues faced by children who have had a sibling recently hospitalized are summarized by Simon (1993). She indicates that the siblings who are at the greatest risk for adverse effects are younger and experiencing many changes, perceive their parents to be treating them differently as compared with before their sibling's hospitalization, have received little information about their ill brother or sister, and are being cared for outside of the home by care providers who are not relatives. It can be concluded that life events or crises that affect one child in a family inevitably affect the others. And more so than at any other time in the lifespan, what affects the parents resonates through all the children.

Overall, these findings show that siblings are important suppliers of companionship, affection, and intimacy for one another. In today's society where parents spend considerable time working, children are often left to fend for one another and play even more important roles in each other's lives. Anthropologists (Weisner, 1982, 1989; Whiting & Whiting, 1975) have documented the widespread incidence in different cultures of older siblings serving as caregivers for their younger brothers and sisters. This phenomenon may not be as widespread in North America, but it is becoming more common. Moreover, the economic strains on families today that result in larger percentages of children in the United States and Canada growing up in poverty, and the increasing number of adults who choose not to have children, means that many adults are either underwhelmed or overwhelmed with regards to the emotional and social capital they commit to children (Kahn, 1988). Siblings may have little choice but to depend on one another. Through a shared history and common bonds, siblings have the potential for providing each other with intense emotional experience, support, guidance, information, and companionship. Given the significance of the sibling relationship, then, it is not difficult to understand why the death of a child can have profound effects upon brothers and sisters—effects that permeate the lives of surviving siblings.

☐ The Impact of Sibling Bereavement

Earlier in this chapter, I cited Doherty's observation about literary artists clearly portraying the nature of sibling relationships. To end the chapter, I refer to literary and other artists to illustrate the ongoing impact of sibling bereavement in childhood.

Edvard Munch (1863–1944)

Edvard Munch was the most internationally important Scandinavian artist of the early modern movement. He is best known for *The Scream*, a powerful expression of the anxiety-ridden existence of modern man. The central theme in a series of Munch's paintings derives from the death of his sister Sophie. Among his brothers and sisters, Sophie was the one to whom Munch felt most attached. She died when she was 15 years old; Munch was a year younger. The first of the series, *By the Deathbed, Fever* (1895), shows what the dying girl would have seen as she looked up from her deathbed—her family standing silently around her bed, heads bowed. Another, *The Sick Child* (1896), portrays the agonizing grief of Munch's mother as she sits with the dying Sophie. A third painting, *The Death Chamber* (1896), shows the scene at Sophie's death. The girl sits in a chair with her back to the viewer, with family members standing together in the room, but alone, each portraying the solitary lonely anguish of bereavement.

In the Munch museum in Oslo, it is written that Sophie could have become a great painter if she had lived. The descriptive notes suggest that Munch felt that he was not as good an artist as she and continually strove to match what he thought would have been her standard. The impact of Sophie's death became the focus of his most significant art in which he tried to convey the depth of human experience.

Pablo Picasso (1881–1973)

Picasso's story illustrates that the child's response to sibling death is influenced by several factors, including his own personality and his own history. For Picasso, who was a child troubled by new situations, the death of his sister emphasized his tendency to withdraw and want to stay close to home. Further, the impact of the death on his parents emphasized how critical a variable this is on sibling bereavement.

The Tragedy (1903) is one of Picasso's most memorable works of art. The painting shows a mother, father, and preadolescent boy standing at the edge of the sea. The parents appear so overcome by grief that they seem divorced from the outer world; their heads are bowed, their arms are folded, their eyes are downcast. Only the bereaved little boy continues to reach out, as he tentatively touches his father with a comforting pat. The death of the painter's little sister, Concepcion, may well be the tragedy to which this picture refers (Gedo, 1980, p. 50).

Concepcion died from diphtheria at age 8, when Picasso was 14. Her loss permanently upset the family balance, since Picasso's father (and perhaps his mother as well) never recovered from this tragedy. In a biography of Picasso, Gilot (cited in Gedo, 1980) noted that the artist continued to seem torn by guilt and remorse over this tragedy 50-odd years after the event. Huffington (1988) describes how Pablo watched the desperate comings and goings of the doctor during this sister's approaching death. In his anguish, the young boy made a pact with God. He offered to sacrifice his abilities and never pick up a brush again if God would save Concepcion. And then the boy was torn between wanting his sister saved and wanting her dead so his gift would be saved. When his sister died, Pablo was convinced that it was his ambivalence that had made it possible for God to let her die. He suffered incredible guilt, without anyone apparently talking with the lad to reassure him that he was not responsible for his sister's death.

Salvador Dali (1904–1989)

Dali's story illustrates the impact that a sibling's death can have even on children born after the first child's death. His story also underscores how parental reactions are influential in how children grieve. Dali describes the role that his brother's death played in his early development:

> At the age of seven, my brother died of meningitis, three years before I was born. This shook my mother to the very depths of her being. This brother's precociousness, his genius, his grace, his handsomeness were to her so many delights; his disappearance was a terrible shock. She was never to get over it. My parents' despair was assuaged only by my own birth, but their misfortune still penetrated every cell of their bodies. . . . Many is the time I have relived the life and death of this elder brother, whose traces were everywhere when I achieved awareness—in clothes, pictures, games—and who remained always in my parents' memories through indelible affective recollections. I deeply experienced the persistence of his presence as both a trauma—a kind of alienation of affections—and a sense of being outdone. All my efforts thereafter were to strain toward winning back my rights to life, first and foremost by attracting the constant attention and interest of those close to me by a kind of perpetual aggressiveness.
>
> The dead brother, whose ghost was there at the start to welcome me, was, you might say, the first Dalinian devil. My brother lived for seven years. I feel he was a kind of test-run of myself. . . . I learned to live by filling the vacuum of the affection that was not really being felt for me with love-of-me-for-me. In being born, my feet followed right in the footsteps of the adored departed still loved through me, perhaps even more than before. (Salemson, 1976, p. 12)

Oscar Wilde (1864–1874)

Oscar Wilde was a teenager when his young sister, at age 9, died from meningitis. Oscar was very distressed and paid regular visits to her grave. The author of Wilde's biography speculated that the "melancholy which he [Wilde] always afterwards insisted underlay his jaunty behaviour may have been first awakened by this early death" (Ellman, 1988, p. 25). The intensity of Wilde's grief is clearly portrayed in his poem, *Requieset,* written about his sister:

Tread lightly, she is near
Under the snow,
Speak gently, she can hear
The lilies grow.
All her bright golden hair
Tarnished with rust,
She that was young and fair
Fallen to dust.
Lily-like, white as snow,
She hardly knew
She was a woman, so
Sweetly she grew.
Coffin-board, heavy stone,
Lie on her breast,
I vex my heart alone,
She is at rest.
Peace, peace, she cannot hear
Lyre or sonnet,
All my life's buried here,
Heap earth upon it.

Charlotte Bronte (1816–1864)

Charlotte Bronte was the third of six siblings, with two older sisters, Maria (b. 1813) and Elizabeth (b. 1815). When Charlotte was 5, her mother died; when she was 9, both older sisters died. In his biography of Bronte, Keefe (1979) says that "the death of her two older sisters was traumatic for Charlotte. We know that she talked of . . . [them] . . . obsessively through her adolescence, and that she structured a major portion of *Jane Eyre* around Maria's character and death. . . . Maria's death, then, had a formative influence on Charlotte's psyche which outweighed the effects of later losses. . . . Death had become the central phenomenon of her life, its pall a filter through which she saw all of existence" (Keefe, 1979, p. 3). The impact of her sisters' deaths was lifelong for Charlotte Bronte in "the creation of literature, the incessant building up of structures which could not be torn down by death" (Keefe, 1979, p. 10).

Elvis Presley (1935–1977)

Famous as the "king of rock and roll," Elvis Presley provides an example from a more recent era of one who suffered from the guilt of having lived when his brother died and from his mother's reaction to her other son's death. Elvis was troubled throughout his life by the stillborn death of his twin brother, Jesse. At times, Elvis consciously blamed himself for Jesse's being stillborn; the guilt surrounding his brother's demise tormented him. He felt that his vocal gift and his life itself were not truly deserved. He persistently felt detached and lonely, as if something were missing from his life. In later life, he visited the area where Jesse's unmarked grave was supposed to be and often talked to his lost twin brother, as if in prayer (Pierce, 1994). Later still, he created his own cemetery for his brother and his mother on his Graceland property. Despite his remarkable talent, Elvis succumbed to drugs and an early death, still searching for the reason he lived while his brother had not.

Munch, Picasso, Wilde, and Bronte faced sibling bereavement in their early years. Dali and Presley, though never sharing life with their siblings, also faced the impact of their brothers' deaths. Developmentally, it is during the early years that sibling relationships have their primary effect (Watanabe-Hammond, 1988, p. 358). "Blueprints" for character are created, where each individual's beliefs and meanings are laid down. To experience a sibling's death during these years has potential lifelong effects. The impact of sibling bereavement can indeed be profound. Yet, the systematic study of sibling bereavement only began in recent years. An overview of research into sibling bereavement is presented in the next chapter in order to lay the groundwork for the research findings presented in the subsequent chapters.

2

CHAPTER

The Evolution of the Study of Sibling Bereavement

☐ Publications Addressing Sibling Bereavement

This chapter attempts to go beyond what is presented elsewhere (Davies, 1995c) and to provide a broad perspective on the evolution of sibling bereavement literature. The study of children's reactions to the death of a sibling is a relatively new area of investigation. For example, a bibliographic compilation of 20 years ago (Fulton, 1977), entitled *Death, Grief and Bereavement: A Bibliography 1845–1975*, contains 309 citations classified under the general heading of "children." Of these, only 15 are listed under the subheading of "reactions to the death of siblings," and seven of these pertained to adult sibling bereavement, not to children's experience. A few years later, a major Institute of Medicine report (Osterweis, Solomon, & Green, 1984) stated that lack of information on sibling bereavement precluded incorporating a section devoted to sibling grief. How has the study of this topic reached the point at which it is today?

The earliest publication that specifically addresses sibling bereavement[1] was written by Rosenzweig in 1943. His paper discussed the relationship between sibling death and schizophrenia. No other articles appeared until the 1960s when four were written (Cain, Fast, & Erickson, 1964; Hilgard,

[1]References that explicitly referred to sibling bereavement in the title were selected for categorizing into chronological order.

1969; Pollock, 1962; Rosenblatt, 1969). Two of these papers (Pollock, 1962; Hilgard, 1969) followed a similar theme as Rosenzweig's paper: the effect of childhood bereavement on adult patients being treated for psychiatric disturbance. Cain and his colleagues reported on their observations of disturbed reactions in children following the death of a sibling. Similarly, Rosenblatt described the disturbed reactions of a young boy to his sister's death. All authors were psychiatrists and published their work in psychiatric journals. A strong psychiatric orientation was obvious in the focus on "disturbance" or "psychopathology." This is not surprising, however, because the subjects of all papers were individuals undergoing psychiatric treatment.

During the next decade, of the six publications located, four were published in psychiatric journals and were authored by psychiatrists. Blinder (1972) presented three case studies to illustrate the potentially profound effects of sibling death on children. Binger (1973), based on children in 20 families whose sibling had died from leukemia, focused on the aftermath of such an experience. Tooley (1973), although focusing on maternal bereavement, addressed the possibility of surviving siblings becoming scapegoats in maternal bereavement. Pollock (1978), building on his earlier work, discussed sibling loss and creativity; he was the first to consider that sibling bereavement may have creative outcomes, not just be the source of pathology. In Australia, Nixon and Pearn (1977) looked at the emotional sequelae on parents and siblings of the drowning or near drowning of a child. The decade's publications concluded with a paper by Krell and Rabkin (1979) in which they introduced the effects of sibling death on surviving children from a family perspective.

The publications of the 1980s began with a paper entitled, "Siblings—The forgotten grievers" (Zelauskas, 1981), a title that reflected the situation up to that time. The ensuing decade provided a dramatic increase in the number of publications pertaining to sibling bereavement. Thirty-two publications were located. Shifts were noted in the authors' disciplines, which now included other health care professionals who were interested in the well-being of children, particularly nurses and psychologists. Publications no longer appeared solely in psychiatric journals. Instead, papers were in journals focusing on death and dying (*Death Studies, Death Education,* and *Omega*); social work and school health (*School Health* and *Child and Adolescent Social Work Journal*); pediatric medicine (*Pediatric Annals* and *Archives of Diseases in Childhood*); nursing (*Issues in Comprehensive Pediatric Nursing, Cancer Nursing, Archives of Psychiatric Nursing, Recent Advances in Nursing,* and *Pediatric Nursing*); and children's health (*Children's Health Care*). The focus had turned from examining sibling bereavement primarily as a psychiatric problem to looking at childhood bereavement as the concern of many disciplines interested in promoting children's health.

Four of the publications during this decade were doctoral dissertations (Balk, 1981; McCown, 1982; Davies, 1983; Hogan, 1987). These dissertations and the publications that derived from them account for 50% of the publications during the decade. An additional three publications (Lauer, Mulhern, Bohne, & Camitta, 1985; Birenbaum, 1989; Birenbaum, Robinson, Phillips, Stewart, & McCown, 1990; Martinson, Davies, & McClowry, 1987) resulted from the implementation of models of care for children dying of cancer and their families. Some other papers focused on the bereavement responses of a particular age group, heretofore not specifically mentioned—adolescents (Balk, 1983a, 1983b; Mufson, 1985; Hogan, 1988b). Publications of this decade reflected an expanded conceptualization of sibling bereavement, including an examination of various factors that affected bereavement outcome: location of death (Lauer et al., 1985); funeral attendance (McCown, 1984); closeness between siblings (Davies, 1988a); family environment (Davies, 1988b); cause of death (Adams & Deveau, 1987); parental grief (Demi & Gilbert, 1987); time (Hogan, 1988a); and parent communication (Birenbaum, 1989; Birenbaum et al., 1990). In addition, outcomes of bereavement were reported, notably in relation to self-concept (Balk 1983b; Martinson et al., 1987).

The focus on deaths from cancer continued in some of the papers (Davies, 1988a, 1988b; Birenbaum et al., 1989–90; Lauer et al., 1985; Martinson et al., 1987). Other papers were derived from situations in which the deaths occurred from sudden and unexpected deaths as well as cancer. Mandell, McAnulty, and Carlson (1983) were the first to describe sibling bereavement responses when the death had been due to sudden infant death syndrome (SIDS).

Interest in sibling bereavement has continued into the current decade, with several papers and one known dissertation published to date during the 1990s. Accounts of bereaved siblings themselves (Romond, 1990) and clinical descriptions continue to offer insight into the experiences of this group of children and adolescents (Heiney, 1991). A focus on adolescent bereavement has continued with additional papers by Balk (1990, 1991), Fanos and Nickerson (1991), Hogan and Balk (1990), Hogan and Greenfield (1991), and Hogan and DeSantis (1992, 1994). Hogan has contributed the first description of a measurement tool for assessing sibling bereavement (Hogan, 1990). Effects of sibling bereavement on younger children have been described (McCown & Davies, 1995), and research-based guidelines have been suggested for nurses working with bereaved siblings (Davies, 1993a). Now, in addition to looking at the immediate response of bereaved siblings, the long-term effects of sibling bereavement are noted (Davies, 1991; Martinson & Campos, 1991; Hogan & DeSantis, 1992). Explorations into sibling bereavement following death from various causes has continued, although not to a significant degree. Brent et al. (1993) explored the psychiatric impact of the loss of an adolescent sibling to suicide on surviving adolescent siblings; Hutton and Bradley (1994) investigated sibling reactions to a brother or sister's death from SIDS; and Mahon (1993) explored children's concept of death in relation to sibling death from trauma. These last two studies used comparison groups, a step forward in research design. Moreover, methods used to study the phenomenon have expanded to include qualitative methods (for example: Davies, 1991; Hogan & DeSantis, 1992; Mahon & Page, 1995) in addition to traditional quantitative methods. A cautionary note must be added here—qualitative projects must not simply repeat what has already been done but rather should build on work already completed. Finally, in this decade, publications have begun to describe intervention programs for siblings (Gibbons, 1992), although most programs focus on family members, not specifically on siblings (Heiney, Wells, & Gunn, 1993).

Over the past 30 years, sibling bereavement has become a topic worthy of systematic study. But 30 years? "Children have been dying since the beginning of time," one hears others say, "Surely this topic has been studied in great detail?" The answer, of course, is "No." Why is the study of sibling bereavement such a phenomenon of recent interest? Why was it not a significant object of study earlier? The answer lies partly in the attitudes toward children throughout history.

The History of Childhood

The study of children is only a relatively recent interest in the Western world. In fact, it is difficult to locate within the literature any comprehensive account of the history of childhood. The study of sibling bereavement, therefore, must be considered within the context of history and culture. It matters not only where we are born and to whom, but when—a common fact that may easily be overlooked in a culture somewhat removed from its own past and all too preoccupied with its own distinctive habits.

For so long, or so it seems, we have respected the innocence, the insightful intelligence, the soft and sweet gentleness of children, accepting the early years as the most important and the most formative in the life of human beings. We find it almost impossible to believe that those of earlier periods in history thought otherwise. Most readers of today will be startled to learn that the most influential thinkers of the 16th century, and of the preceding centuries as well, agreed that the child is nothing more than a lower animal—"the infant mewing and puking in the nurse's arms," as Shakespeare put it baldly but succinctly. Is it possible that the beautiful child we instinctively want to cuddle and to hold was called by Ralph Waldo Emerson only a century ago "a curly, dimpled lunatic"? It is hard for us to imagine that the death of a child was once regarded so coldly as conveyed by the otherwise civilized English essayist, Charles Lamb, in a personal letter to a friend:

> We have had a sick child, who, sleeping or not sleeping, next to me, with a pasteboard partition between, killed my sleep. The little bastard is gone.

Was the life of a child in any century so expendable as to warrant that unfeeling epitaph (Schorsch, 1979)?

During the 16th century, the answer is yes. The saying, "Who sees a child sees nothing" reflected attitudes toward children during this period. Although there were always exceptions to the rule, medieval communities dealt with their children as they dealt with their animals, and in the same practical and unsentimental way. Both shared the floor, the worms, the dirt, and every manner of disease that being a dog or a child in this period invited and implied. Perhaps in one way children were uniquely different from the animals with whom they wallowed: children were treated as if they were expendable—which they were because they died in droves. A child's death was not necessarily a cause for any public concern. Yet it is difficult to conceive of parents of any century not grieving the death of their own children. Perhaps to compensate for the horrors of an incredible infant mortality rate, parents consciously limited affection and attachment to their children. It was common practice, after all, for parents to "put out" their infants to wet nurses and to put them out again at seven or eight years of age for apprenticeship or service. Childhood was of little consequence and social value. Beyond artistic impressions of the Nativity story itself, there is very little in art or literature that reflects attitudes of affection toward children much before the 17th century (Schorsch, 1979). Consequently, death in childhood was not of major concern.

During the Middle Ages, either the community survived or no one survived. But by the 17th century, humans exchanged communal responsibility for individual freedom. As a result, the value of the individual rose and so did a corresponding interest in childhood. Even during this period, however, the attitude toward children was quite bleak. The new Calvinism of the time envisioned every child as a bearer of natural sin, and physical restriction accompanied the 17th century restraints of the will.

The family as we know it today had its origins during this time. The man of the household replaced the king of the community as the figure of authority and power and as such had complete control over his property, including his wife and children. Before the Reformation when children had been treated as domestic animals, discipline and training were considered wastes of time.

In the reforming spirit of the 17th century, when the nature of childhood was recognized as "curable," discipline and training developed structures of their own. Children were harshly disciplined and not in any way pampered. However, some of the literature of the period presented many tender thoughts about children, particularly when they were perceived as helpless or when they were dead.

During the 18th and 19th centuries, the Industrial Revolution created a western culture that was exploitive of its children, both at home and in the factory. Children worked alongside adults in factories and at home, and in many cases did the work that adults would not do (e.g., chimney sweeps). Scores of children were homeless orphans, without protection or love from someone who cared for them. Corporal punishment was then an accepted form of "teaching," and children were mistreated and even murdered at the hands of their masters. The evils of child labor in England and the fledgling United States affirm the duress under which children lived. They often died without notice by anyone other than the master who was inconvenienced by their untimely death. The plight of children as exposed by the pen of Charles Dickens was only too true not only in England but in early America as well.

In the 19th century, laws and public institutions—orphanages, foundling homes, asylums, schools—replaced masters and factory and land owners as the guardians of poor children. The first factory act in England (1802) legally separated orphaned apprentices from other workers and protected them simply because they were young. Eventually child labor laws were enacted in England and America to protect children from overwork and a life of illiteracy (Schorsch, 1979).

The 20th century has seen a dramatic change in the attention paid to children compared with what had gone before. Only within this century has our western world begun to value children as individuals who are worthy of care by their parents and of protection by law. Contributing to this century's emphasis on children's well-being and development was Freud who opened up new avenues of thought into the human psyche. In so doing, he motivated exploration of the significance of early childhood experiences for subsequent development. The child, as the precursor to the adult, took on new significance. In addition, human experiences took on new significance—mourning as one such experience was described for the first time in the literature (Freud, 1957). Several decades were yet to pass, however, before mourning in childhood became a topic relevant for study. The exploration of childhood bereavement could only evolve as the field of death, dying, and bereavement emerged as an area worthy of systematic exploration.

The History of the Study of Death, Dying, and Bereavement

The study of bereavement, although a universal experience, was not a topic of extended or systematic study until the second half of this century. World War II presented to the modern world a picture of death and destruction never before experienced: the holocaust in Germany and the use of the atomic bomb in Japan. The cruelty of human beings to their fellow man was an assault to the modern perception of civilized life. How individuals could survive physically, emotionally, and spiritually in the face of such horror was incomprehensible. Curiosity, and perhaps fear, inspired many to learn more about the experience of these individuals and about how they coped with such devastation and despair. The repugnance was made greater by the realization that groups of vulnerable individuals at either end of life's continuum (children and the elderly) who were usually protected were not immune to warfare, as Anne Frank's story made poignantly clear. The war and its effects also inspired the first written accounts of children's understanding of death (Nagy, 1948, 1959) and their awareness of death (Anthony, 1940, 1972).

Between 1940 and 1960, interest in the field of thanatology was growing. The historical origins of this interest, outlined by Benoliel (1994, p. 4), indicate that in the "aftermath of war, interest in death and dying as subjects for scientific investigation was stimulated by a number of factors: the rapid expansion of the organized sciences and societally funded research, the appearance of the mental health movement with a central focus on suicide prevention, a depersonalization of many aspects of human existence associated with new technologies, and a powerful death anxiety that has been attributed to the use of atomic weapons at Hiroshima and Nagasaki."

The horrors of the war motivated a desire to prevent such pain and suffering from ever occurring again. Perhaps there was also a need to compensate for the atrocities. Children especially should be saved from suffering. This orientation occurred at the same time as tremendous new developments were occurring in the fields of science and medicine. Medical technology advanced rapidly and provided hope for cure and prolongation of life. Recently discovered penicillin and newly developed antibiotics were saving children's lives from those illnesses that had previously killed them; the wonder drug, the Salk vaccine, was saving children from the ravages of polio. Leukemia and other childhood cancers took over as the most frequent cause of death in children, often resulting in slow and painful deaths. Focus turned to these children and to their families—how they cope and how health care professionals can help them win the battle against this disease as successfully as other diseases had been conquered. At the same time, as mentioned earlier, there was a growing interest in the psychosocial realm of experience and the effects of childhood experiences on the psyche. This context helps account for the early psychiatric interest in sibling bereavement and for the subsequent focus on siblings following a child's death from leukemia. Since cancer remains the major cause of death from illness in childhood, an ongoing avenue of sibling bereavement research continues into the experiences of children when a brother or sister dies from cancer.

The end of World War II also saw the rapid expansion of migration to urban areas. Children growing up in the 1950s and 1960s had relatively little contact with rural life—they no longer directly observed life and death as everyday events and had little opportunity to learn to deal with these situations accordingly. Today, with almost a quarter (25.87%) of the population in Canada, and even fewer (24.45%) in the United States, living in rural areas (United Nations, 1995) on farms, natural scenes of calves, colts, and kittens being born and dying have largely been removed from the personal observations of most children. So, when U.S. President Kennedy was assassinated in 1963, the event had a notable effect on children in classrooms, and their teachers struggled with the best ways to help them. Interest in helping children cope with death and bereavement moved a little closer to the forefront.

During the 1950s, 1960s, and into the early 1970s, death was not generally an issue for open discussion, especially when one was dying. In their book, *Sickness and Society*, Duff and Hollingshead (1968) described what happened when patients were dying. Of the 161 patients they studied, 25% died. In most cases, the physician and family decided to keep the patient from knowing the truth about his or her condition and its expected outcome. Around the same time, Glaser and Strauss published their books, *Awareness of Dying* (1965) and *Time for Dying* (1968). The trend to tell patients about their illnesses and their prognoses was only beginning.

If it was rare to tell adult patients about such things, it was taboo to discuss such topics with children. In fact, experts advocated that children younger than 10 years had no cognitive grasp of the meaning of death and were not capable of experiencing or expressing feelings about death (Knudson & Natterson, 1960; Morrissey, 1963a, 1963b, 1965; Richmond & Waisman, 1955). It was only with Waechter's hallmark study (1968, 1971) of the fatally ill child's awareness of death that researchers began to attempt to study this sensitive but profoundly relevant area of inquiry. Others followed with added documentation that children do have an understanding of the meaning of death and dying (Easson, 1970; Spinetta, Rigler, & Karon, 1973, 1974; Raimbault, 1981; Bluebond-Langner, 1977, 1978; Spinetta, 1972).

Their results indicated that children do in fact know that they are very ill, and they benefit from openness about their situation.

The decade of the 1970s saw the field of thanatology flourish in the academic world. Courses in death and dying were offered in colleges and universities; workshops were held for the general public. Kubler-Ross's book, *On Death and Dying* (1969) reached beyond academic circles to the lay public and kindled awareness of death as a topic for open discussion. Attempts were made to establish communication networks among those interested in the field—indeed, three professional journals on the topic were started (*Omega: The Journal on Death and Dying* in 1970; *Journal of Thanatology*, which was later to become *Advances in Thanatology*; and *Death Education*, which later became *Death Studies*). Informal networks were established that provided opportunities for multidisciplinary investigations involving academicians and clinicians in shared research endeavors. Formalized networks came into being in the form of the *International Work Group on Death, Dying and Bereavement* (1974), and the *Forum on Death Education and Counseling* (later the *Association for Death Education and Counseling*), and the *National Hospice Association* in 1978. Numerous books were compiled, and the literature flourished with articles about death, dying, and bereavement. Given the growth of thanatology during this decade, however, relatively little investigation was directed toward children. The major focus of the few publications that existed had to do with the experiences of dying children, primarily from cancer, and of their parents. The limited number of publications that addressed bereavement in children focused primarily on responses following the death of a parent (e.g., Furman, 1974). Literature pertaining directly to sibling bereavement was scant.

It took until the early 1980s for a more open attitude to emerge toward talking with children, siblings in particular, about their experiences with the death of a brother or sister. To talk with children about their own impending death was now at least considered feasible, but to broach the subject with surviving children was still considered dangerous—to openly ask questions might be harmful to their emotional well-being. When I sought the approval of the ethics committee for my own dissertation research in 1980, my request to interview the siblings directly was turned down on the grounds that it was not ethical to subject children to the stress of such a discussion. I was given approval to talk only to parents about their surviving children. Parents were then approached by the members of the clinical teams caring for them to ask if they might be willing to participate in the study and to have me contact them to provide further information. When I telephoned parents who had agreed to be contacted, in the course of the conversation in which I was explaining the study, they would say, "If you are interested in studying the siblings, wouldn't you like to talk to *them*?" I would explain that the ethics review committee prevented me from doing that, and they would respond, "If we ask you to talk with the children, or if we request that you also meet with our children, would you do that?" So, I met not only with the parents but also talked with the bereaved siblings, either along with their parents or sometimes separately. I asked each of them to respond to a question at the end of the interview about what effect, if any, resulted from their participating in the interviews. Without exception, the families and the children reported that the experience had aroused sad memories, but the experience was positive. Some families reported that the interview was the first time that family members had sat together to discuss the death. After completing that study, I was able to reassure other ethics committees for subsequent studies that previous experience indicated that there were no negative consequences that arose from talking to children about death and bereavement, and, in fact, such conversations had been reported as helpful by those families who had participated in the first study.

Overcoming such hurdles was only one step necessary for the systematic study of sibling bereavement. Given the historical insignificance of children until the 20th century, and given the recent development of death, dying, and bereavement as a field unto itself, it is no wonder that the number of studies pertaining to the topic was so small prior to the 1980s.

☐ Published Literature Reviews Pertaining to Sibling Bereavement

During the past 10 years or so, as sibling bereavement has become a topic worthy of study, six "literature reviews" have been published. Waechter's was the first, initially written in 1964 (Waechter, 1964) with limited availability, and then published in a book that was edited as a tribute to Waechter in 1985 (Krulik, Holaday, & Martinson, 1987). Waechter focused on a broad overview of the literature pertaining to death, dying, and bereavement. Waechter did not specifically address the needs of grieving children in this review, but she indicated that the death of a parent or sibling "is a shattering experience for the child and may have far reaching effects." She explained this effect in relation to the child's understanding of death at various ages. Waechter was building an argument for studying dying children directly, since until this time it was emphasized that to talk to a child about his or her diagnosis and prognosis was harmful.

In a paper written as a follow-up to Waechter's, Betz (1987) reviewed the research and theory generated in the field of pediatric thanatology during 1970–1985. She reviewed four major areas of inquiry: children's conceptions of death, the fatally ill child, and children's and parents' bereavement responses. In the section about children's bereavement responses, Betz includes discussion of bereavement responses following the death of parents and siblings. Betz briefly discusses nine studies pertaining to the study of sibling bereavement and concludes with suggestions for future research.

Stephenson (1986) reviewed the literature on grieving children with special emphasis on those who have lost a sibling. Instead of summarizing or critiquing the literature, he bases recommendations for helping grieving children on the review. More recently, Opie (1992) and Walker (1993) published critical reviews. Opie reviews nursing studies in particular and identifies limitations due to small samples and designs that include nonrepresentative samples, lack of comparison groups, and unclear definitions. Walker categorizes the literature into early studies identifying pathological grief responses (1950 to 1985) and later studies identifying grief responses (1985 to present). In this latter grouping, she categorizes studies into developmental age-specific studies, impact of family environment on grief responses, and intervention studies. Her review encompassed a final sample size of 24 research reports and 15 clinical papers obtained from a Medline computer search from 1982 to 1992 and searching the reference lists from articles citing related works. Even with this extensive search, however, there are significant research papers published during this time frame that have been excluded from Walker's review. She provides a concise summary of each paper reviewed and makes conclusions about the future research similar to those put forth by Betz (1987) and Opie (1992).

The sixth review (Davies, 1995c) provides a comprehensive review of the "state of the art" of sibling bereavement research. This paper divides the literature into general topics that characterize the research to date: behavioral responses (both problematic and positive responses) and mediating variables, which include individual, situational, and environmental characteristics. Aspects of this paper will be incorporated into the subsequent chapters of this book that deal with each of these issues.

These reviews indicate that the field of sibling bereavement research continues to evolve. As stated earlier, the first studies of sibling bereavement (1960s to mid-1970s) focused on the psychiatric implications for adults of experiencing a sibling's death in childhood. Even the first studies of bereaved siblings themselves focused on problematic outcomes among bereaved siblings undergoing psychiatric treatment. From the middle of the 1970s to the middle of the next decade, oncology, instead of psychiatry, provided the setting for many studies. In the early 1970s, Martinson and her colleagues initiated the first home care program for dying children, representing the beginning of a changed emphasis to intervention programs for children with cancer (Martinson et al., 1978; Martinson, 1980). This allowed some investigation of the impact of such programs on the siblings. During the 1980s, attention was given to sibling bereavement associated with a child's death from diseases other than cancer, including cystic fibrosis and SIDS, and from other causes, such as suicide. The focus also was directed to specific age groups, especially adolescents. The literature also conveyed the difficulty that exists in attempting to isolate factors that affect sibling adjustment and bereavement outcome and acknowledged the contribution of environmental factors, such as the family, to bereavement outcome.

It is enlightening to look back over the published research pertaining to families and sibling bereavement. Cobb's (1956) was the first published paper that addressed the effects on the family of a child's death. Cobb's paper, a clinical description, derived from her own experience as a pediatrician caring for families in which a child was dying. In the next decade, the titles of three papers specifically mentioned the effects on families of having a child with leukemia (Natterson & Knudson, 1960; Lewis, 1967; Binger, Ablin, Feuerstein, Kushner, Zoger, & Mikkelson, 1969). None of the papers focused specifically on the siblings but did mention the special needs of siblings. The family focus broadened during the 1970s—five publications referred specifically to family functioning following the death of a child. As with publications directly related to sibling bereavement, publications pertaining to families reflected the ongoing interest in childhood cancer and leukemia, but two papers with a family focus introduced deaths from other causes: suicide (Rudestam, 1977) and cystic fibrosis (Kerner, Harvey, & Lewiston, 1979). The focus on family functioning and childhood cancer prevailed into the 1980s as well.

It is interesting to speculate on this persistent interest in cancer deaths. Accidents are the primary cause of childhood death, but cancer is the leading cause of death from disease among children. When children are mortally injured as a result of accident or trauma, they are usually rushed to the nearest hospital. Many such children are dead on arrival and are therefore not admitted to the hospital. If their condition requires hospital admission, it is usually to an intensive care unit where they survive for a short time before succumbing to their injuries. Emergency and intensive care staff struggle with how best to help the families of such children during their short contact with the hospital. A cancer diagnosis in a child initiates a very different relationship with hospital staff. Numerous admissions to the oncology unit and visits to the oncology clinic continue over several years. Staff form close, ongoing relationships with these children and their families. Moreover, a diagnosis of cancer in a patient of any age often connotes despair, dismay, and death, which is only emphasized when the patient is a child. Staff struggle on a day-by-day basis for many months, and sometimes years, to help these children and their families. Physicians and nurses bear witness to the children's long struggle and, as the end approaches, to the suffering of these children. This was especially true 25 years ago when treatment was less developed, and nearly all children with cancer died. The process of dying for children who die in the emergency room or the intensive care unit from accidental causes, while no less serious, is shorter lasting than for children with cancer who suffer in the long term. Clinicians, in their attempts to find new ways to help children with cancer and their families, and in their attempts to cope themselves with the suffering of children, have focused on this population. Only recently, realizing the potential impact of a child's sudden death on a family, have clinicians and researchers begun to explore bereavement in families after a child has died from causes other than cancer.

The focus on families following the death of a child continues to receive attention, although not as much as one would expect. Parkman (1992) addresses the needs of families when a child dies in an intensive care setting, and others describe the need for family-centered bereavement intervention programs (Gibbons, 1992; Heiney, Hasan, & Price, 1993; Heiney, Wells, & Gunn, 1993). This trend toward including the family is likely part of the ongoing evolution of sibling bereavement research. The focus now needs to turn to assessing the complex interactions of multiple factors affecting sibling bereavement, to assessing bereavement interventions for siblings and their families, and to continuing to document the long-term outcomes of sibling bereavement. In addition, the focus needs to broaden beyond the boundaries of our own western world. Most importantly, the focus needs to be guided by the fact that there is no one right or proper way for siblings to grieve. Researchers and clinicians must guard against limiting their research and their practice by predetermined frameworks and, instead, remain open to learning what siblings themselves have to teach us.

As a reference for other researchers, clinicians, and educators, summaries of the literature pertaining to sibling bereavement research are included in the appendix. Only journal articles are included (excluding chapters in books). Articles were located through library searches and by following up on other articles cited in reference lists. Only articles referring explicitly to the concept of sibling bereavement in their titles were included. An attempt has been made to be as comprehensive as possible, but there are, no doubt, articles that have been inadvertently omitted. The first appendix includes papers that are personal accounts or clinical descriptions of sibling bereavement and literature reviews pertaining to some aspect of the topic. The second includes papers that are systematic descriptions or studies of more than one case of sibling bereavement. It is obvious from the list of summaries that studies vary considerably in many respects: sample size, age range of siblings included, time since death, and cause of death. There is also wide variation in design and type of analysis. My goal, however, is not to offer a comprehensive critique of the research presented here. It is simply to offer a compilation of reported research in the field. The research to date has answered some questions; it has also raised many issues yet to be explored. The research represented in these summaries lays the foundation for further research that will continue to offer insight into the experiences of bereaved siblings.

The third and final chapter of this first section of the book continues to set the context for presenting my research findings. Chapter 3 focuses on children's understandings of the concept of death.

3

CHAPTER

Children's Understanding of Death

Why did Johnny have to die?
Did I make him die?
Will I die too? Will you die, Dad?
Will Johnny come back for his birthday?
How can Johnny breathe in the ground?
What happens to your body when you die?

Such are some of the questions that children ask following the death of a brother or sister. How to answer such questions challenges even the most knowledgeable and articulate parents and other adults who interact with grieving children. When parents are overcome with their own grief, it is often difficult even to think clearly, let alone respond "appropriately" to their other children. It is helpful, however, to have some understanding of how children conceive of death since their conceptions differ from those of adults. Knowing how the child is understanding death helps adults to understand "where the child is coming from." Keeping the child's point of view in mind helps adults prepare for children's inevitable questions and to respond more appropriately than if adults expect children to have adultlike interpretations of death.

Death is a complex concept that presents challenges to all human beings as they try to grasp its meaning and struggle with its effects. The acquisition of a concept of death is a gradual process developed over a lifetime. How children learn to understand death has been a topic of considerable, though not always very satisfactory, study during the past half century.

☐ Developing a Concept of Death

The study of healthy children's understanding of death began with the pioneering work of Schilder and Wechsler (1934), although Anthony's (1939, 1940, 1972) work continues to be the more frequently cited. Anthony, using parental reports and other methods to assess children in England in the late 1930s, concluded that there was a five-stage developmental sequence through which children acquire an accurate concept of death:

1. Three-year-old children are apparently ignorant of the meaning of the word "dead";
2. by five years of age, children have a limited concept;
3. by the time children are about 7, they define "dead" by focusing on associated phenomena (such as the ability to move) or by referring specifically to humans but not to other living things;
4. one year later, children have a correct but limited understanding; and
5. nine-year-old children can provide general, biological, or logical explanations for "dead."

In the mid-1960s, Peck (1966) attempted to replicate Anthony's results. He found the same stages but concluded that each stage was reached at an earlier age than Anthony had described.

Nagy's work (1948, 1959), completed prior to the end of World War II (but not published until after the war), is also frequently cited. She interviewed 378 children, 3 to 10 years of age, in and around Budapest and subsequently described three stages in children's learning about death:

Stage 1. Children younger than 5 years of age attribute life and consciousness to the dead, perceiving death as temporary and reversible; death is considered to be a different form of living.

Stage 2. Children of 5–9 years of age may not recognize that death can happen to them; death is personified and imagined as a separate person. (This finding, although frequently cited, has not been replicated by other researchers [Mahon, 1993].)

Stage 3. Children older than 9 years of age recognize death as the cessation of bodily activities, as universal and irreversible.

Melear (1973) attempted to replicate Nagy's work: he interviewed 41 children, 3 to 12 years, and asked them to comment on themes found by Nagy. Although 3–4-year-olds were vague about the meaning of death, there were associations with violence and with death as a different form of life. Children 4–7 years old understood death as temporary and reversible and believed that dead people were cognizant and had biological functions. And 5–10-year-olds believed that death was final and irreversible but that biological functions continued. None of the children in any particular age group completely recognized that death meant the cessation of biological functioning.

☐ Developing a Concept of Death by Cognitive Level

The most common developmental framework for understanding children's concept of death is that of Piaget (1959), who studied how children acquire and explain knowledge. Piaget's stage theory of cognitive development describes the development of the child's intellect (thoughts, perceptions, judgment, and reasoning) as an orderly hierarchical sequence of three major periods, each integrating and extending the previous one. In the first stage, sensorimotor, infants learn via motor and sensory actions, which lay the foundation for behavior. Children of this age are unable to think or form concepts. Infants respond not to the concept of death but rather to the feelings resulting from separation from those to whom they are attached.

The second period comprises two components. The first is preoperational thought (2–6 years of age) when the child cannot separate internal and external worlds (egocentricity) and has thoughts that do not follow logical rules. At this age, the child believes that death is reversible and temporary; it is a departure or sleep. During the stage of concrete operations (7–12 years of age), the child gradually becomes less egocentric, with decreases in animistic and magical thinking. The child comes to realize the personal nature of his or her views. Language and communication skills increase markedly, and the child's thinking becomes logical. The child is concerned with the actual, rather than the hypothetical, and the child's beliefs are influenced by the observable. Many of the cognitive skills acquired before or during the stage of concrete operations are foundational for developing an accurate concept of death.

The stage of formal operations begins around the age of 12 years and continues to adulthood. Previous structures and functions are integrated to form full intellectual capacities, including the ability to deal effectively with the world of abstract ideas. This is true in terms of achieving a cognitive understanding of many concepts, including death.

Research into children's concepts of death has since supported Piaget's original work, with some significant variations. Steiner (1965), for example, explored the concepts of life and death with 60 white non-Catholic students in three age groups: 4 to 5 years, 7 to 8 years, and 11 to 12 years. Consistent with Piaget's findings, children in the middle age group recognized death as final but mistakenly guessed that their own deaths would be at a very old age. In addition, there was a shift from death as a result only of violence (found in the youngest group) to death as a result of violence and accidents. Children in the youngest age groups believed that death is gradual, temporary, and reversible. Children in the middle age group recognized death as final. Children in the oldest group recognized both the universality and inevitability of death. Koocher (1973, 1974) did seminal research with children and their concept of death. He also supported Piaget's findings, but, in addition, he found that age alone was not a reliable indicator of response; however, the higher the children's cognitive functioning, the higher their level of abstract thinking about death.

Studies in cognitive development by Piaget and others allow us to understand how children respond to death, for children understand ideas at their own cognitive level. There is general consensus that as children get older, their concepts of death become more adultlike. But, of course, there are inconsistencies across studies as to the specific age at which children achieve an "adult" concept of death since this is essentially a developmental issue, not a chronological one. Peck (1966), for example, found that Anthony's stages applied at younger ages. Koocher (1973, 1974) found that age was not a reliable indicator of response. Mahon (1993) found that children had an accurate concept of death earlier than predicted by either Nagy (1948) or Melear (1973). Forty-five percent of 5-year-olds in Mahon's study had an accurate concept of death, and at least half had an accurate concept of finality and universality. It could be speculated that children are learning more at younger ages. However, it is more likely that the stage theory of how children learn about death may be limited. Such theories offer stereotypical descriptions and result in potentially misleading relationships between chronological age and cognitive development.

☐ Developing a Concept of Death as Subconcepts

An alternative approach is offered by Speece and Brent (1984, 1992) and discussed by Deveau (1995). Speece and Brent completed a comprehensive review of the available empirical research conducted between 1934 and the early 1990s to investigate children's understanding of death (Speece & Brent, 1984, 1991, 1992; Speece, 1986, 1995). They compared and contrasted age and developmental staging information. They concluded there is general consensus among the studies that as children get older, their concepts of death become more adultlike. There are, however, inconsistencies across studies as to the specific age at which children achieve an "adult" concept of death. A major reason for the ambiguity stems from variable definitions of the concept of death. (Considerable variation also occurred across studies with regard to methodology, timing of when studies were conducted, design, and control for variables such as socioeconomic level and religious background.) Speece and Brent point out that the concept of death is not a single concept but rather a complex concept composed of three components or subconcepts. They suggest that dividing the concept of death into its various components permits a clearer picture of what children at different ages understand about death. The three most widely researched subconcepts or components are irreversibility, nonfunctionality, and universality. These components are defined as follows.

Irreversibility (finality, irrevocability) concerns the understanding that once a living thing dies, its physical body cannot be made alive again. It is important to keep in mind that this component is limited to the physical body and, thus, should be kept separate from beliefs about a spiritual afterlife. Prior to understanding irreversibility, young children typically view death as temporary and reversible. Dead things come alive again. For these children, death is seen as almost identical to sleep (in that you will wake up) or to a trip (in that you will return). Three-and-a-half-year-old Martha had been told her 6-year-old sister, Maggie, had died (in a bike accident). Yet, for weeks, Martha still eagerly awaited her big sister's return from school each day. She scurried to the front window after waking from her afternoon nap, accustomed to Maggie's arrival at that time of day. Martha continued to ask her mother, "Maggie come home soon?" "Where's Maggie?" Martha could not comprehend that Maggie was gone forever. Martha needed to hear the same information again and again: "Maggie died, and when you die, you can never come back. Maggie won't be coming back."

Nonfunctionality (cessation) refers to the understanding that all external (eating, breathing, moving) and internal (feeling, thinking, dreaming) life-defining functions cease at death. Before children understand that death involves the cessation of life-defining characteristics, they attribute various functional abilities to dead things. While saying good-bye to friends who were the last to leave their son's viewing in the funeral chapel, the parents of 4-year-old Suzie noted she was sitting quietly by the open casket of her baby brother. They overheard her whispering, as she placed her small, stuffed rabbit beside him, *"You can play with Bunny when you're deaded."* Suzie perceived her brother could hear her and that he would be playing with Bunny.

Gradually, children's understanding changes so they conceive death as somewhat different from life in that dead things do not possess all of the functional capabilities of alive things—dead things cannot eat, but they can still hear; or they have diminished functions—they cannot hear as well as alive things. Again, it is important to point out that this component concerns the physical body and not beliefs about the spirit and its capabilities.

Universality (inevitability) concerns the understanding that all living things die—death is inevitable, including the reality that they, too, will die

(Speece & Brent, 1984). Before children understand that death is universal and inevitable, they often believe that there are certain actions that can be taken to avoid death, such as being clever or lucky. Most children also think that certain people do not die—mothers, other children, or themselves (Speece, 1986). Having experienced a sibling's death, however, young children are particularly concerned that they, or their parents, will also die. Six-year-old Sarah's sister had died from cancer. Three months later, Sarah was in bed with a fever and chills. She was restless, irritable, refused to sleep, and insisted that her mother stay by her side. Her mother sensed Sarah's fear and gently asked, "Sara, are you afraid you'll die like Casey did?" "The look on Sarah's face was a dead giveaway," Sarah's mother said. She began to cry and she just sobbed, "Casey had a fever too." Sarah's mother reassured her that Casey's fever was from a different cause—"Casey had leukemia; you have a flu bug." Within a short while, Sarah had fallen into a restful, much needed sleep.

These three subconcepts (irreversibility, nonfunctionality, and universality) have been the focus of much of the research pertaining to children's understanding of death. Speece and Brent concluded that a "model age" for acquiring each subconcept is 7, with approximately 60% of children achieving a mature understanding of all three concepts between the ages of 5 and 7 years. Two other subconcepts are not as clearly defined: causality and belief in an afterlife. A mature understanding of causality involves an abstract or generalizable and realistic understanding of both internal and external events that bring about death. In additional research, Brent and Speece (1993) have shown that the belief in some type of continued afterlife is also characteristic of children's (and adults') concept of death. Whether or not this aspect is actually a component of the concept of death is still under discussion among researchers in the field.

Lazar and Torney-Purta (1991) examined how children related four subconcepts (irreversibility, universality, nonfunctionality, and causality) to people and animal deaths. They interviewed 99 6- and 7-year-old children, 7 months apart. They concluded that children first learned the subconcepts of irreversibility and universality, and that one of these two subconcepts must be understood before a child understands the subconcepts of either nonfunctionality or causality. The children's understanding of the subconcept of nonfunctionality changed over the 7 months, so that 60% understood this concept with respect to animals, and 47% with respect to humans. Lazar and Torney-Purta and Speece and Brent agree that additional research is necessary to investigate the four subconcepts separately, in relation to one another, over a period of time, and with both animal and human referent objects, in order to understand the development of children's concepts of death.

These findings can serve as rough guidelines for dealing with bereaved siblings. The guidelines provide a set of expectations regarding what children understand about death, including likely misconceptions. They also highlight part of what death education for young children should emphasize—the universal and inevitable nature of death and the differences between the states of being alive and being dead.

☐ The Role of Children's Experiences in Developing a Concept of Death

It is assumed that children's experiences may also influence how they understand death. Clinical experience indicates that terminally ill children are often far beyond their years in understanding what is happening to them. Yet the extent to which experience can advance development independent of developmental level continues to be debated. Only one study has been located that addresses this specific question (Mahon, 1993). Mahon examined the relationship between children's experience of a sibling's traumatic death and their acquisition of an accurate concept of death. Experience of sibling death did not make a significant difference in children's acquisition of an accurate concept of death. The experience did, however, make for differences in the way in which children supported their belief statements when they responded to the question, "Why do you think that?" Bereaved children were much more likely than those not bereaved to draw on their own experiences. When one 5-year-old was asked, "Could this happen to someone else?" she responded "Yes." When asked to explain her answer, she replied, "Because it happened to my brother so it can happen to anybody else.... My brother was killed, so what's the difference?" (Mahon, 1993, p. 341). Nonbereaved children were less likely to support the reasons for their answers with explanations based on direct experience. Rather than saying that someone else could die from cancer because their grandmother had, these children were more likely to say, "Because everybody dies."

Developmental level was a highly significant predictor of concept acquisition, whereas the experience of sibling death from trauma was not. Therefore, it is essential to consider developmental level when interacting with children about the topic of death.

☐ Understanding Siblings' Concept of Death

Children whose siblings die, like all children, are going through the process of developing an understanding of death. They see the world from the vantage point of their own developmental level, although there is no single mold into which all children fit. The more advanced children's cognitive functioning, the higher is their level of abstract thinking about death. This conclusion fits well with the conceptualization put forth by Speece and Brent and by developmental and stage theorists. They all support the view that, as children mature, they move from concrete intellectual operations to more abstract or conceptual ways of thinking. Age alone is not a reliable indicator of children's understanding of death, but it remains the most *practical* guideline for understanding children's conceptions of death. Following is a summary of children's understanding of death according to phase (Faulkner, 1993), age, and developmental level and including reference to the components of the concept of death.

Separation Phase—Infants: Children Less than 2 Years of Age

These children are in Piaget's sensorimotor stage of cognitive development. What adults refer to as death, young children see as a separation from love and important people in their lives. This is particularly true for infants, who for many years were thought to be incapable of grieving. Yet even young children will respond to separation from a loved figure, especially their mother. Young children also seem to miss a deceased sibling: after the death of his 4-year-old sister, 18-month-old Derek would go to her room searching for his sister under the blankets and under the bed. Verbal skills in children of this age are limited, so their concerns are primarily expressed through crying, separation anxiety, and attachment. Their need for close and continuous physical contact is paramount.

Structural Phase—Toddlers and Preschoolers: Children between 2 and 5 Years of Age

Children in this group are in Piaget's stage of preoperational thought. For these children, things are as they appear to be, and will remain so. These youngsters interpret very literally what is told to them, as one mother illustrated in her description of her 30-month old daughter:

> I didn't tell her what had happened to the baby (SIDS) for the first two days, and she thought that one of Daddy's friends had come and got him. My mother told her that we lost him. So she looked under the beds and everywhere until I explained that he died because of an illness.

These children attribute life to all things that move. On the other hand, the absence of movement can denote a quality of nonaliveness or death

(Gordon & Klass, 1979). They recognize death in terms of lying-down immobility but may not recognize that being dead and being alive are mutually exclusive. I recall scenes of a father playing with his 3-year-old daughter where the father would lay very still and close his eyes as if asleep. The child would demand, "Wake up, Daddy." When there was no response from the father, the child poked him with repeated admonitions to "Wake up, Daddy!" With still no response, the child would back away slightly, beginning to look fearful. Daddy would then twitch his nose, and the child would laugh with joy and, seemingly, with relief. The lack of movement was frightening to the young child.

The thinking of children who are between 2 through 5 years of age is characterized by their egocentric view of the world and by magical thinking. Their egocentricity also makes them feel all-powerful. This is aptly illustrated by the young child who, watching the moon through the moving car's window, exclaims, "Look, Mommy, the moon is following me." Seeing themselves as the center of the universe, in combination with magical thinking, makes young children particularly vulnerable to feeling responsible for events, including the death of a loved one. Even just wishing, in a moment of jealous frustration, that an ill sibling would "go away" is sufficient cause for young children to feel responsible for the sibling's subsequent death. Or they may perceive naughty behaviors as the cause of a death: Jennifer, now 18, was 3 years old when her sister died of SIDS:

> For several years, I thought my sister's death was my fault. This was because when she was alive I was watching her sleep one day, and I felt mischievous. I plugged up one of her nostrils, and then the other, and she started to cry. Later on, I naturally associated my plugging her nose with her breathing stopping forever a couple of weeks later. That is the only thing I remember now about our relationship when she was alive. (Mandell, Dirks-Smith, & Smith, 1988)

Children of this age perceive that the dead will return; they do not see death as irreversible. This perception is frequently reinforced by cartoons on television where the same characters return to life again and again after disastrous deaths. Preschool children think that the dead are simply living under altered circumstances—they are just living somewhere else. Consequently, young children expect that the dead could come back ... if they really wanted to. When a deceased sibling does not return, the surviving child may wonder what it is that he is doing to prevent his brother or sister from wanting to come back. Moreover, children of this age perceive that the dead remain functional; this explains the child's questions of "How will Mary eat in her coffin?" or "Will there be toys in heaven for the baby to play with?" Children of this age require repeated simple explanations, reassurances, and much physical contact.

Functional Phase—School-Age Children: 6 to 12 Years of Age

Children in this phase are in Piaget's concrete operational phase. During the early years of this phase, children rapidly acquire a specific and concrete understanding of death. Thus by the age of 7, most children will have acquired a concept of death that recognizes all the components of irreversibility, universality, nonfunctionality, and causality (Speece & Brent, 1984).

Younger school-age children (between 6 and 8 years of age) are curious about the world. In addition, they are still often fearful of thunder and lightning, monsters under the bed, and ghosts in the closet. They are beginning to overcome such fears by figuring out how things work, like what makes thunder and lightning and how shadows are created. They begin to ask why things happen rather than what things are. They begin to learn about cause and effect. Death is now seen not as interchangeable with life but as something linked to cause and effect. They sometimes attribute death to monsters, "things that come and take you away," and they find comfort in believing that they can run away from such monsters. They are also learning that old age, and sometimes illness, are causes of death. They usually do not see themselves or other children as dying, because death does not take children, or because children are young, they can run away. Consequently, the death of a sibling can be very frightening for young school-aged children. At this age, children are also very much concerned about rituals surrounding the death, such as funerals and burials. And they see the dead as nonfunctional; that is, the dead don't breathe or eat or move.

Young school-age children's worlds expand increasingly further beyond their own home. They gain more independence and become more involved with their peers. It is a time of venturing out a little more bravely into the world, manifested in games such as "Follow the leader" or "I dare you." They become aware of time as something that stretches out before them, and they become aware of the passage of time. Death is now seen as the end of life, which is a very scary notion for children. With that awareness, they increasingly understand the universal nature of death. They understand that children can die.

As children progress through their early school years, they become much more logical in their thinking. They are intrigued with how things work. They are increasingly interested in the details of death, often asking questions about graveyards, funerals, and decomposition. They understand the seriousness of terminal illness, but death is not yet a personal reality. However, if children themselves are ill, or have been exposed to illness in a sibling, they know only too well that children can die. In these populations, the conception of death seems related to experience with illness and its treatment rather than the child's chronological age or stage of cognitive development. Health care professionals should be reminded to use information about the relationship between age and concept of death only as starting points in the dialogue with individual children who are dying or whose loved one is dying.

Abstract Phase—Adolescents

Children over 12 years of age are in Piaget's formal operations phase of cognitive development. They begin to accept the reality of personal death, at least in a theoretical sense. Young people realize that they can die but do not usually believe it can actually happen to them. Their thinking is consistent with reality and logical; in addition, they are able to speculate on the implications and ramifications of death (Faulkner, 1993).

There is a paucity of research about adolescents' concepts of death, with investigators believing that adolescents fluctuate in their beliefs about death. Adolescents are struggling with developmental tasks pertaining to gaining their independence; they are feeling all-powerful and capable of doing anything that they want. They are very future oriented, so while they can conceive of their death in the future, it is generally difficult for them to appreciate death as a present possibility. They are filled with dreams and hopes and expectations. To realize that death can end all that in one fell swoop may be overwhelming for young people. They sometimes react with reckless behavior to prove, mostly to themselves, that they are as invincible as they feel. Adolescent concerns center around a new awareness of their bodies and of body image. The destructive nature of death is frightening to them as a result. Young people are also keenly aware of their peers and their reliance on peers for companionship and support.

☐ Sibling Responses at the Time of Death

Several factors affect how siblings react to the news that their brother or sister has died, but the children's reactions must always be considered in light of their age, developmental level, and understanding of the concept of death. Siblings may react in a variety of ways—they may be fearful or confused, they may cry or not, they may want to be alone and withdraw physically or emotionally, they may seem to be indifferent, and all usually have questions, although not all may verbalize their questions. Their questions, of course, are strongly related to their capacity to understand death.

Other factors also impact upon the siblings' responses to the news, and they too must be taken into account. One factor that influences their response is whether the death is sudden and unexpected or if the death follows a downhill trajectory of illness. Children who die from cancer or other progressive, life-limiting illnesses usually have undergone a long course of treatment, often over many months or years. As a result, it is often concluded that the family has had time to prepare for the child's eventual death. But even with preparation time, the actual death is often a final surprise. While 10-year-old Carly was at school, her sister, Cassie, aged 15, died quietly from the cancer that had ravished her body during the last year. Upon hearing the sad news, Carly cried, "But I thought she'd wait until I got home from school—I finished the basket I was making for her today!"

All parents of an ill child hope that their child is the one who will recover. Family members struggle to put aside their fears of death. This is not an unrealistic strategy given that dramatic advances in therapeutic techniques in the past few decades have changed the typical course of diseases (e.g., childhood leukemia) from being acute and usually fatal to being chronic and requiring long, complicated treatment. Similarly, siblings tend to revise their appraisals of the sick child's state of health in a positive direction unless they continue to be exposed to negative indicators and reminders (Brett & Davies, 1988). Thus, even when the child's death is imminent, parents and siblings report the actual occurrence as "unexpected." There is always an element of the unexpected in a child's death, even if it is only "We thought that she would make it until Christmas Day," or "We knew the end was near, but we didn't expect him to die this morning," or like Carly, "I wanted to show her what I did in school today." No degree of education or anticipatory grief adequately prepares family members for the reality of death that occurs when all bodily functions cease permanently. Anticipatory grief does not replace the grief that follows the actual death. In this respect, hearing the news about the death can be very traumatic for the siblings, and how they are told can either complicate or facilitate their subsequent course of grieving.

Shock and Indifference

Children may respond to the news of their sibling's death in ways that adults are totally unprepared for. Although predictable patterns characterize the responses of various age groups, all children are individuals and will respond in their own ways. Therefore, adults must be prepared for each sibling to react to the shock differently. Not fully comprehending the meaning of death, the younger child may not show any visible signs of sadness and is just as likely to continue playing or to ask to go to the playroom.

Older children attempt to gain some control by seeking refuge in solitude. These children, struggling with independence and with the embarrassment of expressing strong feelings, may respond to the news by running from the room or escaping to a quiet corner or the outdoors. Such reactions are sometimes difficult for parents and other adults if they do not understand that these are normal responses for children. As adults do, children resort to familiar patterns when they hear bad news or when they are afraid or anxious. To return quickly to the familiarity of playing, or the safety of solitude, is a way of gaining some control over what seems like a very scary, uncontrollable situation. Most importantly, adults must not judge children's immediate responses as "good" or "bad." Adults must not jump to the conclusion that seemingly indifferent children do not care or did not love the ill child enough.

Telling the News to Siblings

Depending on the circumstances, health care workers, chaplains, or other adults may find that they are the ones to give the news of the death to the other siblings or to guide parents in how they might inform the other children about the death. Nurses are often the ones who are present at the time of death and find that they are the ones to tell the siblings. Several guidelines can be helpful in informing children that their brother or sister has died.

First, if it is possible, parents are the best ones to tell the siblings, but sometimes parents are too overcome with their own grief to be able to deal with their other children. At such times, professional caregivers can be most helpful by supporting the parents in this emotional task either by being with parents as they tell their children or by telling the children in the parents' presence. When parents feel as if they cannot deal with their other children at the moment, caregivers can give the news to the children, explaining to them that their parents are very saddened and then reuniting them with their parents as soon as possible: "Your mom and dad are feeling very sad right now. They want to be with you, but they couldn't tell you themselves. Everybody has a different way of reacting to sad news, and that is okay."

When telling children about the death, find a quiet and private place, away from the curiosity of others. Begin with a "warning" of the news that is to come: "I have some sad news for you, Mary" or "You remember that Johnny had difficulty breathing last night?" While conveying the news, sit close to the children, perhaps with a gentle touch, thereby offering reassurance that they are not alone.

Provide the children with a brief but accurate description of what happened. Do not use euphemisms or refer to religious beliefs. Simply say that the child died: "Johnny was sleeping on his bed by the window. Your mother and I had lifted him higher up on the pillows, and we were sitting beside him, when he took one deep breath, and then he died . . . about noon," or "Kathy was driving home from school with her friend, Jane, and there was a bad accident. What we know is that Kathy's head was hit very hard and she died."

Sharing your own feelings with the children is helpful in letting them know that you too are sad and that it is okay to talk about the shock and the sadness: "We all knew that Johnny would not get better, but I still can't believe that he has died. I will miss him very much," or "Kathy went to school today just like any other day. It's so hard to believe what has happened."

Reassure children that their feelings and reactions are okay: "Sometimes we don't know what to do or say, or even how we feel, when we hear this kind of news." Sit quietly with the children, and give them time, if they want, to talk or to just absorb the news. If the children want to return to their play, or to be alone, to cry, or to scream, respect their wishes, knowing that such responses are "normal."

☐ Remember the CHILD[2]

The five letters of the word, child, used as an acronym, serve as a useful reminder of what to keep in mind when talking to siblings about death. These guideposts are useful in helping adults to assist children in coping with the death of any loved person, although they are used in this book to emphasize their utility in helping siblings cope with the death of a brother or sister.

C - Consider

Consider the child's age, developmental level, and capacity to understand thoughts and feelings. Younger children interpret what they are told literally, so explanations must be simple and appropriate. One woman, now 34, still remembers what she, at 4 years of age, was told when her sister died:

> "Well, your sister's gone to the sky, and when you see little stars out there, she's one of them." As soon as she would put me to bed, I would get up and open the curtain and wait and wait until the stars came out. So as soon as I would see the first star, it was, "Oh, there she is. Now I can go to bed." I remember always going to bed with cold feet because the floor wasn't carpeted.

A couple of years later, the child was taken to the cemetery and told the truth about where her sister was buried. She continued, "I would just stand

---

[2]Adapted by permission of Oxford University Press from Davies, B., & Eng, B. (1998). Special issues in bereavement and support. In D. Doyle, G. Hanks, & N. MacDonald (Eds.). *Oxford textbook of palliative medicine* (2nd ed., pp. 1077–1084). Oxford: Oxford University Press.

in front of the gate and stand there and stare at the grave of my sister, just stand there everyday . . . just waiting and waiting and waiting . . . for her to come back." This young girl was mislead with the first story, and then, after learning that her sister was not really a star, she had difficulty in understanding why her sister was not coming back. Sensitive honesty with children is vital to avoiding making a difficult situation even more confusing.

Because of differences in children, adults must realize that no two children in the family will respond in the same way to the death of their sibling. Bobby, age 8, ran from the room when his parents told him of his older brother's sudden death in a car accident, slamming the door behind him. He ran along the gravel road in front of his house, picking up a handful of rocks and throwing them as hard as he could down into the ditches. He returned to the house in an hour, exhausted, confused, and crying. He didn't want to talk about the death or about his feelings or thoughts. Bobby's younger sister, Suzanna, was 4 years old. Upon hearing the news about the death, she got out a box of crayons and drew pictures of the hospital. When asked about her drawings, she said to her mother, "Billy went to the hospital. Can we go to see Billy there?" Two children, two reactions. Child care professionals must consider such variations in siblings' behavior, and must also consider the challenges that parents face in dealing with their children's varying responses.

Child care professionals must be sensitive to their own tone of voice and body language in dealing with parents and children. Consider the effect on children and on grieving parents of ignoring their questions, pretending just not to hear them, and hoping that they will not repeat the questions. Consider the effect of reprimanding or making fun of children for their questions. For example, when a child asks, "Will I die too?" responding impatiently with a sharp tone, "Of course not! Everyone dies sometime but not all at the same time!" reveals primarily the adult's own discomfort. The words themselves are actually helpful ones for a child to hear, . . . but it is the tone of voice and the facial expression that facilitates or hinders the child's understanding of what has happened. The same words spoken gently and directly are reassuring to the child whose question is rooted in feelings of insecurity. The same, of course, applies to how professionals answer parents' questions.

H - Honesty

In talking about the death, advise parents to use the "d" words: death, dead, dying. Recall the earlier example of the child who looked under beds for her "lost" brother. Telling children the truth, as completely as possible, though simply, is critical. Reassure parents that it is all right not to have all the answers—it is better to say, "I don't know," than to try to save face by making up an answer or by berating the child for even asking the question in the first place. Provide simple answers and explanations: "When you die, your heart stops beating; you stop breathing; your body doesn't move, or eat, or sleep anymore." In response to the common question, "Why did my brother have to die?" it's best for parents to reply with a simple, "I don't know, honey. There are some questions that we can't answer, and that makes us very sad and sometimes makes us mad." Advise parents to let children know what has happened to their sibling, as best they can. Preferably, such honesty occurs right from the time of diagnosis if the sibling has a life-limiting illness. Give children factual information about the causes of death. Reassure children that their bodies are healthy (if they are) and that it is very unlikely that they will die also.

I - Involve

Encourage parents to allow the child to participate in family discussions about the death and subsequent events. Give children choices about their preferred degree of involvement in death-related activities, such as helping to choose the casket, planning the funeral, passing cookies at the wake. Encourage children to draw a picture or write their own feelings and thoughts that can be shared at the funeral or wake. More will be said about sibling involvement in later chapters.

L - Listen

Let children tell their parents, or child care professionals, what they do or do not now understand about death. Concentrate on discussing the stumbling block of the moment—too often when the subject is sensitive, adults want to rush ahead to explain and reassure in order to finish the conversation. Rather, let children talk through what is on their mind. Let children know that it is okay not to talk about the death anymore at the moment, if that is what they want. Give children other forms of communication to express their questions and concerns—art, drawing, writing letters, composing poetry or songs, playing, throwing a football, or hitting golfballs on the driving range. Clarify that the child's own thoughts and actions do not cause death. Be attuned to magical thinking in younger, and sometimes even older, children.

D - Do It over and over Again

Remind parents that children can take in only so much information at a time, so that they, or you, may have to repeat or emphasize various aspects of previous discussions over time. As children reach new developmental phases and their concept of death develops, they will have additional questions to ask from the perspective of each new phase. What seems like the "same old questions" may sound the same, but the answers will need to be altered so that they fit with the child's new level of understanding.

Children respond to a sibling's death, each in their own unique way. The challenge for parents and child care professionals alike is to individualize their interactions according to each child's response. The next chapter discusses the various reactions of children to a sibling's death.

Sibling Responses to a Child's Death

The earliest studies of children's reactions to a child's death focused on pathological responses to the death of a sibling. Several classic retrospective studies are frequently cited as evidence that siblings of a child who died are at significant risk of severe psychological problems. Using case studies of families with a terminally ill child, Cobb (1956) was the first to draw attention to the detrimental effects on siblings of being separated from their parents and their reactions to the death. Nearly 10 years later, Cain, Fast, and Erickson (1964) retrospectively reviewed the mental health case records of 58 children, aged 2 1/2 to 14 years, who were undergoing psychiatric treatment and had lost a sibling. The authors reported that a majority of the children's mental symptoms were related to the death. Disturbed reactions included guilt; distorted concepts of illness and death; disturbed attitudes toward physicians, hospitals, and religion; disturbances in cognitive functioning; reactions to the change in family structure; and reactions to death. A few years later, Binger and his colleagues (1969) described sibling reactions in 20 families where a child had died from leukemia. They found that in half the families, one or more previously well siblings evidenced significant behavior problems, including both physical problems (for example, enuresis, headaches, and abdominal pains) and emotional problems (such as poor school performance, school phobia, depression, and anxiety). Binger (1973) concluded that the physical and emotional symptoms were associated with grief and for a number of siblings, were enduring symptoms and distortions in character structure. Other researchers reported similar sibling reactions in families where a child had died from cancer (Kaplan, Grobstein, & Smith,1976; Townes & Wold, 1977; Tietz, McSherry, & Britt, 1977; Payne, Goff, & Paulson, 1980). Siblings in these studies developed academic, psychological, or social problems after the death. In looking at sibling response to the drowning death of a brother or sister, Nixon and Pearn (1977) found that 32% of siblings were significantly affected by the death—sleep disorders and feelings of guilt were common problems.

In contrast, no obvious increase in problems among surviving siblings was reported by other investigators. In their study of 21 families interviewed during the illness of a child with leukemia and after the child's death, Futterman and Hoffman (1973) found that most (18) coped well. Similarly, Stehbens and Lascari (1974) found few adverse reactions in the 64 surviving siblings in 20 families where a child had died 6 months to 3 years before. Seventy percent of these siblings were considered by their parents to be "back to normal" within a week, and the remainder experienced "transient problems" but were "back to normal" within a year. The range of problems reported therefore shows considerable variability and raises questions about whether the behaviors evidenced by grieving siblings represent pathology or typical bereavement response.

Early descriptions (Cain et al., 1964; Binger et al., 1969) of siblings' responses as pathological are not remarkable since the samples for investigation were selected from children already identified as having psychiatric or emotional problems. When the majority of children in other populations of bereaved siblings did not demonstrate the same behavior problems, questions were raised about how bereaved siblings' behavior compared with that of nonbereaved siblings. McCown (1982) and Davies (1983, 1985) were among the first to make such comparisons. They both used a standardized child behavior checklist (CBCL) which allowed a comparison of not only behavior problems but also of behavior competencies. Their results were similar—children who had lost a sibling demonstrated significantly more behavior problems when compared with the standardized norms. The means for behavior problem scores of bereaved siblings were all higher than the standardized mean of 50. Conversely, the sample mean for the total social competence scores was less than the standardized mean. The bereaved siblings had significantly more behavior problems, especially internalizing behaviors (that is, turning inward kinds of behaviors), and less socially competent behavior than the standardized normal population of children (Davies, 1983, 1985, 1988a, 1988b). Birenbaum et al. (1990), using the CBCL to investigate 61 children's responses to the dying and death of a sibling from cancer, reported identical results. The CBCL is sensitive to behavior problems in siblings; bereaved children demonstrate behavior problems. But whether these problems are typical or atypical bereavement responses is not clear.

Bereavement literature indicates that sadness, irritability, feelings of being alone, complaints of bodily discomforts, sleep disorders, and loss of appetite are common to both children and adults. Under seemingly normal circumstances, the presence of such symptoms can be indications of stress in both adults and children. If however, these behaviors are considered to be components of normal grieving responses in children as they are in adults, then their presence in bereaved children is not cause for undue alarm. Rather, they underscore the need for better understanding the needs and reactions of bereaved siblings. This raises the question of whether these behavioral problems in bereaved siblings are in fact indicators of maladjustment.

There is no rigid distinction between problem behaviors and other behaviors. The difference is a matter of degree. Problematic behaviors are essentially exaggerations of, deficiencies in, or a maladaptive combination of behavior patterns common to all children. In contrast to an emotionally disturbed child who suffers from severe and fundamental personality defects, a behaviorally disordered child shows an inability to cope with a current or ongoing situation (Taylor, 1982). When behaviors occur with sufficient frequency and intensity in bereaved siblings to interfere with daily functioning and interacting, they might be considered warning signs that such children should be referred for mental health assessment. Davies (1983, 1985) identified behaviors that were reported for at least 30% of the children in her samples. Twenty-seven behaviors were identified and ranked according to their frequency of occurrence. Of the most frequently occurring behaviors, four were reported for at least half or more of the sample. They included the following: argues a lot, occurring most frequently (for 73.5% of the children); nervous (52.9%); likes to be alone (50%); and unhappy, sad, or depressed (50%). Both Davies (1983, 1985) and Birenbaum (1989) and Birenbaum et al. (1990) found that about 25% of the children demonstrated behaviors with sufficient intensity and duration to be indicative of psychopathology.

Focusing on behavior problems ignores the possibility that sibling bereavement has more than potentially negative outcomes. When interviewed directly, siblings also described positive outcomes as a result of their experience. Their grief, although painful, serves as an impetus for psychological growth. Many surviving siblings perceive themselves as more mature than their peers, as being more sensitive and empathic to the situation of others, and as being better prepared to handle personal distress (Balk, 1983a, 1983b; Davies, 1987a, 1991, 1995a, 1995b; Hogan, 1988a; Hogan & Balk, 1990; Martinson et al., 1987). Enhanced self-concepts were derived from the siblings' perceptions of personal maturity and from the lessons learned about death and life.

Siblings' responses or reactions to the death of a brother or sister do not occur in isolation. Even the earliest studies (Cain et al., 1964) suggested

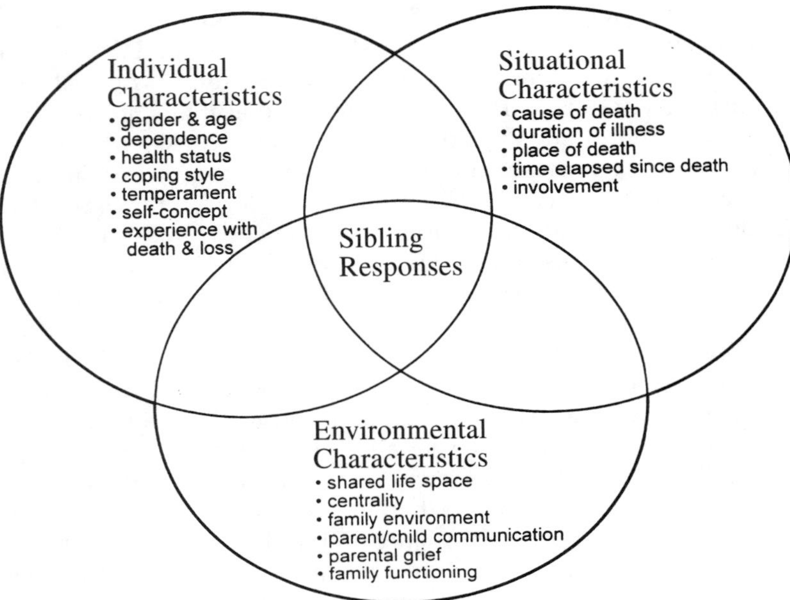

FIGURE 4.1. Conceptualization of the mediating variables that impact the phenomenon of sibling bereavement.

that children's responses were affected by characteristics of the children's environment. In addition to environmental factors, characteristics of the children themselves and of the situation, or circumstances, surrounding the death also impact on sibling responses following the death of a brother or sister. These various factors, conceptualized as individual, situational, and environmental characteristics, interact with one another, coming together to impact on siblings' response to the death of a brother or sister (Figure 4.1). The remainder of this chapter focuses on children's reactions to a sibling's death. The next three chapters focus, in turn, specifically on the individual, situational, and environmental factors that impact on sibling bereavement.

Common Reactions of Grieving Siblings

What follows in this chapter is a discussion of the most common responses of children to the death of a sibling (see Table 4.1), illustrated with direct quotes from siblings who participated in a variety of research projects.

The responses are the expected behaviors of grief. They are not considered "problem" behaviors, in the sense that they indicate maladjustment in

TABLE 4.1. Most frequently occurring behaviors in bereaved siblings

Acting-out behaviors
- Argues a lot
- Shows off
- Disobedient

Sadness and Depression
Crying
Loneliness
Anxiety
Guilt
Psychophysiological Behaviors
- Aches and pains
- Enuresis
- Sleep disturbances
- Eating disturbances

Poor School Work

the child. Referring to siblings' bereavement responses as "problems" emphasizes the behavior as something that must be "fixed." The *Oxford English Dictionary* (1971) defines a problem as a "difficult or puzzling question proposed for solution." To label children's responses as behavior *problems*, therefore, implies that the responses must somehow be resolved, rather than interpreted as normal manifestations of grieving. Children themselves, however, may experience their responses as problematic, and concerned adults, particularly parents, may perceive the children's responses as troublesome.

Rather than assessing children's response to a death by identifying the presence or absence of any of the following behaviors, it is more important to consider the degree of intrusiveness created by the grieving in the child's life (Webb, 1993). Specifically, we must determine the extent to which children can carry on with the normal activities of their lives and proceed with normal developmental tasks. When the grief interferes with children's social, emotional, or physical development, then the resultant behavior may justifiably be considered a problem, or to use Webb's term, the behavior may be considered "disabling."

Some children will not demonstrate any of the following behaviors. As Bowlby, whose work focused on the possible devastating effects of separation and loss in early childhood, cautioned, "Not every child who experiences either permanent or temporary loss grows up to be a disturbed person" (1963, p. 527). The absence of typical behaviors is not necessarily cause for alarm—not all children are affected to the same degree by a sibling's death. Parents, in fact, need to be advised that each child in the family will react differently. Many factors come into play to affect bereaved children's responses. On the other hand, most children avoid distressing feelings and can tolerate discomfort only in small doses. Consequently, children's reactions may not become evident until later, sometimes after a considerable period of time has passed.

Acting-Out Behaviors

> *My grades dropped off.... I remember I had a terrible time finishing things. Then, I started arguing a lot with mom, and I fell into a terrible crowd, and that made it worse.... I got into quite a bit of trouble the year after he died.*
> Luke, now 19, remembering his reaction as a 10-year-old to his brother's death from cancer

Behaviors that could be classified as acting-out behaviors (argues, brags, demands attention, disobedient at home, feels unloved, shows off, stubborn, moody, teases, temper tantrums, and unusually loud) occurred in varying proportions of the bereaved siblings. "Argues a lot" occurred most often (in 73.5% of the children), while the other behaviors occurred in approximately 20 to 40% of the children (Davies 1983, 1988a, 1988b; McCown & Davies, 1995). These behaviors may be interpreted as manifestations of the irritability and anger that are part of normal grieving. Such anger may result from the deceased siblings' absence or from an inability on the part of the surviving child, the parents, or others to bring back the missing sibling. Anger may also stem from the disruption that follows a child's death: "Why did Johnny have to die anyway! If he hadn't died, then things would still be normal around here!" Such anger is particularly common after a death from suicide: "I was so angry at him [brother] for making so many people so sad and for being so selfish and for just being foolish." Anger may also be rooted in the frustration of having so many strong feelings and not knowing what to do with them. As 9-year-old Sally recalled of her younger years, "When my brother died two years ago, I would just get mad lots of times. I don't know what made me mad, but I'd throw my animals and dolls and stuff on the floor." Young children cannot easily put words to these feelings but exhibit more aggressive behavior as a way of expressing them. They may push and shove other children and yell and scream. In a combined sample of bereaved siblings, McCown and Davies (1995) noted the highest incidence of aggressive behavior among bereaved siblings was reported for 4- to 5-year-old boys. They speculated that these aggressive behaviors may have been less motivated by anger than by the desire for attention. Parents, struggling with their own grief, may pay less attention to bereaved children; the children may respond to intrapsychic feelings of loss by seeking attention from their parents through these aggressive behaviors.

Older children are better able to verbalize their distress than are younger ones. Unlike Sally (above) who could verbalize only two years after the death, 13-year-old Barry exclaimed at the time of the death:

> I get so mad sometimes because my brother had to die. Why him? Why? I get really mad when people keep asking me dumb questions about it all, and I try not to let mom and dad see how mad I am. But, sometimes it just all comes out—just the smallest thing will set me off, and I yell and scream and I just want to explode!

Moreover, older siblings have a more mature understanding of death as a final, universal, and personal event and are better able to understand and benefit from cultural rituals associated with death. This mature understanding may contribute to less aggression in some siblings. In other older children and adolescents, acting-out behaviors may manifest as risk-taking behaviors, particularly in boys. Adolescent drivers, for example, normally take more risks than drivers in other age groups. Jonah (1986) suggests that this has to do with a common adolescent perception that taking certain risks serves a useful purpose, such as impressing peers or expressing strong emotions. As 17-year-old Larry described his response to his sister's death, he boasted with a macholike pride, "I drive like I'm crazy, but I never worry about having a car accident or anything."

It is not easy to deal with a child's acting-out behaviors at any time, but is particularly challenging for grieving parents whose personal resources are already at the limit. Acting-out behaviors are often a normal reaction to grief in children, and with time, most often diminish on their own. Encouraging parents to set limits and stick to them is important, although this may be difficult for them to do. Having lost one child, parents are often acutely aware of the value of their surviving children, and they may play out this feeling by relaxing the rules. In the long run, not abiding by the limits does more harm than good because the children end up feeling like mom and dad do not care anymore.

The overly aggressive child can be disruptive to the family and in school, causing parents and teachers great anxiety as they try to cope with outbursts of anger. This behavior may cause discord with adult caregivers and peers, eventually causing the child to become isolated from friends or involved in acts outside the legal limits of the community. Parents have several options. They may permit certain behaviors (such as slamming the door as a way to vent anger), attempt to change the aggressive behaviors (through lecturing, scolding, or punishing the child), tolerate certain behaviors for the time being but not actually accept them (such as irritability or argumentativeness), or use anticipatory planning to avoid situations that elicit the child's aggressive behavior (going home early from an outing, before the child gets overly tired). It may be helpful to allow for controlled release of aggression, such as through sports or by teaching children to modify asocial aggressive acts by substituting more acceptable responses (such as verbal expression of anger instead of hitting). One father put up a basketball hoop on the driveway so that his son could burn off some of his anger by tossing the ball. Acknowledging that it is okay to be angry, but not okay to hit others when you are angry, helps to affirm the child's emotions but limits his or her behavior. Parents need to set consistent limits, to show affection, to reward with expressions of approval for social acts, and to assist in verbalization of frustration and anger. In terms of discipline, "time outs" instead of physical punishment may be best. Advance warning about consequences when parental tolerance limits are about to be breached and immediate discussion of the child's and the parent's perceptions of what happened and what precipitated the incident are also helpful strategies in assisting grieving children with acting-out behavior. Sometimes parents require assistance from child care professionals in dealing with the challenge of living with a child who acts out aggressively.

Sadness and Depression

> *I miss my sister. . . . We were real close. I miss her for the things we did together. Like watching cartoons together on Saturday mornings . . . and I would come down, and do it, but it just wasn't the same. The things that I do . . . that we did together—it's not the same anymore. I try not to think about it . . . but I miss her. It's hard to be happy when I think of her, and because I miss her. I just pretty much keep to myself now.*
> Eleven-year old George, 24 months after his sister's death from cystic fibrosis

Half of the bereaved siblings were sad, unhappy, or depressed (Davies, 1983, 1985, 1988a, 1988b, 1996). Sadness has been described as a normal component of the grieving process; the response has been described in terms of pervasive sadness, a painful dejection, and a painful yearning (Bowlby, 1980; Freud, 1957; Peretz, 1970). Although sadness is a common manifestation of grief, early studies of bereaved siblings did not specifically describe sadness as a behavior problem, with the exception of Binger and his colleagues (1969). They reported depression in bereaved siblings, but their sample was composed of children under psychiatric supervision.

Bowlby (1980) suggests that it is important to distinguish between sadness and depression. Sadness, he says, is a normal and healthy response to any misfortune. Most, if not all, intense episodes of sadness are elicited by the loss, either actual or expected, of some loved person, place, or role. Sad people know who or what they have lost and yearn for the return of what is gone. Despite great sadness, hope is still present; sad people are receptive to support and comfort from others, and their sense of competence and personal worth remains intact. When sadness is accompanied by feeling abandoned, unwanted, and unlovable, pathological depression results.

Adults need to differentiate between normal periods of depressed moods, which are brief and fade away, and depression that persists and tends to get progressively worse. Traditionally, depression was thought to occur only after about age 15; however, health professionals are increasingly recognizing the existence of depression in younger children. Risk factors for depression can be genetic or environmental. Depression is known to occur in families, but it is difficult to separate out the relative influence of genetics from environment. If one parent has a depressive disorder, the risk of depression for the offspring is 27%; with two affected parents, the risk increases to 74% (Aylward, 1985). There is also evidence that children who come from families with a history of alcoholism are at greater risk for depression. Psychosocial factors also play a part in putting a child at risk for depression. Contributing factors include the loss of a loved one, rejection by parents, and low self-esteem (Aylward, 1985).

The signs of depression in young people may take many forms—sometimes children or adolescents will appear withdrawn, will talk freely about feeling sad and lonely, rejected and depressed. Some, overwhelmed by feelings of despair and hopelessness, may express suicidal thoughts. More often, however, depression may take the form of somatic complaints such as changes in eating patterns, changes in sleeping patterns, or changes in productivity such as problems in school. Bereaved children may, in fact, use aggressive behavior to ward off depression, giving rise to masked depression (Lewis & Volkmar, 1990). Sometimes depression manifests as behavioral changes in the form of destructive, aggressive, or acting-out behaviors. These symptoms are the same as those evidenced during grief. It is difficult, therefore, to differentiate children who are depressed from those who are experiencing the "normal" sadness of grief. We return to this differentiation in the last section of this chapter.

Withdrawal and related behaviors were reported for at least one-fifth and for as many as one-half of the children in Davies' (1983, 1985) studies. Feeling unloved was reported for 35.3% of the children; 26.5% felt worthless; and 47% felt self-conscious. These behaviors—sadness, withdrawal, feeling unloved and worthless, and feeling self-conscious—then suggest that many of the bereaved children were not only sad; they were also depressed. Moreover, the frequency of sadness for the bereaved children was more like the frequency of sadness among nonbereaved children who required psychiatric and psychological intervention than like the frequency for nonbereaved children not requiring such services. Sadness then is a normal manifestation of grief among bereaved siblings. However, sadness in combination with other negative feelings about themselves increases the potential for depression in bereaved siblings.

Dealing with sadness in children can be a heart-rending experience. Adults feel helpless when they cannot alleviate a child's sadness. But when adults acknowledge that sadness is a normal response in grief, and when they share their own feelings of sadness, they give children permission to be sad and to share their sadness too. As 10-year-old Susan said when describing her response to a sibling's death, "Sometimes when I'm sad, I talk to my parents and it helps a little bit to be sad together" (Romond, 1990, p. 7). Talking about sadness is not always easy to do, so it may help to encourage children to draw or write instead. Regardless of the medium, expressing sadness provides only temporary relief for the recurring feeling. But not to express it only compounds the feeling. Adults also need to remember that sadness comes in waves—children may be sad for a while, and soon after may be heard laughing and giggling. It is important not to criticize a child for laughing or having what seems like fun during a tragic time—the moment is only transitory.

Crying

> *I don't think I had a dry eye at the wake, and I don't think I had a dry eye all night. All summer, I cried myself to sleep every night.*
> Sixteen-year old Sam, recalling his brother's death from cancer

About one-quarter of the bereaved siblings studied cried "a lot" (Davies, 1983, 1985, 1996). Payne, Goff, and Paulson (1980) described excess weeping as a common behavioral problem of bereaved children. But, in other studies, wide ranges of crying behavior were described. Marris (1958), for example, said that some children cried hysterically for weeks, and others, especially younger ones, did not cry at all following the death of a parent. Kliman (1968), in his work with children whose parent had died, noted that there seems to be a clear tendency for weeping to increase with age. Little information is available about crying behavior in grieving siblings.

Tears are a normal expression of sadness. Bowlby (1980) suggests that crying is a biological response to loss since it serves as a means, either consciously or unconsciously, of attracting and recovering the missing person. As such, it is considered to be a normal component of grief. Tears are thought to fill an important function in the work of grieving, yet some grieving siblings do not feel a need to cry, others inhibit the response because of environmental demands, and others want to cry but cannot.

Tears are a necessary part of the healing process. The enzyme that is released in tears of anger and grief is physiologically and emotionally cleansing. Yet our society generally condemns crying, even by such descriptive terms as "falling apart," "losing it," or "going to pieces." Grieving children are chided for crying: "You're still crying?" or for not crying: "Why don't you cry?" Drawing attention to the child's tears may stifle them, but it is important to acknowledge the feelings behind the tears. "Feeling a little sad?"

or "Missing Johnny?" may be helpful phrases. Some children will pull away from a hug if given too quickly, so it may help to touch the child gently on the shoulder or arm. The child may nod, or respond with a firm "No! Leave me alone!" In either case, it is important to let the child know that it's okay to feel sad, or angry, and to cry. It is equally important to let children know it is acceptable if they cannot cry. Their lack of tears may be of concern to them, as it was for 15-year-old Zelda:

> I couldn't cry when he died—I wished I could. I would see other people crying, and I wanted to cry too. I used to have a dream about not crying at his funeral . . . and that his classmates had a party and they'd invited me, and then they'd start telling me that "You didn't cry at your brother's funeral. You mustn't have loved him."

To encourage dialogue, it helps to sit beside children or to get at their eye level which appears less judging and feels less authoritative than standing in front of or above them. For adults to share their tears and feelings, as appropriate, helps children to learn that such reactions are a normal part of grief. Providing an accepting, safe, compassionate, and private environment can allow this flow of release. It is also important to remember that boys and young men (as well as fathers, uncles, and grandfathers) have the same anatomical tear duct construction as females do, although children themselves have difficulty in seeing men cry. Zelda remembered her brother's funeral:

> I remember seeing an uncle of mine cry. I hadn't seen too many men cry. That was . . . I don't know what it is about men crying. You grow up with, "Boys don't cry." When you do see it then, it's harder than to see a woman cry.

It also helps to recognize that laughter can release defenses against crying; consequently, laughter may easily turn to tears, sometimes to the surprise of children themselves:

> And then my cousin came to hug me. She was just over a year older than me—I was thirteen—and we hadn't seen each other for a long time, and when she went to hug me, we snapped heads and, of course, we both cracked up and started to laugh, and then we started to cry even worse, and then we didn't know what to do.

Children, and particularly adolescents, who cry easily may be embarrassed over this "weakness." Cultural mores forbidding or discouraging crying are difficult to overcome, but it is not impossible if a supportive and sensitive environment is provided.

The crying behavior of children seems closely related to their individual coping styles and to the general attitude toward crying in their families. In some families, crying was recognized as a normal and inevitable response to sadness and was tolerated and even encouraged. Parents who cried easily worried about their children who did not seem to cry as much. In one family, for example, everyone cried a lot, but the tears were not perceived as problematic. Relationships among family members were particularly close; warmth characterized their interactions with one another and with me during the interview. The father stated,

> We have all cried so much, and what is wrong with that? We have had a lot to cry about, and it is so much better to release the tension by letting the tears flow than to keep them inside. But, we do have a rule about crying in our family: You can cry as much as you need to, but you cannot cry alone.

Family members agreed that tears were an expected part of grieving; moreover, they believed that tears were better shared—a hug or a listening ear from another family member would not erase the sadness, but the experience would not be quite so lonely.

In a second family, an opposite view prevailed. Upon arriving home from his son's funeral, the father declared to his tearful family that, "There will be no more tears now—there has been enough crying today to last forever. We have to be brave and get on with our lives." Consequently, the children did not share their tears with each other or with their parents. The parents reported that the children did not cry. The children confided that they did cry—silently in the quiet of their beds at night, afraid that their father might hear them. One daughter said that she did not cry: "I can't cry even though I sometimes really want to. I see people on TV crying, and I wish that I could cry like that too." Interestingly, the mother confided that she cried "buckets" but only when she was alone in the house. The expression of sadness through tears in this household was not well tolerated, and so tears were either blocked or hidden.

Loneliness

> *The worst thing is being lonely . . . you know how other people have brothers and sisters . . . just I don't have one now. You know, Christmas morning . . . being the only child . . . it's really lonely.*
>
> Laura, now 13, who was 4-years-old when her only sister died

There is no doubt that grief is lonely. For surviving siblings who had spent a lot of enjoyable time with their brother or sister, the loneliness is profound. Forty-four percent of the children were reported as being lonely, and loneliness was a frequent topic of discussion during the interviews (Davies, 1983, 1985, 1996; Davies & Kalischuk, 1997). It occurred particularly among those children who had shared a close relationship with their sibling before his/her death. David provides the following example.

David was the surviving twin after his brother died. The two brothers had shared nearly every moment of their lives and loved each other's company. As twins often do, they had developed their own special ways of communicating and interacting. No one could match the running skills of these two boys. They had combined their secret communication skills with their running abilities to devise a way to chase and catch lizards in the desert where they lived. They would spend hours out in the sun enacting an elaborate ritual of cornering, catching, and then releasing the lizards. After his brother died, David was extremely lonely—he missed his brother in every aspect of his life and summed it up with the few disconsolate words: "No one can run fast enough. I have no one to catch lizards with anymore." Loneliness is acute for sole surviving siblings, but even children with other surviving siblings were also lonely, particularly if the deceased child was the one with whom they shared a close relationship.

In the same way that parents know that no other child can ever take the place of the one who died, so too do siblings know that no other child can take their brother's or sister's place. Some parents think that having another child, or adopting one, or taking in a foster child, will allay their surviving child's loneliness. This is not the case. In fact, as discussed in Chapter 7, adding another child to the family often makes the surviving children feel displaced, thereby compounding their grief.

Encouraging children to play with their friends or to make new friends helps to some degree, at least for short periods of time. Parents must guard against using the children to help allay their own loneliness, at the children's expense. Although parents may not wish to socialize much, they should not assume that their surviving children also want to remain quietly in the house. Children cannot grieve 24 hours a day, and require some normal activity in their lives in order to adapt to their loss.

Anxiety

> *I used to think it [cancer] was contagious and then when I was sick, I'd ask if I was going to die. I was really scared that everyone in the family might get it too.*
> Fifteen-year-old Sarah, remembering her reactions as a 7-year-old to her brother's death from leukemia

Fears are common to every child's experience. Children are afraid of different things at various developmental levels, including the dark, imaginary creatures, certain animals, and natural events such as storms and tornadoes (Prugh, 1985). Most of these developmental fears are transitory and do not interfere with the child's daily functioning, but such fears may be magnified in grieving children. Over half of the children exhibited nervousness and 41% were worried (Davies, 1983, 1985). One-fifth were "too fearful or anxious," as was 6-year-old Mary. Her mother said, "There were some dogs that she had to pass on her way to school. She didn't like these and was frightened of them, and she frequently said she was scared and wanted to stay home with me. At school, she tended to be one who clung to the walls or stayed on the outside." Other children were anxious because they missed the companionship of their deceased sibling. Joanie, for example, "had a difficult time doing things for the first time. Like when she started school and had to go on the school bus, she would make comments like, 'I wish Jimmy were here to go with me.' "

Anxiety is often a manifestation of feeling insecure. The loss changes the child's world so that new behaviors are required. They may become more clinging and reluctant to leave mom's side; their usual fears may be overpowering. They are afraid of being left alone, of illness, of dying too. As 8-year-old Molly said, "I get so scared in the night.... Sometimes I dream that mom and dad have died too, and I am all alone when I wake up in the morning."

When children are anxious, they should not be forced to do whatever is making them anxious. They need to be assisted in stages to overcome their fears. We return to 6-year-old Mary and her fear of big dogs. On her way to school, Mary had to pass by a house with two German shepherds in the yard. The dogs were tied up behind a fence, but Mary was still timid. After her sister died, Mary's fears were more pronounced and she refused to return to school after her sister's funeral. Mary's mother let her stay home for three days, thinking that it was best not to force Mary to return too quickly. For the next four school days, Mary's grandfather walked with her to school, each day talking to the dogs as they passed their house. Then, for another two days, her grandfather accompanied Mary only as far as the dogs' house, waiting until she had passed by their yard and reminding her to say hello to the dogs as she walked by. The next day, Mary went on her own. Mary's grandfather didn't make fun of Mary's fear; he understood that she needed reassurance and time to overcome it. Above all, he didn't get angry with Mary for her anxieties—"Oh, you are such a baby!" or "Come on, that's enough.... You know those dogs won't hurt you and you have to go to school—NOW!" Such comments only serve to ridicule children's fears, destroy their confidence, and reinforce their anxieties.

Guilt

I sometimes wish we hadn't argued so much . . . that I had told him that I liked having him for a brother. But brothers argue . . . that's normal . . . isn't it?

Twelve-year-old Bobby, 18 months following his brother's death from a car accident

Since competitive and hostile feelings among siblings are common, varying degrees of guilt may be expected in the surviving children following a sibling's death. Surprisingly, I found few parents reported that their children experienced guilt. This finding contrasts with earlier studies where over half of the children were reported to feel very guilty (Cain et al., 1964; Binger et al., 1969). These researchers, however, were focusing on children who were under psychiatric supervision and so their reactions may have been more profound in order to require that form of supervision. Guilt usually results from the assumption of responsibility for the death. For example, Nixon and Pearn (1977) found a high degree of guilt in their subjects following the accidental death of a sibling.

Although parents might not report "guilt" as a common behavior in their grieving children, this finding does not necessarily mean that guilt was absent. Since guilt is an emotion not always expressed in directly observable behaviors, it may be that parents have difficulty in assessing this response accurately. However, when the bereaved siblings were asked directly about their sense of guilt, few acknowledged that this was a feeling they had. Most of them took some time to ponder the question and then replied thoughtfully, "Nooo, I don't really feel guilty because I couldn't stop the cancer" (Davies, 1983, 1985, 1996; Davies & Kalischuk, 1997). Fourteen-year-old Garry commented,

> People think that all the time. I can tell from how they ask me questions. But I don't feel guilty. My brother, for some reason, decided to kill himself. That wasn't my fault and I couldn't stop him. I miss him, and I wish he hadn't done it. I wish we could've done something, but we couldn't.

Such siblings recognized the dangers and the potential of feeling guilty for the death but also seemed able to separate out their own behavior from the situation that caused the child's death. When children cannot do this, and instead assume responsibility for the death, then guilt is a more common response. On the other hand, it was years later that some siblings realized they had felt guilty at the time of the death (Davies, 1996). Children may not be able to identify, or admit, to harboring guilty feelings at the time.

Guilt in children, as Wiener (1970) describes, may be expressed in other types of behavior such as nightmares, depressive symptoms, or aggressive behaviors. It may be possible that siblings' sleep disorders and sadness may be the result of unexpressed guilt, but this seems unlikely in "normal" cases. Children, like adults, may not always be clear about their own feelings of guilt or the reasons for their behavior. The possibility exists that some children do feel guilty at some level but are unaware of those feelings as the source of their discomfort or their behavior. Yet some children were able to state that they did feel guilty. For such siblings, the guilt was usually over words said in anger or over some action occurring before the child died. Even then, the feeling was more of regret than of guilt, wishing that they had not said or done what they did. For example, Mark's brother died in a car accident on the way home from a dance. Mark had wanted to use the family car that same night, and had been annoyed that his brother was using it. The two brothers had argued over the use of the car. Mark said,

> I feel really bad that we argued that night. The last conversation I had with him was about the dumb car. . . . I feel really bad about that. I wish I could just have a chance to say something else to him, instead of what I said. He will never know how sorry I am.

When asked if he had any feelings of guilt, he replied,

> No, I don't feel guilty—I couldn't stop him from dying, but I wish we hadn't argued, or at least I wish I would have won the argument and then he wouldn't have been driving that night. Is that guilt? I don't know. . . . It doesn't feel like it to me.

It is important to reaffirm for siblings, particularly younger ones, that their thoughts or behaviors were not responsible for the child's death. Children may not verbalize their fears, so it may be important for parents to say something like, "I know that, sometimes, children feel like something they said or did caused their brother's or sister's death. We all feel like this sometimes . . . remembering something we said and wished we hadn't. I want you to know that any thoughts any of us had didn't kill Johnny. And if you ever have any questions about that, I want you to ask me." The child may not overtly acknowledge the comment but nevertheless will have heard the reassurance. As 7-year-old Marcus described, "I took the baby's blanket . . . and he died. But, my mom told me that we couldn't have made the baby die. . . . I was scared that the baby got too cold and died because I had the blanket."

In cases where children were in some way responsible for the death, interactions can be very difficult. Not only do the children feel responsibility for the death, they feel very alone, assuming that their actions now mean that they have not only lost their sibling but also their parents' love. There is no doubt that it is difficult sometimes for parents to acknowledge any love for the surviving children—they are angry with what has happened and rightly so. But at the same time they need to remember that their surviving children need their love more than ever. It is not easy for parents to manage their own grief and still respond to their other children in optimal ways. Yet that is what must happen for the benefit of the other children if parents want to avoid the double losses that Sam Jones experienced. His two teenage sons were out sailing together when their boat capsized in a sudden storm. Peter drowned, and Adam survived. Three years later, Mr. Jones lamented:

> I lost both sons that day, but I didn't know it at the time. Adam blamed himself for his brother's death, and I let him know that I did too. It took longer to lose Adam. Peter's death was a sudden loss, but with Adam, my anger slowly pushed him further and further away. He's had trouble in school; he's a real loner—but he didn't use to be, not before his brother died.

In such cases where the sibling was involved in the child's death, issues of forgiveness eventually rise to the surface. Families usually benefit from professional assistance in learning how to forgive one another.

Psychophysiological Responses

> *I always had a stomach ache after she died. I couldn't figure out why—I wasn't hungry either and that was a worry for my mom who knew teenagers were ravenous. The stomach aches lasted all summer.*
> Lana, now 18, recalls her reactions as a 15-year old to her sister's death from cancer

> *I would dream about it for ages. . . . I still do sometimes. Mostly, I had this bad dream where he was in a bird cage, and I couldn't get him out.*
> Kelli, age 9, 6 months after her brother's death following heart surgery

Complaints of bodily discomforts, sleep disorders, and loss of appetite are common to both children and adults during bereavement. Under seemingly normal circumstances, the presence of such symptoms can be an indication of stress in both adults and children. In children, such symptoms are often thought to be indicators of major problems. If, however, these responses are considered to be components of normal grieving in children as they are in adults, then their presence in bereaved children is not cause for undue alarm. As with adults, what would be significant is the intensity and duration of the response and the presence or absence of other behavior problems.

Aches and Pains

Approximately one-fourth of the children in the samples studied (Davies, 1983, 1985, 1996) complained of psychophysiological responses in the form of headaches, generalized aches and pains, and stomach aches and cramps. Such complaints can be found in nonbereaved children as well. For example, recurrent abdominal pain is a fairly frequent problem in school-age children. Approximately 1 out of 9 children will have at least 3 attacks of abdominal pain over a period of 3 months (Bain, 1974), and an organic cause can be found in 10% or fewer children (Leebman, 1978; Versano, Zeidel, & Matoth, 1977). Abdominal pain in children has been found to be related to socioemotional factors which may play a role in grief situations as well. In 32% of the children in Leebman's work (1978), abdominal pain was related to perfectionism and high expectations; Versano et al., (1977) found that almost 50% of children with abdominal pain had marked dependency needs. In my studies, "needs to be perfect" was a behavior reported for 35.3% of the children; "too dependent" was reported for 23.5% of the children. It may be that the occurrence of these behaviors partially explains the occurrence of abdominal pain in bereaved children. Leebman also found that marital turmoil, parental oversubmissiveness, or excessive punishment patterns existed in many of the families of children with recurrent abdominal pain. Therefore, patterns of family dynamics may also need to be taken into account when bereaved children complain of abdominal pain.

On the other hand, children's complaints of aches and pains may be a manifestation of normal grief behaviors. Complaints of physical distress are commonly reported by grieving adults. Such complaints were frequent among widows in studies of adult bereavement (for example, Parkes, 1972; Parkes & Brown, 1972). Headaches, tension, and fatigue are common, as are feelings of emptiness in the stomach and sensations of lumps in the throat. Adults will often talk about epigastric distress as a "hollow feeling" or "feeling empty in the pit of my stomach." Perhaps children experience these same sensations but describe them differently—as stomach aches or cramps.

Grieving siblings may also complain of physical symptoms that are similar to the cause of death in the deceased child. Twelve-year-old Martha, for example, complained frequently of an ache in her right arm after her brother's death from cancer, which originated as osteogenic sarcoma in the right upper arm. The appearance of symptoms in another child is usually cause for great concern among parents whose first thought is, "No! It cannot be happening again!" Memories of the first child's illness are rekindled and fanned by fear. It is easy, therefore, for parents to overreact to the child's symptoms and become overprotective in their concern. However, parents should not overlook such symptoms or too easily dismiss them. Without proper attention to their symptoms, children feel as if their concerns don't matter—they feel dismissed. Adults must remember that it is common for any grieving person to have symptoms similar to the cause of death in a loved one. Therefore, children's symptoms should be assessed as part of their total response to grief and not be isolated as a particular symptom.

Listen to what children are saying, and encourage parents to do the same. Acknowledging children's complaints reassures them that they have been heard. A distracted "Umm hmm" does not give children the reassurance they need. Instead, repeat what the child has said, "Your tummy hurts?" Wait for a response, and take it as a cue for your next response. It helps if parents let the child know that they have had similar sensations, especially when they are missing the child who has died. This acknowledges children's physical discomfort, lets them know that they are not alone in having this response, and gives them a clue about what might be causing the discomfort. If the aches and pains persist, it may be helpful for parents to take the child to their family physician or local clinic for a checkup just to rule out any physical cause and to ease the parent's concern.

Enuresis

Enuresis is defined as the involuntary passage of urine by a child over the age of 3 years (Parker & Whitehead, 1982). It can occur during the day or night. Four per cent of all children between the ages of 6 and 12 years have enuresis. For children between 13 and 17 years, the prevalence is much less (Gross & Dornbusch, 1983). Enuresis has been described by some as a common problem among bereaved children (Binger et al., 1969). However, it is reported primarily when study participants are preschool children. When young children experience stress, it is common for them to revert back to behaviors characteristic of an earlier developmental phase. Most often, enuresis is caused by developmental or maturational delay in the child, and spontaneously disappears in many children as they get older. Keeping this fact in mind assists adults in coping with the problem, knowing that it will diminish with time. When enuresis occurs, it should be handled matter-of-factly, without berating the child. It helps to reassure him that it will be better as he gets older.

Sleeping Difficulties

Close to one-third of the bereaved siblings (Davies, 1983, 1985, 1995b, 1996; Davies & Kalischuk, 1997) were reported to have sleep disorders, including trouble sleeping, nightmares, or walking/talking in their sleep. About one-fifth were reported as being overtired. Other researchers have also reported sleep disturbances in their bereaved child subjects (Nixon & Pearn, 1977; Payne et al., 1980; Stehbens & Lascari, 1974).

Although frequently not wanting to go to bed, children usually fall asleep quickly once in bed. Dreams are not usually frightening, but recurrent nightmares may signal distress. Older children and adolescents have the ability to describe their dreams. Several recalled dreaming that their deceased sibling needed help in "getting out" of somewhere, as did Kelli whose words were quoted at the beginning of this section. Ten-year-old Luci had nightmares about her deceased sister: "We'd be in the house that she died in ... the room she was in ... and the nightmare is that ... she was yelling at me to let her out." Insomnia is rare in children and, if present, signals a problem (Wieczorek & Natadoff, 1981). Difficulties with sleeping and feelings of exhaustion are nearly universal in adults who are grieving and might, therefore, be expected manifestations of grief in children as well.

A child's resistance to sleep may be exasperating for all parents, even when they are not having to deal with grief. It is helpful to point out to parents that many of the normal fears of childhood are encountered at bedtime. Children's fears of separation, of the dark, and of noises all happen in relation to going to bed. Adults must recognize that children's fears are real and should not be ridiculed, and that most fears can be dispelled with help and patience from parents. Even for older children and adolescents, going to bed can be the most troublesome time during grief. As one 13-year-old described, "I was afraid to go to sleep after my sister died. I was afraid I wouldn't wake up. I didn't really understand that I was a healthy person and if I went to sleep, that didn't mean I wasn't going to wake up."

There are several techniques that might help children of all ages who are having difficulty sleeping. A routine bedtime schedule is probably the most important. If younger children are afraid of the dark, leave a night light on. It is better to take children's fears into account rather than forcing them to "learn to live with it" by making them go to sleep in a dark room. Refraining from stimulating play or activity before bedtime also helps; quiet, relaxing activities such as story telling, listening to gentle music, and quiet conversation are much more conducive to helping children get to sleep. This is especially true for toddlers whose incessant activity and curiosity leave them irritable, overtired, and highly stimulated if some effort is not made to provide a quiet period before bedtime.

Grieving children may have additional concerns that reinforce their normal fears at bedtime, and it is important to get at the root of these concerns. For some children who shared a room, or even a bed, with their now deceased sibling, it may be comforting to continue to sleep in the same room or bed. For others, it may be very disturbing. It is advisable to ask children what they prefer and to engage them in the process of resolving their discomfort, as did Mr. Smith with his son, Peter.

The Smith family lived in a tiny house, and 8-year-old Peter had always shared a room with his older brother, Bill. After Bill died, Peter felt very much alone in the room. Mr. Smith sensed the difficulty his son was having but felt at a loss for what to do since the house only had two bedrooms, a living room, and a kitchen. There was no space to create another bedroom for Peter. Mr. Smith acknowledged his dilemma, and Peter said, "I don't need another room, Dad—let's just get rid of the beds." Mr. Smith explained that they couldn't immediately afford a new bed for Peter. "I know that," responded Peter, "so let's just put both mattresses on top of one another until we can get a new bed." The bed frames were removed, the "mattress bed" created, and Peter soon returned to his regular sleeping patterns. In another family, Jon who was 11 when his brother died, remembered a similar experience: "We shared a room ... bunk beds. I didn't sleep in that room for quite a while. I slept on the floor in mom and dad's room . I think it was even until they ... moved the bunkbed out ... that I even slept in my room ... maybe a month."

Calming music or a warm drink before bedtime is also sometimes conducive to helping children sleep. Sleeping with mementos of the loved sibling may also help. One 16-year-old girl adopted her sister's teddy bears after her sister died and clung closely to one of them every night. For other children, having such a memento has the opposite effect, so children's individual preferences must be considered. Listening to relaxing tapes is often helpful for older children and adolescents who, in their search for independence, enjoy this kind of activity that remains within their own control. Setting too firm limits is not usually helpful for children who are having difficulty sleeping after the death of a sibling. As one young teenage girl described,

> I had trouble sleeping, so I slept with my mom for a long time. And then she said, "This has got to stop." It had only been a couple of weeks, and she said, "You have to learn to live with this. You have to sleep in your own bed." And the warmth and compassion was turned off just like that. And so I'd stay up until four o'clock in the morning reading in my room. I was going to school on three hours sleep off and on for six months.

It would have been much more preferable in helping this girl if her mother had discussed sleeping difficulties with her daughter and found some mutual solution.

Eating Difficulties

Nearly one-quarter of bereaved siblings in my studies were not eating well. Eating disturbances also are described as normal grief responses for adults who experience loss of appetite and loss of interest in food. The child's age must be considered when assessing the grieving sibling's difficulty with eating. The slowed physical growth of toddlers and preschoolers, for example, decreases their requirement for food and is reflected in a pattern of fluctuation in the amount and type of food they eat. Children of this age are often more interested in playing with their food to discover how it feels, tastes, and splashes, than with eating seriously. When grieving, children of this age may not only seem to lack interest in eating but also show more or less interest in playing with their food.

Children's appetites vary according to periods of growth. Children tend to grow in spurts and have healthy appetites during these times. Children between the ages of 6 and 16 years are growing rapidly and require sufficient nutritional intake. Healthy appetites are the norm for these children, and poor appetites can be an indication of distress. School-age children often become too busy or involved to eat properly. It is normal for any child to want more food on some days than on others (this occurs in adults too), but some adults tend to think that children should always eat a specific amount of food each day.

In addition to a decreased appetite occurring as a normal aspect of grief, siblings' eating difficulties are sometimes related to the special diet, or lack of appetite, that an ill sibling had before he died. Sometimes the deceased child's favorite foods or fun foods trigger memories of that child and either stimulate or depress the sibling's appetite. For two weeks after his brother died, Martin refused to eat any of the food his grandmother prepared for the family's evening meals—all he wanted was pizza. Pizza was the only food his brother craved during the last weeks of his life.

There are several ways to encourage children who are having difficulty eating. It helps to have a schedule for eating meals at regular times, ensuring that children do not have to eat alone. It also helps to prepare food in attractive ways, to provide children's favorite foods in small amounts at frequent intervals, or to plan diversions at mealtimes, such as inviting guests to dinner or watching television. The latter, however, needs to be monitored because a consistent pattern of watching television while eating inhibits children's ability to pay attention to their food which, in turn, can contribute to overeating. Serving small portions with seconds allowed, or permitting children to serve themselves, is preferable to serving more food than the child can eat.

Preparing meals, let alone adding extra touches that make the food attractive, and paying attention to the individual likes and dislikes of each child can be exhausting for grieving parents, who are sometimes overwrought with just having to shop for groceries. Some siblings find it helpful to assist their parents with meal preparation or to take turns in making the main meal each day. This works well for older children and has the added benefit of giving them some real responsibility for family functioning with the result that they feel very much a part of the family's experience and healing. The same results can be achieved for younger children who can help out by setting the table or helping to clear it.

Some grieving children have difficulty with weight gain or loss. Eating can range from being a distasteful duty one does to survive to being a frantic effort to fill an empty void. For children to lose or gain excessive weight adds to their problems by affecting body image in negative ways. Parents must guard against fast food and junk food which are easy to prepare—a blessing for parents whose energy levels are low. But their high caloric, salt, and fat content makes them less than ideal as a regular diet. Parents can overreact to their surviving children's eating problems, perhaps because such behavior reminds them of previous challenges with the deceased child if he or she was ill prior to death or perhaps because parents feel guilty when their surviving children will not eat. Parents who have lost a child often go through a period of time when they feel inadequate as parents: "If I had been a good parent, or a better parent, my child wouldn't have died. I should have been able to somehow protect my child." To have other children not eating meals that are prepared becomes further "proof" that the parent is inadequate: "Why can't I get this child to eat!" Such parents can benefit from support for their own grieving, with information about normal eating patterns in children and reassurance for their own parenting skills.

School Performance

> *My grades dropped off. . . . I remember I had a terrible time with not finishing things. I'd . . . I wouldn't even write my name on the sheet, you know. I wouldn't take it home. It'd lay in my locker and the next day when it was due, I'd say, 'Well, I forgot it.'*
> Lyle, now 17, remembering his reaction as an 11-year-old to his brother's death from cancer

School performance, along with the child's social interactions, such as involvement with friends and participation in activities and hobbies, compose behavioral competencies. The majority of bereaved siblings studied (Davies, 1983, 1985; Davies & Kalischuk, 1997) were doing well in school and actively participated in school, sports, and extracurricular activities. Some children (about 15%) had lower scores on the social scale, but not all of these children seemed to be having difficulties. However, when children scored low on the social scale in combination with school problems, then this was an indication that children were having difficulty coping.

A decline in school work was reported for one-quarter of the children (Davies, 1983, 1985, 1996; Davies & Kalischuk, 1997). Poor school work has been widely reported in other studies of sibling bereavement (Binger et al., 1969; Binger, 1973; Cain et al., 1964; Kaplan et al., 1976; Stehbens & Lascari, 1974; Tietz et al., 1977; Townes & Wold, 1977). In a study of bereaved children following the death of a parent (Van Eerdewegh, Clayton, & Van Eerdewegh, 1985), one particular symptom drew the researchers' specific attention: the widespread drop in school performance in all categories of bereaved children. Potentially, lowered performance may lead to rejection of school, underachievement, and school dropout.

Some bereaved children showed an opposite response—they became nearly obsessed with school work, showing a reaction of overachievement. Adults tended to see these children as good copers, with less of a problem responding to the loss. Their excellent academic records were praised by parents and teachers alike and valued by the children themselves. Consequently, their behavior was positively reinforced, sometimes to the neglect of their grief. As adults looking back, they were able to describe the pain of their grief and their feeling that the only refuge they had was to work hard in school. They did not regret their achievement; they only wished someone had recognized that their focus on school work was, in reality, an escape from their pain.

Problems in school are an indication of adjustment problems in children (Achenbach & Edelbrock, 1981) and probably serve as a good barometer of inner turmoil with the child and family unit. School-related difficulties, therefore, are a critical variable in identifying children who are having difficulty adjusting to their sibling's death.

Problems with school work may be related to an inability to concentrate, a problem reported for 44% of the children (Davies, 1983, 1985, 1996). They could not sit for any length of time, either in the classroom or while doing their homework. They sometimes forgot more easily and got directions confused. It is helpful to advise parents and teachers alike to give children simple and clear directions and to expect that repetitions may be necessary. Having a memo board in the kitchen where all family members record messages and reminders facilitates retention. It is also a good place to record schedules: "Tuesday—Mom at the dentist after work." This not only helps mom remember her dental appointment but helps the other family members recall why mom is not home at her usual time and allays unnecessary anxiety.

Posting "things-to-do" lists for all family members also helps siblings keep track of what needs to be done and by whom. It has the added advantage of relieving parents of constantly reminding their children about what needs to be done. When jobs are completed, it is always important to acknowledge the child's success and contribution.

Difficulties in concentrating can seriously affect a child's school performance. First, it is critical for parents to inform the staff at the child's school about what has happened. At the very least, the principal and the child's primary teacher should know about the death, as well as the guidance counselor, if there is one at the school. Being informed increases the likelihood that school personnel will be able to respond sensitively to the child.

In some situations, parents and teachers may disagree about the best time for siblings to return to school following the death. There is no right time that is best for every child. Some children feel uncomfortable staying home at all, as described by 13-year-old Jan:

> I stayed with my sister-in-law at their apartment while my dad and my brother came into town to make the funeral arrangements, and it was so weird. I was lying in the pool thinking that I had a holiday from school because my sister died. It was just so bizarre that I could take a day off from school. It just seemed like the opposite of what I should be doing.

Fourteen-year-old Marla went to school in the afternoon on the day her brother died—"I wanted to be with my friends; I wanted to feel normal." Six-year-old Mary, however, stayed home for three days before returning to school. Other siblings have stayed home for a week, or even two, before they feel ready to return. The longer siblings stay away from school, however, the harder it is to return. Siblings themselves indicated that a week "was about the most time" to stay away from school. Sometimes children need encouragement to return to school, and sometimes even a firm approach from parents is necessary to engage children again in the activities of daily living.

Alcohol and Drug Problems

> *After his death, I started using more drugs than I did before. I didn't really get into the hard drugs . . . but marijuana and speed and stuff like that.*
>
> Ray, now 25, recalling his reaction as a 16-year-old to his brother's death from cancer

Drug and alcohol abuse refers to the inappropriate use of alcohol or drugs. Substance abuse is primarily a problem of adolescents. Young people may abuse psychoactive substances for many reasons. These substances may provide "false courage" in threatening social situations or "make the world seem more bearable" when social anxiety causes withdrawal from peer interactions. Such patterns may be emphasized when young people are grieving.

Problems relating to drug and alcohol use are not often reported or found to be a problem in the literature on childhood bereavement. In my earliest work (Davies, 1983), problems related to alcohol and drugs were reported for only two children. In one of these cases, the problem was discussed during the interview, and the parents explained that the child had been falsely accused at school of being involved in a drug-related incident. Only Martinson (1980) referred explicitly to drug use being a problem for grieving children but for only one child. Bowlby (1980) noted that alcoholism became a problem for grieving adults only in cases where it had been a problem before the death; he indicated that it is a manifestation of disordered grieving. This was the case for Ray (quoted at the beginning of this section), who had been experimenting with drug use before his brother died. With drug and alcohol use among young people increasing generally in our society, it may occur with increasing frequency among bereaved children in the future.

Child care professionals who suspect alcohol or drug abuse should encourage the child or the parents to get professional help. Encourage the family not to buy alcohol and to use caution with medications. This is especially important if there is a history (family or individual) of alcohol or drug use.

For older children who are on prescribed medication, it is important to be aware of who is prescribing medication for the child. Is there more than one prescriber? How much medication is prescribed? Can the prescriptions be readily renewed? Is the child following the prescribed dosage? Is the child combining the medication with other medications or alcohol? Has this young person had problems with drugs or alcohol in the past?

The messages adults give to children are also significant in setting patterns for their own coping behaviors. Parents who drink or take medications to ease their own suffering teach children that these are acceptable ways of coping. There are times when medication is appropriate, but inappropriate use of medication gives messages of "Don't grieve. . . . You don't need to grieve. . . . Don't bother me with your pain. . . . Take this and everything will be all right."

☐ Identifying Children in Trouble

Finding that bereaved children exhibit behavior problems is not surprising. To find no changes in their behavior would be to deny the significance of the event and the resultant impact on the children after losing someone who was an integral part of their lives. The question that is often asked however is, "How do I know if the child's behavior is part of the normal grief response or if the child's behavior is a sign of trouble and he should be referred for counseling?" This is a difficult question to answer, because there is no clear-cut way to identify those children who are in need of mental health services. The challenge is compounded when we realize that the expression of grief can take many forms (Wolfelt, 1983, 1996; Rando, 1991) with varying duration.

Few of the early studies of sibling bereavement determined to what extent the problems described for the children were related to normal or complicated bereavement. In one study (Cain et al., 1964), for example, the sample was drawn from a population of children who were all under psychiatric supervision; in another (Binger et al., 1969), 50% of the families had at least one member who needed psychiatric help. In contrast, in a study of families who had home care for their dying children (Martinson et al., 1978), only one of 32 families had a member who received psychiatric help after the child's death.

I attempted to differentiate normal from complicated grieving responses among the bereaved siblings in my earlier studies (Davies, 1983, 1985). Total behavior problem scores and the percentages of occurrence for behavior problems of the children studied were compared with those of referred and nonreferred children (Achenbach & Edelbrock, 1981). Referred children were those under the care of child mental health professionals; nonreferred children were not receiving such care. Nearly one-quarter of the bereaved children had total behavior problem scores high enough (equal to or greater than the 90th percentile) to be more like children referred to mental health clinics than like children who had not required referral to mental health professionals. In the general population, only 10% of children have such high scores.

Five behaviors occurred with sufficient frequency among bereaved children to be indicative of possible psychopathology: "argues a lot"; "lonely"; "nervous"; "unhappy, sad, or depressed"; and "worrying." An additional four behaviors, although occurring with frequencies that overlapped those for both referred and nonreferred children, occurred with frequencies closer to those for referred children. These behaviors were "likes to be alone," "nightmares," "secretive," and "shy and timid." Taking these nine behaviors as a group, all but one (argues a lot) were internalizing behaviors, reflecting a turning inward, an inhibition of activity and expression, and depression. Depression can also be manifested in children through acting-out behaviors; arguing can be seen as such a behavior. Given that these behaviors occurred with frequencies comparable with those of referred children, it can be concluded that these behaviors occurred in the bereaved siblings in high enough proportions to be reflective of possible psychopathology.

Fifteen percent of the bereaved children also had social competency scores in the maladaptive range. A combination of behavior problems and diminished social competence is a warning that the child may need further assessment and assistance.

These findings indicate that a pattern of responses may signal that a child is in trouble and could benefit from referral to a mental health professional. No one problem by itself is necessarily an indication that the child is in trouble. Grollman (1967) points out that

> The line of demarcation between "normal psychological aspects of bereavement" and "disordered mourning reactions" is thin indeed. The difference is not in symptom, but in intensity. It is a continued denial of reality even many months after the funeral, or a prolonged bodily distress, or a persistent panic, or an extended guilt, or an unceasing idealization, or an enduring apathy and anxiety, or an unceasing hostile reaction to the deceased and to others. Each manifestation does not in itself determine a distorted grief reaction; it is only as it is viewed by the professional in the composition of the total formulation. (p. 21)

Watch for children who are persistently sad, unhappy, or depressed; who may be persistently aggressive or irritable; who complain of being lonely and who have withdrawn from their involvement with activities, hobbies, or friends; who seem to worry a lot; are persistently anxious or nervous; who

TABLE 4.2. Criteria for major depressive episode

A. Five (or more) of the following symptoms have been present during the same two-week period and represent a change from previous functioning; at least one of the symptoms is either (1) depressed mood or (2) loss of interest or pleasure.
Note: Do not include symptoms that are clearly due to a general medical condition, or mood-incongruent delusions or hallucinations.
  (1) depressed mood most of the day, nearly every day, as indicated by either subjective report (e.g., feels sad or empty) or observation made by others (e.g., appears tearful). **Note:** In children and adolescents, can be irritable mood.
  (2) markedly diminished interest or pleasure in all, or almost all, activities most of the day, nearly every day (as indicated by either subjective account or observation made by others)
  (3) significant weight loss when not dieting or weight gain (e.g., a change of more than 5% of body weight in a month), or decrease or increase in appetite nearly every day. **Note:** In children, consider failure to make expected weight gains.
  (4) insomnia or hypersomnia nearly every day
  (5) psychomotor agitation or retardation nearly every day (observable by others, not merely subjective feelings of restlessness or being slowed down)
  (6) fatigue or loss of energy nearly every day
  (7) feelings of worthlessness or excessive or inappropriate guilt (which may be delusional) nearly every day (not merely self-reproach or guilt about being sick)
  (8) diminished ability to think or concentrate, or indecisiveness, nearly every day (either by subjective account or as observed by others)
  (9) recurrent thoughts of death (not just fear of dying), recurrent suicidal ideation without a specific plan, or a suicide attempt or a specific plan for committing suicide.

B. The symptoms do not meet criteria for a mixed episode.

C. The symptoms cause clinically significant distress or impairment in social, occupational, or other important areas of functioning.

D. The symptoms are not due to the direct physiological effects of a substance (e.g., a drug of abuse, a medication) or a general medical condition (e.g., hypothyroidism).

E. The symptoms are not better accounted for by bereavement; i.e., after the loss of a loved one, the symptoms persist for longer than two months or are characterized by marked functional impairment, morbid preoccupation with worthlessness, suicidal ideation, psychotic symptoms, or psychomotor retardation.

Reprinted with permission from the *Diagnostic and Statistical Manual of Mental Disorders,* Fourth Edition, Washington, DC, American Psychiatric Association ,1994.

may be having ongoing eating difficulties or have recurrent nightmares; who do not seem to be feeling very good about themselves; and, who at the same time, may be doing very poorly in school.

Additional factors may make some children more vulnerable to pathological bereavement reactions. If there are questions about suicidal risk, or if the child was in some way involved in causing the death, then the child should be referred to mental health services. An additional four groups of "vulnerable or troubled" children who may require special assistance have been identified by Fox (1985):

1. children who themselves have a life-threatening or terminal illness,
2. children who have already been identified as emotionally disturbed,
3. children who are developmentally disabled and who may have difficulty understanding what has happened,
4. children who remain "frozen" and in shock long after most grievers have returned to the usual daily activities.

Children in each of these groups deserve the attention of someone who has been trained in the broad field of mental health, so if intervention is indicated, it can begin promptly. As Rando (1991) advises, whenever there is a question about how children are managing grief, it is better to err on the side of going for professional help.

Based on her experience as a child and family therapist, Webb (1993) has noted that the DSM-III-R criteria (now the DSM IV) describe in detail many of the behaviors and responses that occur in grieving children, especially those whose grief has become "disabling" (p. 25). According to the American Psychiatric Association (1994), the criteria to diagnose a major depressive syndrome in children are the same as for adults and are presented in Table 4.2. All child care professionals who work with bereaved children would find it helpful to become knowledgeable about these criteria.

This chapter has focused on the reactions of children to the death of a sibling. The most commonly occurring responses have been described, with suggestions for how to handle such responses in children. The issue of determining when children's behavior might indicate mental health assessment was discussed. Despite the importance of children's responses, they cannot be looked at it isolation. Individual, situational, and environmental factors impact on siblings' responses. Individual factors are discussed in the following chapter.

Individual Variables Affecting Siblings Bereavement Responses

Sibling grief following the death of a brother or sister is manifested in children's responses or reactions—their own ways of coping with the event. But it is not sufficient to look only at children's responses. Adults who are concerned about helping siblings with their grief must also consider a range of variables that may contribute to sibling adjustment and bereavement outcome.

Aside from emphasizing children's levels of cognitive development and their associated understanding of death, there is very little in the literature relating individual characteristics to bereavement outcome in siblings or in any other group of bereaved individuals for that matter. Attempts to isolate factors that affect sibling grief response are complicated by the number of variables investigated and the difficulty of establishing adequate control or reference groups. Systematic study of mediating variables has been limited. Findings are therefore not always consistent and few definite conclusions can be drawn.

Paying attention to individual characteristics is rooted in respect for the personhood of children and adolescents: "Respect for an individual person requires an understanding of not only how persons in general thrive or are vulnerable but also the particulars of the life of the individual" (Attig, 1995, p. 43). Respecting bereaved children and adolescents requires understanding of what makes each child or adolescent unique. It requires knowing about the child and those factors that influence the child's vulnerabilities to loss. Those individual characteristics include physical characteristics (such as gender and age, dependence, and health status), coping style, social-emotional characteristics (such as temperament and self-concept), and experience with death and loss.

☐ Physical Characteristics

Age and Gender

Blinder (1972, p. 173) suggested that the effect of sibling death on the surviving children is "influenced by the factors of age and sex which in a more general way influence the intensity of association, identification and competition generated." But, until fairly recently, no explicit examination of relationships between age and gender differences in siblings and bereavement outcome has been included in studies of sibling bereavement.

Studies that have included age as a variable report inconclusive results. In one study of 32 children ranging in age from 2 to 19 years, Betz (1985) reported that significant differences in reactions were associated with age. Interview data obtained from parents and children following the death of a child indicated that school-age children most often reported withholding feelings, remembering the deceased, noncommunicativeness, and acknowledging spiritual presence. In a study of long-term consequences for adolescents surviving a sibling's death from cystic fibrosis, those who were between 13 and 17 years of age at the time of the death were more anxious, depressed, and guilty than survivors who were between 9 and 12 years or were 18 years at the time of the death (Fanos & Nickerson, 1991). McCown (1982, 1987) found that younger children tended to demonstrate more problems. Boys and girls in the 6–11-year age group showed significantly more behavior disturbance when compared with norms on a standardized test. This finding was not true of children in the 4–5-year or 12–16-year groups. On the other hand, Davies (1983) reported that behavior was not significantly associated with the age of the bereaved children, although older children tended to have fewer behavior problems and greater social competence.

McCown and Davies (1995)[3] combined their data to look more closely at sibling bereavement responses in relation to age and gender. They found that the highest incidence of behavioral problems occurred in preschool and school-aged children. The youngest children, aged 4–5, were almost uniformly "argumentative," "irritable," "demanding of attention," and "disobedient." Behaviors that occurred more frequently in school-aged children

---

[3]The following discussion is adapted from McCown, D. & Davies, B. (1995). Patterns of grief in young children following the death of a sibling. *Death Studies, 19*, 42–53.

than in other age groups were "stubborn, sullen, or irritable" and "being easily embarrassed." The majority of behaviors appeared to decline with age, with adolescents showing the relative lowest incidence of behavioral problems. Few behaviors occurred in more than half of the 12- to 16-year olds, but the ones that did were most frequently observed in girls and included "secretiveness" and a "preference for being alone."

The single most frequent behavior observed in bereaved children—"demanding a lot of attention"—occurred in 100% of the 4–5-year-old males studied. The youngest boys also topped the list with 88.9% noted to "argue a lot" and to be "disobedient at home." The most common behavior for females ("stubborn, sullen, or irritable") occurred in 85.7% of 4–5-year-old girls. The three behaviors that were found to be consistently high (over 50%) across all age groups included "argues a lot"; "stubborn, sullen, and irritable"; and "self-conscious or easily embarrassed." These researchers concluded that the aggressive behavior of young children was not an expression of the anger which is a common component of grief in adults, but rather indicative of attention seeking. It appears that young children may respond to feelings of loss by seeking attention from their parents who are absorbed in their own grief. Similar findings were reported by Walker (1988) in her qualitative study of young bereaved siblings.

The younger children studied by McCown and Davies (1995) showed more aggressive behavior than the older children. This finding corresponds with the increased cognitive ability of teenagers to understand death as a final, universal, and personal event, and to understand and benefit from symbolic and cultural rituals associated with death. This mature understanding contributes to usual grief responses of withdrawal, sadness, and sullenness observed in the teenagers studied. It is also possible that the teenagers' enlarged interpersonal peer group network, which extends beyond the family, provides the external social support needed to facilitate behavioral adjustment in the older child.

Other studies of bereaved teenaged siblings showed differences in the expression of anger according to age. Balk (1983a, 1983b) investigated three overall categories of bereavement reactions among 33 adolescents whose siblings had died between 4 and 84 months prior to data collection. Age differences were reported in relation to the expression of anger. Older adolescents (17–19 years of age) reported anger at the time the sibling's death happened and at the time of the interview; younger subjects (14–16 years of age at the time of the interview) did not.

The influence of age on the bereavement experience of siblings is perhaps most noticeable in the expectations that accompany various ages. Young children, simply because they are "young," are left out of explanations and events: "My sister and I felt really alone, even though lots of people came after he [brother] died. I felt like we were out of the way, like we were the youngest and so were sort of put away and no one paid any attention to us." Conversely, other children, by virtue of being the oldest, are given more responsibility than perhaps they can manage comfortably:

> So after my brother's funeral, my dad came home and gathered me up and said, "Your mother is going away for a few days. You are the oldest one, and so you will have to be really strong now for the little ones." I was 8, and the other five were all younger.

Children are often surprisingly resilient, but it is wrong for adults to assume that the children will be "okay" just because they are youngsters. As one woman, now in her late forties, reflected,

> That attitude is not a very good one—that it [death] won't affect the children much. And you hear people saying all the time, "Oh children are so flexible, they'll get over it"—whether it's the death of a puppy, or a move to a different town or whatever. Children are very resilient, but there's a limit to how resilient they are.

Age then influences the child's responses because of the effect of cognitive development on the child's understanding of death. Age also makes a difference in how the child's grief may be manifested: for example, younger children are more aggressive because they are dealing with their anxiety and responding to the changed behavior of their parents. Older children may be more aggressive, but this may be an indication of depression. And age may be associated with various expectations or assumptions about how children cope.

Although there is a growing body of literature concerning children's understanding of death, there is a dearth of research that is systematically designed to examine gender differences in children's understanding of, and reaction to, death (Stillion, 1995). Most studies that examine children's death concepts, death attitudes, or grief and coping behavior do not report their results by sex. Stillion suggests three reasons for this lack of attention to gender. First, researchers in the field of death and dying may be more interested in the commonalities of human reactions to various aspects of death than in differences by gender. Second, sample sizes are most often too small to examine reliably by gender. Third, it simply may not occur to most researchers of children and death that gender is a salient factor that should be routinely examined when the size of sample permits. Whatever the reason, the result is that there are very few well-designed studies that examine gender differences with respect to death and childhood. Consequently, there is little to be reported about how gender may affect sibling grief other than we know that grief responses appear to be manifested differently in boys and girls. Although both sexes in one study (McCown & Davies, 1995) showed predominantly aggressive behaviors characterized by instrumental attention-seeking actions, girls also frequently demonstrated internalizing, depressive behaviors. In contrast, boys reflected a high frequency of externalizing, hyperactive behavior.

We cannot ignore that gender makes a difference in how children are socialized, and this may have an effect on siblings' expression of grief. Socialization begins at birth. From the minute a newborn baby girl is wrapped in a pink blanket and her brother in a blue one, the two children are treated differently. The difference starts with the subtle tone of voice of the adults cooing over the cribs and continues with the father's mock wrestling with his baby boy and gentler play with his "fragile" daughter. Researchers have observed sex differences in behaviors of male and female babies at amazingly young ages, most directly traceable to parents' differential treatment of infant boys and girls (Weitzman, 1982). Both boys and girls learn to distinguish male from female roles by observing the men and women around them: their parents, brothers and sisters, aunts and uncles, neighbors and friends. In addition to serving as models for the young child, these adults and older boys and girls often provide explicit instructions on proper behavior. In contemporary Western society, we have traditionally socialized males to be more "independent, assertive, dominant, and competitive" than females. In contrast, we have stressed that females should be "more passive, loving , sensitive, and supportive in social relationships" (Hetherington & Parke, 1993, p. 533). Studies have shown differences between males and females in death anxiety. College-aged females show higher death anxiety than males (Stillion, 1985). Thus, differential socialization in expressiveness may permit female children to admit fears, discuss them with significant others, and be comforted more easily than male children. Male children, on the other hand, may strive to live up to the norm of independence and emotional toughness and repress emotions associated with death. Interview comments by bereaved siblings often supported these gender differences. Several siblings noted surprise or discomfort when their fathers, uncles, or other males cried. When siblings did witness tears among the men, however, the effect was often beneficial: "I realized that my dad was human after all." Male siblings seldom cried during the interviews, although female siblings often became tearful. Adolescent males more often expressed concern about "being in control" or about "breaking down" in front of their parents or peers. Adolescent females, more often than males, talked about the support they received through talking with a close friend.

It can be concluded that age and gender seem to make some differences when looking generally at the bereavement responses of siblings. Knowing the child's age and gender, then, may provide some clues as to what to expect in grieving siblings, but these characteristics serve only as broad guidelines. Age and gender are perhaps the most visible characteristics and the easiest to examine, but we must consider other characteristics as well.

Dependence

Sometimes it is easy to forget one of the most obvious individual characteristics of children that influence how they cope with the death of a sibling—their physical dependency. Children cannot survive on their own. They need parents, or parent substitutes, to provide them with the basic necessities of life: food, shelter, and love. When a brother or sister dies, children and adolescents feel threatened—"Will I die too?" "Will mom or dad die?" "Will I be left alone?" "Who will look after me?" If children are disabled or handicapped in some way, their dependence is even greater, and their sense of vulnerability is also greater. Mrs. Janes described the reactions of her two sons to the news of their sister's death:

> I sat both of them down on the couch and explained that Sarah had died that morning. I knew it would be difficult for Mark (age 13, mentally handicapped since birth)—and for me to try to make him understand. I started to cry, and Pete (age 15) also cried when he realized his sister was gone. Mark just looked at me, and then at his brother, and back at me. He began to cry too, but it was from seeing us cry . . . he was scared . . . he knew something was wrong but couldn't understand what it was. He didn't even know what I meant when I said Sarah had died.

When children themselves are ill, their coping abilities are limited. Chronic illness affects all aspects of the child's development, sometimes leaving them with limited resources to deal with the grief of losing a brother or sister. Children with progressive, life-threatening illnesses, such as cystic fibrosis, may be profoundly affected by a sibling's death from the same disease. Jerry, age 12, sighed, "Seeing my brother die like he did—I know what lies ahead for me too. Cystic fibrosis is a slow stalker—it seems to me. It's hard to keep on going—now that he's gone, and all I have to look forward to is the same thing." Jerry's father concurred: "Jerry is having a hard time with his brother's death—and who wouldn't? He's been depressed and withdrawn—I think it's because he knows what's in store for him too, and that makes it hard for him." Even children who have the flu or a bad cold are not as hardy as they are on days when they are well. Such factors must be taken into account when assessing the individual child's response to sibling death.

□ Coping Style

Murphy (1974) described coping as a process that consists of a variety of behaviors used in a flexible way to deal with the challenges in the environment. Lazarus and Folkman (1984) define coping as those changing cognitive and behavioral approaches used to manage specific external or internal demands that are viewed as taxing and in excess of the person's resources or both. The repertoire of coping strategies used by children expands from birth through to maturity, although there is little clear evidence that coping changes from one developmental level to another. We know that as young children begin to understand their world, they also become aware of more complex and emotion-laden ways of coping. Murphy (1974) and Murphy and Moriarty (1976) have suggested that although changes occur in coping behavior (from primitive reactions to more complex cognitive processes) the basis for shutting out, exploring, and aggression develops at an early age and continues to influence how an individual copes over time. The techniques one utilizes to bring about relief or equilibrium in relation to a perceived problem are coping strategies (Weisman & Worden, 1976).

Coping strategies used by children will vary greatly with their age and cognitive development. The infant uses coping behaviors that center primarily on motor activity—thumb sucking, hand–mouth activity, crying, fussing, body rocking, and clinging to familiar objects and people. Toddlers, with their increasing communication and locomotor skills, often cope in stressful situations by regressing to earlier familiar infant coping strategies. Also, toddlers use protest (temper tantrums), withdrawal, fantasy, controlling behaviors, and ritualization as coping mechanisms. Temporary use of any of these behaviors in a stressful situation is indicative of healthy childhood coping. Once children reach the age of 6 or 7, they have sufficient ability in cognitive functions such as memory, speech, language, and reality testing to begin to have an understanding of what is happening and how they can manage the situation. School-age children and adolescents cope successfully by finding satisfaction in a variety of compensatory activities, both physical and intellectual, and identifying with other young people undergoing similar experiences. The appropriate expression of anxious, sad, impatient, and angry feelings is an essential and healthy aspect of coping.

Bullard and Dohnal (1984) suggest that children do not "work through" a problem, nor do they "get over" it. Rather, they develop patterns of psychosocial adjustment that they will utilize for the rest of their lives. Some children want to know about what is happening—they are full of questions. Others are more physically active—play acting, letting off steam. Others will simply want to avoid the stress by withdrawing into themselves or into an active fantasy life. What is important is to realize that children have different ways of coping with their worlds, and these individual ways must be taken into account. Coping patterns are closely related to temperament, which is discussed in the following section.

☐ Social–Emotional Characteristics

Children come not only in an unending array of sizes, shapes, and physical capacities, they also vary in levels of social and emotional development and capacities. Some are less able than others to deal with the emotional issues that arise in themselves and their family when another child dies. Some can express their fears and ask their questions directly; others cannot. Or, if they can state their concerns, they are misunderstood or dismissed by the adults in their lives. Those who express themselves nonverbally are even less likely to be understood. Some children have a strong sense of who they are and what they are about; others are confused and uneasy about their abilities, their place in life, and their contribution to their family.

Some children and adolescents are more passive by nature; others have more outgoing and energetic dispositions. Some feel that they are helpless in the face of what happens to them; others learn that they have choices in how to respond to events that are uncontrollable. Many children lack models for how to deal with loss and particularly with death. When children experience the death of a sibling, their parents are also relatively young, many without any previous experience in coping with death, dying, or bereavement. Such parents have difficulty managing their own grief for their deceased child, let alone the capacity to deal effectively with their other grieving children.

Some children are better able to reach out to others. They respond well to support offered by others or they initiate contact themselves. They are receptive to suggestions and assistance from adults and peers. Other children are naturally more withdrawn into themselves—they do not reach out for support or comfort or information. They may be shy and fearful of being rejected or simply not even be aware that others can be a source of comfort and caring. Some reject any support that others may offer, thereby pushing themselves even further away from the potential support and caring that might exist for them. How children are in the world has, in recent decades, been described as "temperament."

Temperament

Chess and Thomas, known as the pioneers in temperament research, define temperament as the way in which individuals behave or respond to their environment and note that it is bound in those genetic or constitutional traits that cause individuality (Thomas, Chess, & Birch, 1968; Thomas & Chess, 1977, 1980; Chess & Thomas, 1984). Simply put, temperament refers to the child's behavioral style—the "how" of behavior as opposed to the "what" (abilities) or the "why" (motivations) (McClowry, 1995). The characteristics of one's temperament are evidenced from birth and are predictive of one's adult personality. The different temperamental constellations represent the wide range of behavioral styles exhibited by people and are all variations within normal limits. An individual's temperament is relatively

TABLE 5.1. Characteristics of temperament (Thomas, Chess, & Birch, 1968)

1. Motor activity	The intensity and frequency of activity or mobility
2. Rhythmicity	Regularity of repetitive biological functions, such as sleep and wakefulness, eating patterns, bowel and bladder patterns
3. Approach to the new	Withdrawal from or acceptance of it—the child's initial reaction to a new stimulus
4. Adaptability	The ease or difficulty with which initial response to new stimuli can be modified
5. Intensity of response	Degree or amount of energy invested in reacting to stimuli
6. Threshold of responsiveness	Level of external stimulation necessary to evoke an overresponse
7. Quality of mood	General cheerfulness or unhappiness, about pleasant and friendly behavior as opposed to unpleasant and unfriendly behavior
8. Distractibility	Effectiveness of extraneous environmental stimuli in altering the direction of ongoing behavior
9. Attention span and persistence	Length of time an activity is pursued, whether self-initiated or planned or structured, and the amount of frustration tolerated in activity despite obstacles

consistent over time and significantly influences the spontaneity with which one adapts to new situations, the intensity with which one reacts to one's environment, and the characteristic nature of one's mood tendencies. People tend to be cheerful, positive, and optimistic or to be irritable, negative, and pessimistic in response to life situations.

Based on their New York longitudinal study, which has been ongoing for more than 40 years, Chess and Thomas (1984) described nine characteristics or dimensions of temperament. They are: motor activity, rhythmicity, approach to the new, adaptability, intensity of response, threshold of responsiveness, quality of mood, distractibility, and attention span and persistence (see Table 5.1). These traits tend to combine to form three clearly different personality structures: easy children, difficult children, and slow-to-warm children.

Easy children are well adjusted psychologically and physically and adapt rapidly. They are friendly and enjoy company. They seek out people during stress. They usually sleep and eat well, with highly regular biological rhythms. They display low to mild intensity of response to change or stressors. A positive mood predominates, and they tend to find the good in most situations.

Difficult children are slow to adapt to any new situation or stressor but function well once they "learn the rules" of the situation. They like people but are not dependent upon them and sometimes function better alone. They seek activity during stress and need acceptable outlets for their vigor and aggressive motor drive. They seem to be constantly moving and are highly destructive and intense in their reactions to change. They display mostly negative withdrawal responses to new situations, often expressing their frustration in tantrums or boisterous responses which may seem out of proportion to the event. They have irregular biologic functioning—they sleep poorly, lightly, and need less sleep. A negative mood predominates, they fuss or complain a lot, and seem to be often unhappy.

Slow-to-warm children have slow adaptive capacities. They usually quietly withdraw but remain watchful and contemplative all the while. They are primarily loners, usually preferring only one or two close friends, and are socially shy. They seek to be alone during stress and are often avid readers. They may mature late: often seeming oversensitive and immature when compared with most peers. They are poor at relaxing and frequently experience disturbed sleep and eating patterns. They display low intensity of reaction to change. They demonstrate fairly high frequencies of negative mood, although it may not be noticeable because of the low intensity with which it is expressed.

Temperament is an important moderator of children's success in responding to the demands encountered in the various settings of their lives. Children with difficult temperaments are more vulnerable to behavioral problems in early and middle childhood, with 70% demonstrating at least mild reactive behavioral alteration by age 10 years (Chess & Thomas, 1984). They also are more accident prone (Russell & Russell, 1989). Carey's studies (1972) revealed that children with difficult temperaments who had handicaps or mental retardation were at even greater risk, and the difficult-temperament child with a mentally ill parent is at greatest risk for behavioral alteration. It is now generally accepted that temperament is interrelated with many other variables and that negative effects of temperament can be mediated by other psychosocial variables (McClowry, 1992, 1995). Despite the apparent significance of temperament to child behavior, temperament has received little attention in the sibling bereavement literature. Temperament was included in one study differentiating sibling bereavement response according to cause of death (Davies & Kalischuk, 1997) and was described in qualitative studies of sibling bereavement (Davies, 1996).

Child care professionals who recognize these three personality structures or temperaments can use this information to make more reasoned judgments about grieving children's reactions and the approaches that will be most effective. Sharing this awareness of temperamental styles with parents and other adults helps them adapt their responses to best meet children's need (Melvin, 1995). What works with one child will not work with another of a different temperament. For example, children's innate activity levels are not likely to present problems in bereavement if they are of average or low levels. However, high activity levels may compound children's difficulties in concentrating. For the school-age child, for example, this may make it more difficult to settle down to sedentary activities in the classroom (Schor, 1985). For such children, opportunities for regular motor activity are important. Eight-year-old Bobby was described by his mother as "always active. He never could sit still, and even as a baby he pulled away from cuddling." Following his brother's death, Bobby continued to be active, unable to sit still in school, and very argumentative. His mother insightfully continued, "I think part of Bobby's problem is that he just is normally an active, acting out kind of child. And it's all made worse for him since his brother died." She also described her tactics for dealing with Bobby: "I don't insist that he sit still. I talked to his teacher about whether he could have a work station at school on the edge of the classroom so he could stand up or sit down and not get in the way of the other children." This strategy, taking into account Bobby's increased difficulty during bereavement, kept Bobby involved in his school work and out of trouble.

Children who have personalities characterized by high approachability respond well to new situations, people, places, and learning demands and are usually a joy for adults. These children may be more likely to openly express their grief and to seek and accept support from others. On the other hand, children who initially withdraw from new situations and are "slow to warm" may be more likely to withdraw during grief. These children need extra time to function optimally and to maintain a sense of dignity and self-worth. Ten-year-olds, Kirk and Kyle, although twins, were very different in temperament. Their father explained:

> Kirk, always curious and open to new experiences, was full of questions about the baby's death [from SIDS]. What he wanted to know, he asked. "Where was the baby now? Why did he stop breathing? What happens when you die? Who will be at the funeral? Will we have another baby?" Kyle is a different story. He's always been quiet and slow to get involved, letting Kirk lead the way. He was even more quiet after the baby died, and still is. We don't know what's going on in his head!

Children with moderate to high intensity of reaction will boisterously demonstrate their grief—they may wail loudly, demand answers to questions, or stomp from the room. However, for those with a mild intensity of reaction, simple observations of their responses will not give accurate evaluations. For these children, adults must be alert for more subtle cues to assess children's reactions accurately and to respond to them appropriately.

Good-natured children with typically positive moods are likely to be treated more positively than ill-natured children with negative moods. Responses to both types of children are likely to reinforce their prevailing quality of mood. Positive-mood bereaved siblings may more likely find something good about each day, even though they feel sad. Bereaved siblings with negative moods may feel "picked on" and find confirmation for feeling that a negative response is appropriate for the predominantly negative world in which they now live.

Professionals who work with grieving children can assess temperament through observation of and interaction with children, through temperament questionnaires or questions included in health histories, or by questioning children's caretakers. Assessment is pertinent from several perspectives. The assessment process provides an opportunity to discuss children's temperament with parents and to educate them regarding temperament implications for understanding their children's bereavement responses and their own parenting approach. Parents of difficult or slow-to-warm children can receive reassurance that their children's behavior may be characteristic of their temperament. Professionals and parents can work together to determine if the children's responses are within the expected responses for the children's temperament. This discussion also affords an opportunity for preventive counseling that might alleviate future behavioral problems stemming from parent–child conflicts because parents did not understand their children's temperament.

Whether the behavior typical of a given temperamental pattern will present in acceptable or aberrant ways depends largely on how the significant others in one's life respond to those characteristics. Additionally, any situation or demand that strongly conflicts with one's temperament produces severe stress, during which time signs and symptoms of behavior problems may arise. Children's feelings may appear irrational at times; nonetheless they are very real. The most loving thing that adults can do is to let children experience the full range of all these feelings—sadness as well as happiness. This deepens children's sense of self and helps them to discover that feelings change. Acknowledging and respecting the feelings children are experiencing allows them to do the same. This acknowledgment and respect also comforts children, because they then know they are not alone in their experience. In the long run, this freedom to express feelings allows children to use their own inner resources to manage the challenge at hand. It alleviates the burden of the feelings themselves and enables them to focus more of their energy on dealing with the problem.

Self-Concept

A key element influencing acquisition of adaptive or maladaptive behavior is the child's self-perceptions. According to Maslow's hierarchy of needs (1968), self-esteem is an extremely important component of healthy living, preceded only by satisfaction of physiologic and safety needs and one's need to be loved. Maslow defines the need for self-esteem as including self-respect, others' respect, self-confidence and feelings of competence, independence, success, and recognition from others.

What I am referring to here is the self-system, that aspect of the human being that accounts for the uniqueness of a person. While some aspects of the self-system may change over time, the central core of this system appears to remain intact and to endure over time (Thomas, 1979). In fact, maintenance and enhancement of this highly stable aspect of self is the major motivational force behind all behavior. Behavioral research consistently demonstrates that maladaptive or antisocial behavior and mental–emotional imbalance can be causally linked with an underdeveloped self-system (Crosby, 1982; Levine, 1983).

Self-concept is a broad generic term that encompasses many smaller constructs (e.g., self-image, self-esteem, self-ideal). Self-concept, then, is the central core of personality development that gives rise to one's uniqueness or identity (Sullivan, 1953). Self-concept is arrived at through self-definition and self-evaluation, which require interpersonal interactions so that the self can be seen through the reactions of others. As children receive feedback from their interactions, they evaluate whether they are a "good person" or a "bad person." Children are not born with an identity or self-concept. This self-system is developed gradually, with different constructs of the system receiving emphasis and maturing at different times. Development of the self-system is always a social process. The child has no built-in mechanisms to assess the worthiness of achievement, the appropriateness of task mastery, or the compatibility of social functioning. Self-concept is strongly influenced by significant others in the child's environment. More will be said about this aspect of bereaved children's self-concept in Chapter 7.

Although much has been written about the significance of self-concept to children's behavior, it has not received much attention by researchers or clinicians interested in bereaved children. Only two studies (Balk, 1983a, 1983b; Martinson et al., 1987) examined this concept in samples of bereaved siblings, using standardized measures. Both studies concluded that sibling death provided impetus for psychological growth. Using the Offer Self-Image Questionnaire (OSIQ) for adolescents, Balk found that his 33 adolescent subjects were similar to their peers in terms of adjustment. He concluded that the crisis of sibling death presented obstacles that the teenagers could surmount and that the death was used by the teenagers as a means of growth. His conclusion was not related to age of siblings; rather, the self-concept scores were related to the time elapsed since the death. Participants whose siblings had died 12 to 14 months prior to the interview had significantly higher mean scores on the moral values scale than did teenagers whose siblings had died less than one year or more than two years prior to the interview.

Martinson et al. (1987) found that bereaved siblings scored statistically higher in self-concept than the normative group of children (using the Piers–Harris Self-Concept Scale). Correlations between the Piers–Harris scores and length of illness, time elapsed since the death, and age and sex of the siblings were not significant.

Analysis of the siblings' interview data indicated that the siblings perceived that they had gained maturity and had grown psychologically as a result of their experience. For example, one 16-year-old boy commented, "I have a better outlook on life now; I mean, I realize how important life is as a result of my sister's death." Twelve of Balk's participants attributed their feelings of increased maturity to having coped with their sibling's death; self-reflection or role changes (for instance, becoming the oldest child) were considered by eight persons to be the reasons for increased maturity. Content analysis of the interviews indicated that the reasons given for the sense of increased maturity were embedded in the psychosocial transition presented by the death of the sibling.

The bereaved siblings felt that positive learning resulted from their experience. The most frequently cited lessons were that there are ways to cope with adversity, irrevocably bad things can happen in life, and people should be valued more while they are alive. Nearly half of the participants believed their peers had not learned these lessons, which they said stemmed from never having experienced a serious life crisis.

Parents' interview data also indicated that the children were perceived as sensitive, caring individuals who matured as a result of their experience. Parents saw their children as more compassionate and aware of other people's problems. In the words of one mother, about her 17-year-old daughter, "She's more mature. She's been exposed to more than most kids. I think she had to grow up a little quicker. She values life. She is very understanding and patient. She puts other people before her own feelings."

Therefore, it would seem true that for many of the siblings, the experience of having lost a sibling was an impetus for psychological growth, and this growth was reflected in the overall higher self-concept scores. These findings offer some reassurance that the death of a sibling does not necessarily have only negative long-term consequences for the surviving children. As occurs with any crisis, there exists also the potential for growth as a possible outcome.

Experience with Loss and Death

Children in the contemporary western world, compared with those in previous times, have fewer personal encounters with natural death. The average lifespan has increased significantly over the centuries so that today, the majority of deaths are of older people. Geographic distance often separates children from grandparents and other older relatives, decreasing the likelihood that children will visit them in hospital when they are dying or attend their funerals. Thus, many children grow to be young adults, or older, without ever experiencing the death of a family member. Discussions about death are seldom held between parents and their children—many parents still consider the topic of death inappropriate, not only for their children but for themselves. But, paradoxically, in a world sheltered from death, children still learn about death. Death pervades the child's world, and the messages children receive help mold the form that the child's experience will take. For children, as well as for adults, learning about death is not something that is odd or extraordinary; it is simply learning about life (Wass & Corr, 1984).

The normal course of everyday life presents many "teachable moments"—opportunities for learning that arise out of ordinary experiences. Such situations are ideal vehicles for helping children learn about death and dying (DeSpelder & Strickland, 1995). Riding in the family car, children see a dead raccoon lying on the side of the highway. They watch their mother discard the dead roses from the vase on the table. They listen to their parents lament an early morning news report about a plane crash that has killed all passengers and crew members. They see the television tribute to a hockey sports broadcaster whose wife of 40 years has just died. They overhear granddad telling their father that Old Uncle Jim died quietly in his sleep last night. They listen to the lyrics of a rock song about suicide. In many ways, and in a variety of places, death becomes part of children's lives. And so it should—death is a part of life. What children learn about death from situations such as these lays the foundation for children's reactions when their brother or sister dies. Jackson (1982) emphasizes that "every death experience for a child can be a learning opportunity. Death is so much a part of the life of a child that it is imperative that it be dealt with in positive ways" (p. 37). Consider the impact of their first experiences with death on the children in the following examples:

> Six-year-old Mary loved her pet budgie, "Tweeties." Before going to school each morning, she carefully replenished his seed and water dishes. Immediately upon her return from school, Mary ran gleefully to his cage. For several noisy minutes, the child and her bird engaged in "conversation" about the day. One day, while Mary was at school, Tweeties escaped from his cage, and

> died suddenly as he flew across the room. Wanting to protect Mary from the sadness of knowing about her bird's fate, Mary's mother rushed to the local pet shop. She felt "lucky" in finding an identical budgie who immediately found himself in a new home, just in time for Mary's arrival. Mary ran to the cage and began her daily recital. The bird did not respond. Anxiously, Mary looked at the bird and burst into tears. "Where is Tweeties?" she wailed. "This isn't my Tweeties!" Her mother then had not only to describe what had happened to Tweeties but also explain her cover-up attempt. Mary went to bed very unhappy that night. The next morning, she didn't want to have anything to do with the substitute budgie.

In contrast, Jacob's canary also died one day while Jacob was at school.

> Jacob's parents were on a holiday; his grandmother was babysitting. His grandmother left the bird in the bottom of the cage, partially covering his body with a handkerchief. When Jacob came home from school, his grandmother met him at the door, inquiring about his day. Looking gently at the young boy, she then said, "Jacob, something very sad happened while you were at school today." Pausing for the words to carry their message of warning, she proceeded. "I went to clean Yellowbird's cage this morning and found him lying on the bottom. He was lying very still, and I knew that he had died." Waiting another few seconds, she asked, "I covered him and left him in case you would like to see him.... Would you?" Crying, Jacob nodded his head. Holding his grandmother's hand, he slowly approached Yellowbird's cage. He noticed that the handkerchief was his grandmother's favorite—the one with all the pretty yellow flowers. Together, they pulled back the handkerchief and picked up the bird. They chatted for a while about what may have caused Yellowbird's death, about how still the bird was, about what it was like when something died. Together, they found a box to bury Yellowbird. Jacob's grandmother suggested that he could bury Yellowbird in the handkerchief if he wanted. Together, they dug a little hole in the back yard and had a little funeral for Yellowbird. Later that night, Jacob's grandmother overheard him telling his parents, "And we buried him in Grandma's favorite hankie.... The flowers matched Yellowbird—he liked that!"

Two children. Two pet birds. Two deaths. Two ways of dealing with the deaths. Both Mary and Jacob learned about death the day their bird died. Mary learned that death is something to be avoided, something to not talk about, something to hide. She learned that her mom could not always be trusted to tell her the truth. Jacob learned that death is sad but not scary. He learned what happens to a body after it dies—it does not move or breathe and is very still. He learned that after something dies, it is treated with respect and love. He learned one way of saying good-bye. He learned that his grandmother could be counted on to help him.

Some children come to the experience of sibling bereavement having endured the deaths of other loved ones. Others may not have had any prior experience and are suddenly caught off guard by this totally new experience, one filled with a myriad of strong emotions and confusing thoughts. Some may have had past losses and learned from those experiences ways of coping that help in the current situation. Others may have had experiences that only add to the distress of the current situation. Some may be in the middle of learning how to cope with one loss when their sibling dies, thereby compounding the losses. For example, Jake's family had just moved to a new city. At 14 years of age, this move was hard for Jake—he had to leave his school friends, who had been his buddies since kindergarten, and he had had to leave the school football team where he was one of the star players. Two months after the move, just before school was to begin, his younger sister was killed in a hit and run accident. Jake was just learning how to cope with his new life when the accident occurred, leaving him with few resources to help him deal with his sister's death. The cumulative effect of losses take their toll and diminish children's capacities to cope with sibling death. Wolfelt (1983) offers an example of a loss inventory as a tool for helping adults to determine the cumulative effect loss events may have had on a child. The inventory considers many situations, including the death of a significant person, and the relative time of the event in order to calculate the cumulative effect. Whatever their experience has been, that is what children bring with them. That is what helps set the stage for the scenes of bereavement that will follow. These experiences must be taken into account.

The various individual characteristics described above impact on children's responses to the death of a sibling. The circumstances surrounding the death also contribute to how children respond. These situational characteristics are the focus of the next chapter.

6

CHAPTER

Situational Variables Affecting Sibling Bereavement Responses

Situational variables refer to characteristics of the situation or the circumstances surrounding the death. These variables include the cause of death, the duration of illness preceding the death, place of death, time elapsed since the death, and the extent of involvement in the death and death-related events.

☐ Cause of Death

It has been widely documented in the literature on adult bereavement that the cause of death is in itself a variable of importance in how survivors respond to a death. Many of the earlier studies of sibling bereavement, however, did not control for cause of death. Those that do control for cause of death are directed to death from cancer (Binger, 1973; Gogan, Koocher, Foster, & O'Malley, 1977; Lascari & Stehbens, 1973; Spinetta, 1977); death from other illnesses (Kerner et al., 1979); and accidental death (Nixon & Pearn, 1977, Appelbaum & Burns, 1991; Brent et al., 1993).

A pilot study (Davies & Kalischuk, 1997) explored the responses of 33 siblings in 18 families to a child's death from long-term illness or from sudden, unexpected causes. Preliminary findings support the view that sudden death is more disruptive to survivors' lives. Surviving siblings of children who died suddenly had significantly lower self-concept scores ($x = 48.7$) as measured by the Piers–Harris Self-Concept Scale than did siblings of children who died following long-term illness ($x = 59.7$, $t = 2.75$, $p < 0.19$). Comparisons of behavior scores, using the CBCL, also indicated behavior problems greater than the norms for both internalizing and externalizing problems. Quantitative findings support qualitative analysis of interview data that indicate that cause of death plays a role in sibling bereavement, as described by one adolescent. Two of her brothers had died, one from cancer and the other in a car accident. She said,

> I think when it's sudden, it has a different impact. It's such a shock, and you have no time to think about it or get ready for it. When it's from illness, then you have time to say a lot of things and to do a lot of things . . . but then you can get very, very close and you lose more then.

Her message is clear—the cause of death has an impact, and there are aspects of both causes which make grief difficult.

Sudden Death

Unlike illness that may have had some chronicity before entering a terminal phase, the results of acute or accidental trauma happen suddenly with no preparation. The impact of sudden trauma and impending death may throw the entire family into chaos, with no one able to coordinate necessary activities. It has been widely documented in the literature on adult bereavement that the cause of death is in itself a variable of importance in how survivors respond to a death. Bereavement following a sudden and unexpected death is more often characterized by greater stress (Carey, 1977; Fulton & Fulton, 1971; Parkes & Brown, 1972; Parkes, 1975; Vachon, 1976). Research investigations reported by Ball (1976–1977) and by Vachon (1976) suggest that young widows, in particular, respond with fewer difficulties when death has been anticipated, rather than sudden. It is not clear how important preparation time is in alleviating the discomfort of grief, but it seems that time to prepare oneself for the possibility of bereavement does have some effect on later reaction. Parkes (1975) insists that time to prepare is particularly important for the relatively young. Parkes' comments refers to young widows, but the same stance applies to those even younger—children.

Whereas children who lose siblings through illness need a clear understanding of the cause of the disease and the changes through the course of illness, Stephenson (1986) observed that accidental or violent death may produce its own particular issues for the surviving siblings, because accidents often imply fault or preventability that may or may not be resolved within the family. Nixon and Pearn (1977) noted that 32% of siblings were significantly affected by the drowning death of their sibling. For these children, sleep disorders and feelings of guilt were common problems. A sudden, traumatic death increases children's sense of vulnerability: *If it (sudden death from a hiking accident) can happen to Janie, who was at school yesterday, goofing off with the rest of us, then maybe it can happen to me too?* Had Janie been ill and then died, her siblings and classmates may have felt less vulnerable.

Children also feel more vulnerable when they perceive the death as painful or violent. Six years after her sister's death in a car accident in Europe, Janis (now 21) still wondered about the way in which her sister died:

> They told us that there was alcohol involved—they had been drinking. And, hard as it may sound, I can deal with that ... if they were drinking, they ... they didn't deserve to die, but I can understand how it happened. But what bothers me still is what happened ... was she conscious? Was she in pain? Did she feel alone? Did she know she was dying and would never see us again? Was she in pain, or did she die immediately and not even know what happened? Those are the things I think about, and worry about ... even still.

When children die violently due to murder, similar thoughts and concerns about how the person died continue to haunt the siblings. Eth and Pynoos (1985) warn that elements of trauma and violence raise anxiety levels and may negatively affect the grief process.

Other authors (Rudestam, 1977; Stephenson, 1986; Brent et al., 1993) suggest that children surviving the death of a sibling by suicide are at risk for subsequent disturbed grief reactions. Not only are the surviving children left to cope with their own grief as well as their possible feelings of rejection by the deceased child, there is the burden of coping with the negative and social stigma of being a suicide survivor. The family of a child who committed suicide often may focus on denying the reality of what has happened, even inventing a new version of the death and suppressing any further discussion of the event. Stigma may affect bereavement outcome when the death is from murder, drug overdose, and illnesses as well, particularly from AIDS.

DeFrain, Taylor, and Ernst (1982) and Williams (1981) identified unique factors exacerbating grief in families following the death of a child from SIDS. Although the authors noted, based on their clinical experience, that subsequent children are at risk for the replacement child syndrome (Posznanski, 1972), only recently have published studies examined siblings' bereavement response following the death of a brother or sister from SIDS (Mandell, McClain, & Reece, 1987; Powell, 1991; Hutton & Bradley, 1994; Dowden, 1995). All studies indicate that bereaved siblings have prolonged and elevated behavioral problems. For example, one study of 16 children whose baby brother or sister had died from SIDS within the past 6–25 months (Davies, 1993b) showed that the siblings' behavior was above the norm for behavior problems (using the CBCL). Most commonly, children's behavior regressed following the death. They reverted to baby talk, clinging to mother, bedwetting, and wanting to drink from a bottle. Parents indicated that they felt able to handle these aspects of their children's behavior, reflecting an understanding of their children's special needs for reassurances and patience. However, parents had more difficulty in answering their children's questions related to the death. The most challenging questions asked why the surviving child had not also died as a baby, and would another baby die.

In summary, there is a marked deficit of published literature pertaining to sibling bereavement responses when the cause of childhood death is other than cancer or cystic fibrosis.

Childhood Life-Threatening Illness

There is not yet sufficient research to determine empirically the relative importance of a child's disability or disease on sibling development, adjustment, and subsequent bereavement. At best, "the impact of childhood disease or disability on siblings may best be conceptualized as a risk or stress factor, the significance of which is mediated by other individual and family characteristics and resources" (Lobato, Faust, & Spirito, 1988, p. 395).

Chronic illness, in and of itself, is a significant challenge to effective family and individual functioning. It is reasonable to assume that this challenge is made even more difficult when it is combined with the unpredictable nature of life-threatening aspects inherent in conditions such as childhood cancer (Adams & Deveau, 1987). The literature on siblings of children with cancer is at an early stage of conceptualization and methodology. Most of the literature has focused on the sibling of the dying child rather than on the sibling of the child with a life-threatening illness, although Bluebond-Langner's (1996) recent book on well siblings of children with cystic fibrosis is a welcome exception. Furthermore, literature has emphasized psychopathology and disturbance rather than coping and adaptation in siblings. Understandably, the majority of research in the area of childhood chronic life-threatening illness continues to focus on children with cancer as this remains the leading cause of death due to childhood chronic illness.

Several studies (Cairns, Clark, Smith, & Lansky, 1979; Lavigne & Ryan, 1979) reported that siblings confronted with a chronic life-threatening illness experience similar stress as their brother or sister who has cancer; in fact, siblings showed more distress than the parents in the areas of perceived social isolation. In addition, siblings perceived the parents as overindulgent and overprotective of the sick child, were fearful of confronting family members with negative feelings, were preoccupied with own their health, and older siblings were overly concerned with failure (Cairns et al., 1979). Similar findings were reported by Spinetta (1981) in a three-year longitudinal study of families with a child with cancer that included 102 siblings. Spinetta summarized the findings by stating "if the patients' scores relative to the controls suggest a need for intervention, then siblings, when they score at the same level as the patients, have the same need for intervention. When the siblings scored at significantly less adaptive levels than the patients, concern is raised regarding the fact that their needs are being met inadequately" (p. 139). Spinetta concluded that siblings live through the experience with the same intensity as the patients and will live the longest with disease-related memories and concerns. If such is the case, the nature of the illness before death potentially impacts the siblings' responses following the death.

Even within the diagnosis of cancer, some researchers hypothesize that there are different types of death. Tietz, McSherry, and Britt (1977) and Hamovitch (1964) reported poorer crisis resolution among the bereaved survivors when the child had been diagnosed with a solid malignancy (i.e., lymphoma, sarcoma) compared with leukemia. Tietz et al. (1977) found high numbers of behavior problems in the siblings in families where the ill child had died from a solid tumor. It was observed that these children suffered a great deal in their terminal stages with the development of paralysis and blindness. In addition, the treatment of solid malignancies usually involved surgery, radiation, and extensive chemotherapy and the disease appeared more devastating and resulted in greater suffering for the ill child. The researchers hypothesized that the child's death may be more difficult to accept when all of the treatment and the pain and suffering was "for nothing" because the child died. However, in my own work (Davies, 1983), I found no difference in sibling bereavement outcome of children who died of leukemia or solid tumors. Stehbens and Lascari (1974) also reported no discernible relationship among type, number, or severity of anticipatory and after-death symptoms. I surmized that the variables that need to be considered are not related to certain diagnoses per se but rather the treatments involved, the extensiveness of the treatments, and the degree of suffering the children actually experienced.

How children respond to the death of a sibling following a long-term illness varies considerably depending on the children's experience during the illness. Some research reports suggest that the well siblings fare as bad or worse than their ill brothers or sisters in overall psychological adaptation (Cairns et al., 1979; Spinetta, 1981; Stein, Forrest, Woolley, & Baum, 1989). Stein and his colleagues retrospectively reviewed the families who used the services of Helen House, the first free-standing hospice for children. Findings suggested that the impact of the illness on the families was substantial. Siblings of the ill children were manifesting considerable psychological distress. A descriptive pilot study by Kramer (1981) sought to determine the healthy children's perceptions of living with a brother or sister with cancer.

TABLE 6.1. Experiences of siblings living with a child with cancer, according to age

Preschool (4–6 Years)	School age (7–11 Years)	Adolescent (12–18 Years)
• Did not retain specific information regarding cancer • Concerned with sibling's physical symptoms (hair loss) or procedures (shots) • Feared for sibling's physical safety • Feared separation from sibling	• Retained information • Understood sibling could die from the illness but believed prognosis was good • Felt sad • Missed sibling and parents during hospitalization • Jealous of parental attention	• Retained information • Were well-informed • Knew sibling could die but believed prognosis was positive for a healthy life • Lonely • Missed sibling during hospitalizations • Found it difficult to answer friends' or relatives' questions when felt they had inadequate information themselves • Felt closer to ill sibling • Worried about sibling dying

Reprinted from Davies, B., & Martinson, I. (1989). Special emphasis on siblings during and after the death of a child. In B. Martin (Ed.), *Pediatric hospice care: What helps*. Los Angeles, CA: Children's Hospital of Los Angeles, pp. 186–199.

From interviews with 11 healthy siblings, Kramer identified three major sources of stress:

(1) emotional realignment within the family,
(2) family separation,
(3) the ill child's therapeutic regimen.

Each stressor resulted in specific negative consequences for the siblings and specific emotional responses, which included feelings of loneliness, resentment, rejection or neglect, frustration, fear, and sadness.

A summary of the common perceptions reported by healthy siblings living with a child with cancer is provided in Table 6.1. While situations may vary somewhat with other critical illness, I believe that many families and children have similar needs and experience similar reactions, regardless of the child's diagnosis. Child health professionals accept the basic concept that any event in children's lives should be examined within the context of the child's level of understanding and development; consequently, these data from our research are presented according to specific developmental groups. The perceptions of the siblings identified in this table concur with many of those reported by the aforementioned authors. Parents' perceptions provide additional insights into the healthy siblings' experience.

Preschoolers

The parents of preschool children (4–6) perceive that their children do not equate the illness experience with death, although they know the child is very sick. Parents reported their well children's fear that the ill child will not come home from the hospital. Parents also understand that the well children fear being left alone.

Parents believe that the experience of having a critically ill sibling leaves well siblings feeling lonesome, causes them to be shuffled around, and triggers needs for more attention and affection especially around times of relapse of symptoms. Although parents experience their preschool children as demanding more attention, the siblings often are unaware of needing more attention. For this age group, parents' perceptions about their well children's understanding of cancer are congruent with the children's reality.

School-Age Children

Parents of school-age children (7–11) perceive that the healthy siblings know that the ill child could die. Parents reported that siblings worry about the child with cancer getting sicker, that they miss their sister or brother, and that they find the situation the hardest when the parents are gone. According to these parents, the siblings also fear that the child will not come home again and retain bad memories of the ill child's physical discomforts. These parents accurately picked up on the healthy siblings' feelings of neglect, jealousy, loneliness, and sadness.

In addition, parents reported an increase in illness episodes and physical discomforts among the siblings and an increase in misbehaving episodes. Siblings, however, report no change in their behavior in these areas. Both parents and siblings agree that separations produce the most anxious times for everyone.

Adolescents

Parents' perceptions of adolescent (12–18) siblings are that they take initiative to discover information about the cancer experience, that they process the parents' information about the child's condition, and that they understand the possible fatal outcome of the illness for the child. Parents believe that adolescent siblings feel slighted by not having enough time with parents, are somewhat jealous of the attention given the ill child, miss their sibling and parents, and want them home.

In general, parents and siblings shared similar perceptions about information given and received between parents and healthy adolescent siblings. Both parents and siblings identified the concerns surrounding feelings of neglect, resentment, loneliness, and being upset about separations. Adolescent siblings identify their difficulties. They also speak of feeling pressured when trying to answer the questions of others, such as from other family members, family friends, teachers, and neighbors. Parents are often unaware of this pressure and of the subsequent anxiety it causes the adolescent siblings.

Duration of Illness

Duration of illness is potentially important to sibling bereavement response. Time before the death allows for a period of anticipatory grief which has been said to lessen the shock of death and facilitates subsequent adjustment to the death (Fulton & Fulton, 1971; Parkes, 1971; Vachon, 1976). In the words of Higgins (1977), "When death is expected, as in the case of malignant disease, its intensity may be reduced by preparatory grief, a process in which separation and loss are anticipated before the death of a significant other, whether parent or child" (p. 693). Blinder (1972), based on clinical case studies of siblings of dying children, also concluded that in comparison with sudden loss by accident, "where a more prolonged illness is involved, anticipatory grief is possible for both the parents and remaining siblings" (p. 173).

Several decades ago, when children diagnosed with cancer lived for only a relatively short time, Natterson and Knudson (1960) stated that it took a minimum of four months from the time of diagnosis to the time for death for the surviving family members to incorporate and cope successfully with the tragic situation. The findings of Schwab, Chalmers, Conroy, Ferris, and Markush (1965), however, indicated that there was a threshold for the beneficial effects of longer-term illness. They reported that grief reactions were significantly more intense when the terminal illness lasted more than one year as compared with less than one year. It might be that these findings are related to the effects of treatment during the 1960s when relatively little could be done for children with cancer, and the longer the children lived, the longer they suffered. However, even with considerable advancement in treatment, similar findings were reported by Payne et al. (1980) two decades later. They found that disruption of the parents' marital relationship was significantly more frequent among those whose child had treatment that extended to more than two years than among those whose child had briefer treatment. In contrast, Spinetta, Swarner, and Sheposh (1981) identified better parental adjustment occurring with longer illnesses; in situations where the child's illness was of shorter duration, the families "did poorly." Neither Davies (1983) nor McCown (1982), however, found significant relationships between length of illness and behavior problem scores.

Several explanations may account for the discrepant findings. Both Davies and McCown studied children between the ages of 6 and 16. One explanation may be that children of these ages may not benefit from a period of anticipatory grief in the same way that it has been documented that adults do. A second is the way in which the variable was defined, which most often was the number of months elapsed between the date of diagnosis and the actual death. This time period may not accurately reflect the time the surviving children had available to them to prepare for the death. This was exemplified by the mother who said,

> Pete grew up with Rebecca's illness—it was a part of his life. His older sister had been told about the illness and the prognosis, but Pete was never told in the same way. It always seemed like such a part of his life that there was no need to.

A suggestion for further study then is to question the parents, or the children themselves, about when they became aware of their siblings' diagnoses and prognosis. When the loss of a sibling is preceded by an illness such as cancer, the pattern of relationship has already been disrupted by the illness itself, and so the disruption caused by the death is not as great as if a sudden death had occurred. It is possible that the greatest impact on children of having a sibling die from cancer is at the time of diagnosis or during the illness. It would be instructive to study children's behavior at diagnosis, throughout the illness, and following the death.

Place of Death

In their evaluation of a home care program for terminally ill children, Mulhern, Lauer, and Hoffman (1983) compared behavior reactions of children whose siblings died at home with those whose sibling died in the hospital 3 to 29 months following the child's death. Using maternal reports on a standardized behavioral checklist, the investigators found that children from the home care program scored within normal limits, whereas those whose siblings died in the hospital had higher scores on fear and neurotic behavior scales. However, caution must be employed in the interpretation of these findings: families who chose home care may have differed substantially from families who selected hospital care for the dying child.

Lauer et al. (1985) subsequently examined children's perceptions and involvement during their siblings' terminal home care or hospital experience and correlated those factors to subsequent adjustment after this sibling's death. Nineteen children whose siblings participated in a home care program for dying children and 17 children whose siblings died in the hospital were interviewed one year after the death. Home care children described a significantly different experience from those whose siblings died in the hospital. The majority of the children who participated in the home care program reported that they were prepared for the impending death, received consistent information and support from their parents, were involved in most activities concerning the dying child, were present for the death, and viewed their own involvement as the most important aspect of the experience. By contrast, non-home-care children generally described themselves as having been inadequately prepared for the death, isolated from the dying child and their parents, unable to use their parents for support or information, unclear as to the circumstances of the death, and useless in terms of their own involvement. Three major recurrent experiential differences noted by the children's self-report in these two groups were preparation for the death, involvement in preterminal and terminal care, and parental accessibility for support.

More recently, Mulhern, Lauer, and Hoffman (1983) examined parental adjustment following a child's death at home or hospital 6–8 years earlier. Long-term data emerging from this study suggest that the early pattern of differential adjustment of home care and non-home-care parents is generally a reliable predictor of long-term bereavement outcome. Parents who provided home care experienced a relatively efficient and enduring resolution of their grief. While this relationship requires further empirical testing among home care and non-home-care siblings population, these early findings provide more definitive support for the role of home care as a determinant of differential profiles of bereavement.

☐ Time Elapsed Since the Death

Elapsed time since the death is another situational variable worthy of consideration. For many years, there was a common assumption that grief is a time-limited process—that by one or two years after the death, the person should be "back to normal." This perception was based on Lindemann's (1944) seminal work on bereavement in which he indicated that grieving individuals were back to normal within a short period of time.

Most studies of sibling bereavement, and in fact most bereavement studies, focus on the months immediately after the death or up to one or two years following the death. Consequently, the longer-term effects of siblings' bereavement are relatively unknown. Several studies (Davies, 1983, 1984, 1985; Rosen, 1986; Spinetta et al., 1981) indicate that grief responses persisted with siblings in the majority of families even two to three years after the death.

Very few researchers have controlled for elapsed time since death. Among those who have are Payne et al. (1980). They found that a variety of problems subsequent to the loss of a brother or sister was evident in a larger percentage (36%) of those children whose sibling had died six months before than of those (22%) whose sibling had died two years before. Similarly, Hogan (1988a) reported that adolescents demonstrated more problems during the first 3–18 months than during the 18–36 months interval after the death. In my earliest study (Davies, 1983), I found that internalizing behaviors were negatively correlated with time elapsed since the death; that is, over time (up to three years postdeath) siblings became more withdrawn, anxious, and sad. The need for longitudinal studies is emphasized. In reporting the secondary analysis of the data collected in Martinson's (1980) study, I (Davies, 1987a) indicate that at 7 to 9 years after the death, siblings reported that they continued to experience effects of the death. Several continued to dream about their deceased brother or sister—such dreams were not disturbing but rather comforting in that they provided a feeling of closeness to the sibling. Feelings of loneliness and sadness persisted, not always in the forefront of their minds but still identifiable. Many of the siblings continued to think frequently about their deceased brother or sister, several as often as once a day. Such thoughts were triggered by internal and external reminders and were more prevalent at certain times, like when they themselves reached the age at which the sibling had died or when they had children of their own. Similar results emerged from an examination of adults who in their childhood lost a sibling (Davies, 1996). Up to 10, 20, or 30 years after the death, siblings perceive that the death had a long-term impact on their lives, often as a constant reminder about the value of life. The long-term effects of sibling bereavement are not necessarily pathological even though periods of intense sadness may recur years later.

These data suggest two contradictions to common assumptions about grief in siblings. First, the data indicate that the time required for the bereavement process in siblings is indeed longer than a year or two. Even many years after the death, siblings are still experiencing pain and loss. Long-term effects are further discussed in Chapter 9. Second, rather than saying things that suggested resolution, the siblings described something different. Instead of "letting go" of the loved one, the siblings and their parents detailed the continuing presence of an "empty space" (McClowry, Davies, May, Kulenkamp, & Martinson, 1987).

☐ Involvement in Illness and Death-Related Events

Perhaps the most significant situational variable affecting sibling bereavement response is the degree to which siblings are involved in events surrounding the death and in the illness experience if the death is preceded by illness. Participating in events relevant to illness and death provides a way for children to incorporate these events into their new life space or environment and thereby offers them an opportunity to understand better the whole transition.

The ability to recognize familiar objects and to orient oneself within an environment implies a degree of mastery of that environment regardless of the extent to which the situation is actively controlled or altered. There is an "active component in perception; in fact, many motor acts are carried out in order to facilitate perception. . . . A person is not the passive recipient of sensations from his life space; he creates his assumptive world by reaching out to his environment and sampling it, he reacts to his life space by moving within it, to keep it the same or to change it" (Parkes, 1971, p. 104). Parkes's idea of active participation in the environment as a way of becoming familiar with it and of easing the process of transition is a significant one—especially when looking at how children adapt to changes in their environment, because children seem to learn best by involvement, participation, and action.

The significance of sibling involvement is supported theoretically, clinically, and empirically. Three theoretical perspectives help in understanding the reason for the value of involving children in significant family events, including illness and death of a sibling.

Involvement, Coping, and Direct Action

First, coping theory put forth by Lazarus, a major contributor to understanding the coping process, indicates that involvement, as a form of direct action, facilitates coping. His earlier theoretical and empirical work (for example, Lazarus, 1966; Lazarus & Folkman, 1984) focused on how a person's cognitive appraisal of a stressful situation influences the emotional responses that are elicited, the coping strategies that are employed, and the ultimate success of the person's adjustment to a crisis. Lazarus's theory states that emotion arises from certain kinds of adaptive transactions a person is having with his environment. This theory implies a two-way interaction involving needs or motives and other psychological properties of persons on the one hand, and environmental settings that provide opportunities for gratification and potential for frustration or harm on the other. The intensity and quality of the consequent emotional reaction, as well as the nature of coping activities designed to master the transaction, reflect the way this situation is evaluated cognitively by the person. The concept of cognitive appraisal thus expresses the evaluation of the significance of a transaction for the person's well-being and the potential for mastery in the continuous and constantly changing interplay between the person and the environment.

Lazarus later elaborated on direct action as a type of coping as self-regulatory behavior. In direct action, individuals try to alter or master the troubled relationship with the environment—for example, when they somehow try to prepare to meet the danger. Children's involvement in visiting their ill sibling in the hospital, in helping to care for the sibling, and in attending death-related events are examples of direct action useful for the child's coping with a stressful environment. To the extent to which such direct action leads to a more benign appraisal of the situation and its potential outcomes, the stress reaction is mitigated and the child can cope more effectively and consequently adapt more easily to the transition. Such self-regulatory processes are normal features of stressful transactions, a continuous feature of living and adapting. As such, they are key intervening processes in the causation and prevention of stress-related behaviors and disorders. In all likelihood, some of these are effective under certain conditions, while others are not.

Involvement, Control, and Predictability

The notion of control is important to the above argument. The child's active participation in selected events related to a sibling's illness and death does not allow the child to gain control over what is happening—the child cannot control the course of events. Direct action, however, does provide a sense of mastery or perhaps, better said, a sense of predictability. Controllability means that the individual can actually *do* something about the event in question, whereas predictability means that the person can merely know something about the event, whether or not the individual can do anything about it.

If children are involved in visiting an ill sibling or in helping to care for the sibling, the children become aware through first-hand experience that the sibling is becoming weaker, less alert, and more ill—the imminence of death is forewarned. The predictability of the outcome is made known. Then, when the sibling actually dies, involvement in the postdeath events provides an opportunity for the child to say good-bye and to begin to predict the realization of the finality of death.

Miller and Grant (1978) indicated that predictability facilitates adaptation to stressful events. In an extensive review of the predictability literature, these authors concluded that there are conditions under which predictable aversive events are "less stressful" than nonpredictable events. Parkes (1971) would concur. He said that if change takes place gradually and the individual has time to prepare, little by little, for the structuring, the chances that coping will follow a satisfactory course are greater than they would be if the change was sudden and unexpected. Involvement in the sibling's illness reinforces for children the predictability of a sibling's death; involvement in the postdeath events reinforces for children the predictability of the finality of death and the continuation of daily life without the sibling. By providing children with some sense of predictability, involvement, therefore, enhances children's ability to cope with the loss of a sibling.

Involvement and Affiliation

The value of the child's involvement in events surrounding a sibling's illness and death can also be framed within the concept of affiliation. In a classic piece of research, Schacter (1959), a social psychologist, conducted an experiment to test the notion that human affiliation had its origins, at least in part, in anxiety or threat. That is, he postulated that to prefer to be with other people rather than alone is a way of coping with threat. He used two treatment conditions, one an experimental group, the members of which were told to expect a severe and painful shock. The painful nature of the shock was emphasized in order to maximize the anxiety and threat. The control group was told about the impending shock in such a way as to minimize the anxiety and threat. Then subjects were permitted to select a comfortable and furnished room in which to wait for the experiment to begin. Subjects were told that some rooms contained other subjects, while other rooms were empty. Each subject was asked whether he preferred to wait in the room with the others or to wait alone. There was a marked tendency for the highly threatened subjects to want to wait with others in contrast to control subjects who had been exposed to low threat. Evidently, the companionship of others seemed to offer potential help in coping with the impending harm. If companionship reduces anxiety and facilitates coping, then to have children involved in both illness and postdeath events along with other family members provides for companionship, thereby helping to reduce children's anxiety and enhancing their adaptive abilities.

Companionship, or linkages with other groups, has been shown to be effective for coping in other situations as well. For example, people who survived imprisonment in concentration camps benefitted from being able to stay together with some members of their family or to remain in contact with prewar peers (Mechanic, 1974). A sense of group belonging was among the factors that seemed to contribute significantly to survival both in psychological and physical terms.

In general, children are better able to cope with crisis situations when normal social support is provided (Viney & Clarke, 1974). When separation from their families is involved, their emotional vulnerability may increase to the point of being unable to adapt to the new social or physical environments (Harding & Looney, 1977). The impending and actual death of a sibling are stressful events. If affiliation with others reduces stress, then again, involvement of children in a sibling's illness and postdeath events (because it provides affiliation with loved ones) facilitates children's coping and adaptation to the death of the sibling.

Involvement and the Clinical Literature

The benefits of involvement by family members in the illness experience of loved ones have been alluded to in the clinical literature. Lascari (1978) reinforces the therapeutic value for parents to actively participate in the care of their ill child:

> It is often very helpful to allow parents to participate as much as possible in the medical management of their child. Giving oral medication, taking oral temperatures, bathing the child, etc. give the parents the sense that they are helping and is often therapeutic emotionally for the parents. (p. 1283)

Cain and Staver (1976) suggested that children's adaptation to recurring partial loss through repeated parental hospitalizations or to the possibility of parental death can be aided by children's involvement: "actively participating in the care of the sick parent also permits some mastery over this type of threatening situation" (p. 576). This same rationale applies to children's participation in a sibling's illness experience. The value of active participation by a young child in a sibling's hospitalization has been documented by a mother's own experience with her daughter visiting the child's terminally ill younger brother: "I think it helped her tremendously to be able to visit David and know where we both were."

In summary, involvement in the events of transition facilitates adaptation to that transition for three reasons. Involvement, as direct action, facilitates a better understanding of the events and enhances coping abilities; it provides a sense of control through predictability of future events; and involvement offers an opportunity for affiliation and a sense of belonging. Children learn well by direct participation.

Empirical Evidence

The foregoing theories and clinical documentation provided the framework for examining whether or not direct action in the form of children's involvement in selected pre- and postdeath events was related to the number of behavior problems demonstrated by children following the death of a sibling. The following data are based on a study with 32 children, aged 6 to 16 years, following the death of a sibling from cancer (Davies, 1983, 1984).

Involvement in Illness

Descriptive data pertaining to the items which composed the involvement in illness index appear in Table 6.2. Five bereaved children had not been able to accompany their siblings on clinic visits because the siblings never attended a clinic. Only 6 children never went along on at least one clinic visit. Two-fifths (41.2%) had accompanied their siblings to clinic visits at least once, and 26.5% had gone often.

Nearly half of the children had been present during at least one of the ill sibling's treatments or procedures. These included such things as observing the taking of blood, the starting of intravenous chemotherapy, or blood administration.

When the ill children were at home and feeling ill—usually during the terminal phase of their illness—most (64.7%) of the bereaved children helped to care for their ill siblings. They helped primarily by "getting things" or bringing nourishment (drinks of water, ice cream) to their weakened siblings. In some families, the well children had not helped at all, either because they were "too young," or because care of the ill child was the "total responsibility of the mother."

The frequency with which the well children visited their hospitalized siblings during their last hospitalizations varied from not visiting at all (8.8%) to visiting every day (20.6%). Of those who did not visit at all, two ill children had never been hospitalized and so the item was not applicable. This particular item was found to detract from the internal consistency of the overall index and was consequently deleted from the index.

Of the 34 children who visited their ill siblings in the hospital, 18 engaged in either solitary or parallel activity during the visit. For example, the well child "wandered away by herself to the cafeteria" or "sat and watched television" with the ill child. Fourteen engaged in interaction: "He [the well child] would play with her toys on the couch and would pull her and her IV in the wagon."

Some children had more contact with their hospitalized siblings than others did, ranging from no contact other than visits to the hospital (12) to daily contact by telephone (11). This item also weakened the internal consistency of the index and consequently was deleted from the index.

The possible range of scores on the involvement in illness index ranged from 1 to 10. The children's actual scores ranged from 2 to 9, with an average score of 6.1. Using the midpoint of the range as a marker, approximately

TABLE 6.2. Descriptive data on involvement in illness index

Index	Item	Category	*N*	%	Mean	S.D.
Involvement in illness	Frequency of clinic visits by surviving child (SC)	Not applicable	5	14.7	1.8	1.0
		None	6	17.6		
		Seldom	14	14.2		
		Often	9	26.5		
	Observation of clinic or hospital procedures	Not applicable	6	17.6	1.3	.76
		No	12	35.3		
		Yes	16	47.1		
	SC's participation in care of deceased child (DC) at home	No	12	35.3	1.6	.49
		Yes	22	64.7		
	*Frequency of hospital visits by SC	Did not visit	3	8.8	2.8	.89
		Less than 1 per week	9	26.5		
		1–3 times per week	15	44.1		
		Every day	7	20.6		
	Interaction with DC in hospital	Not applicable	2	5.9	1.4	.60
		Solitary or parallel activity	18	52.9		
		Interactive	14	41.2		
	*Contacts other than hospital visits	None	12	35.3	1.9	.83
		Indirect	11	32.4		
		Direct	11	32.4		
	Ranges of total scores	2–5 (Low)	14	41.2		
		6–9 (High)			6.1	2.1
			20	58.8		

*Item deleted from the illness index because of low alpha.

Davies, B. (1988). The family environment in bereaved families and its relationship to surviving sibling behavior. *Children's Health Care, 17*(1), 22–31. Reprinted with permission of Lawrence Erlbaum Associates, Inc.

40% of the children were below the midpoint (scoring low for involvement in their ill sibling's illness) and 60% were highly involved.

Involvement in Postdeath Events

Descriptive data on the original eight items in the involvement in postdeath events index are given in Table 6.3. The majority (70.6%) of the surviving children were not present at the time of their siblings' death. In most cases, the ill child died in hospital and the well child was at home at the time of death. Nearly one quarter of the children were with their ill sibling until just before the death—the ill child died at home and so the well children had been with their siblings until they had gone to bed or had gone off to school. Twenty-two of the children saw their sibling after the death, either immediately after the death in the home or hospital or later in the funeral home. Most children (64.7%) did not participate in planning for their sibling's funeral; however, nearly all of the children attended both the funeral (91.2%) and the burial service (85.3%). In both events, most children had observer roles rather than active roles.

On the involvement in postdeath events index, the possible range and the actual range of scores were 3–11. On the postdeath events index, nearly 60% of the children had low involvement and about 40% had high involvement.

Total Involvement

The possible range for scores on the total involvement index was 4–21; the actual range was 7–17 with a mean of 12.4. Forty percent of the children had scores in the lower half of the range (7–11); and 60% had scores in the upper half of the range (12–17).

Involvement in postdeath events and the active-recreational orientation of the family were correlated significantly ($r = .43$, $p < .01$). The greater the emphasis within the family on participation in social and recreational activities, the more involved the children were in postdeath events. No significant relationships were found between either involvement with the illness or total involvement and the family environment subscales (FES).

Total behavior problem scores correlated negatively with each indicator of involvement. In other words, the greater the degree of involvement of the surviving children in their sibling's illness and postdeath events, the fewer the total behavior problems demonstrated after the death. Social competency scores correlated positively with involvement in postdeath events. None of the relationships, however, were statistically significant.

Although significant relationships were not found, the results of this study suggested that involvement in both the illness and postdeath events were

TABLE 6.3. Descriptive data on involvement in postdeath events index

Index	Item	Category	*N*	%	Mean	S.D.
Involvement in postdeath events	Surviving child's (SC's) presence at time of death	Not present	24	70.6	1.4	.60
		Left just before death	8	23.5		
		Present	2	5.9		
	*SC's viewing body after death	No	12	35.3	1.6	4.9
		Yes	22	64.7		
	SC's participation in planning funeral	No	22	64.7	1.4	.49
		Yes	12	35.3		
	**SC's attendance at funeral	Not applicable	1	2.9	1.9	.41
		No	2	5.9		
		Yes	31	91.2		
	SC's activities during funeral	Not applicable	3	8.8	1.1	.56
		Passive observer	23	67.6		
		Active participant	8	23.5		
	SC's attendance at burial	No	5	14.7	1.9	.36
		Yes	29	85.3		
	SC's activities during burial	Not applicable	5	14.7	0.97	.52
		Passive observer	25	73.5		
		Active participant	4	11.8		
	SC's visits to gravesite	Not applicable	2	5.9	1.5	.62
		No	14	41.2		
		Yes	18	52.9		
	Ranges of total scores	3–6 (low involvement)	20	58.8	6.3	1.6
		7–11 (high involvement)	14	41.2		

*Item deleted from index because of low alpha.
**Items deleted from index because of no variability.

associated with fewer behavior problems and that involvement in postdeath events was associated with greater social competence. While codified quantitative data did not support the hypothesis, the interview material testified to the importance of trying to understand better the role played by involvement in resolving grief. Glenn, for example, at 19 years of age was having great difficulty adjusting to life without his brother, Joe. Joe had died seven years ago when Glenn was 12. Joe died from cancer and was frequently in the hospital during the two years of his illness. During these times, Glenn was often left alone; he was not actively involved in Joe's illness. Glenn remembers how he coped on his own:

> When the cats were away, this mouse played. I put boards up against the garage . . . and I went crazy. I took my bike and I went way down the street here, and shifted down in the gears and started just peddling the pants off that little bike, and I went up the boards on the side of the garage right next to the house and I jumped the garage on my bicycle. I jumped over the roof. . . . I wrecked my bike. . . . I didn't get a scratch. I was a tough kid. . . . I handled it my way and I guess it worked out. I learned to be a fool and occupy my time. It kept me from losing my sanity. You had to learn to occupy yourself. You had to learn to do things yourself because mom or dad didn't have the time for that sort of thing. . . . I guess that's why I learned . . . to occupy myself because my folks didn't have time for me.

When Joe died, Glenn was also not actively involved, although he did attend the funeral: "There were nine million people at the funeral. . . . Afterwards, me and my cousin were just standing outside talking kid talk . . . and, like I say, I didn't even know what happened really." Feelings of being left out are common among siblings. Many siblings understand their parents' predicament and can rationalize their parents' absence and lack of attention. But the siblings still feel left out and alone and on the outside looking in.

One explanation for why involvement facilitates adjustment was provided by the theories of Lazarus (1966). He suggested that direct action facilitates understanding of the situation, which, in turn, makes for increased coping abilities. This explanation was supported by the mother who said, "Pete died at home—this made it easier for all the children because they could see it all," and by the mother who described involvement as resulting in a change in understanding and attitude for her surviving daughter: "At first, Carol [surviving child] had the attitude that her brother could 'do it—there's really nothing wrong with him.' Then, as I encouraged her to help him and help me with him, Carol became less that way."

A second explanation had to do with the idea that the children's involvement forewarned them of forthcoming events and thereby enhanced their sense of control. Young Ted, for example, was expecting his brother to die and so it didn't really come as a big shock. He had seen his brother slowly go downhill.

The third and final explanation suggested that increased coping abilities are associated with affiliation; that is, being involved provides an opportunity for being with significant others and feeling as if one belongs to the group and is not alone in the crisis. At the time of the death, for example,

> Caroline was at home sleeping. Her grandparents and great-grandmother and aunt were all with her at home. After we phoned, they went in and woke her up and brought her to the hospital right away. Caroline came into the room where I [mom] was holding Frank's body. She touched her brother and commented that he was cold. When we had all been there long enough and felt it was time to go, the doctor walked us to the car and we all went home together.

Caroline demonstrated few behavior problems after the death of her brother; Lloyd, on the other hand, had been taken to a psychiatrist because of his severe reactions. He had been minimally involved with the death and the funeral:

> Lloyd was sleeping when his sister was taken to the hospital. The next morning he got up and went to school, and when he got home he was told that she had died in the hospital. Lloyd didn't want to go to the funeral; he went to school instead. When he came home from school, everyone was back at the house and he visited and played with the other children who were there. The funeral was never really discussed.

Ten-year-old Sally had attended her brother's funeral, and the mother recalled:

> Important things happened there that made Sally feel a part of what was going on. One family walked over to the car where Sally was—just to acknowledge her especially. Afterwards, that was the thing that Sally remembered most about the funeral . . . that someone had talked especially to her.

Sally had been made to feel supported by others because she was involved in the funeral.

There are conceptually distinguishable forms of involvement that can perhaps best be understood by referring to Chanowitz and Langer's (1980) description of the difference between mindless and mindful involvement. Mindless involvement occurs when a person simply "goes through the motions" of an activity and simply going through the motions does not dictate the sort of experience that will characteristically accompany the activity. The fact that the children were reported by their mothers to have helped care for their ill siblings or to have attended the funeral does not provide information about the nature of the children's experiences accompanying these motions.

Mindful involvement, on the other hand, occurs when an individual is sensitive to what is happening. Mindful involvement promotes the significance and personal meaning of the activities and the development of the self is fostered which enables the person to keep up with the changes. In cases of mindful involvement, children may not only help care for their ill sibling or attend the funeral, but they may also sense that their actions make a difference and, as a result, a greater sense of control is experienced. Glenn, for example, attended his brother's funeral, but he was not mindfully involved. He "didn't even know what had happened really." The study of involvement then needs not only to include what activities were carried out (the outcome), but it must also incorporate some measure of the experience of involvement (the process).

☐ Involving Siblings in a Child's Illness

Caring for a child with a life-threatening illness places great strains on the child's parents. They may feel overwhelmed and have little energy left over to devote to mindfully involving their healthy children. The following section offers suggestions to parents and pediatric caregivers, whether in hospital settings or hospice programs, who can help in meeting the needs of the healthy siblings. Again, these suggestions have evolved out of our work with children with cancer and their families, but they should apply to many situations in which a child has a life-threatening illness.

Suggestions for Parents

1. Treat Children Equally. Treating all children equally does not mean treating them identically. If, for example, noise gives the ill child a headache, the adolescent siblings must be discouraged from playing loud music in the house. Healthy adolescents, however, enjoy loud music; you can purchase head sets for the siblings or permit them to play their tapes in the car's tape deck. Siblings can be expected to "be considerate" much of the time, but their needs must also be met. If they have a sense that you are trying to treat all of the children equally by taking into account everyone's special needs, the well siblings will usually feel less neglected and will be more cooperative.

2. Arrange to See the Healthy Children. Help the healthy children to see you, especially if you are staying in the hospital with the ill child. The "other" children need to know where you are, to know that you are okay, and to feel that they have not been forgotten. You can arrange to have them visit in the hospital (even if it means missing a day or two of school if travelling is involved). Such contacts help the siblings understand the situation through firsthand experience and allay their feelings of isolation and loneliness.

3. Spend "Alone" Time with the Healthy Sibling. Make an effort to find some one-on-one time with the healthy sibling, even it if is very limited time. Something as simple as having a soft drink together in the hospital cafeteria or a bedtime snuggle at home indicates to the healthy children that you still think that they, too, are important.

4. Let Healthy Siblings Lead Normal Lives. Permit the other children to continue with their lives as normally as possible. Because you are sad and preoccupied, you may stop doing such routine tasks as helping with homework or attending soccer games. Often the children worry about being an added burden to you. It is important, therefore, for you to encourage the siblings to continue their daily tasks. You should continue to participate in their children's lives when possible, even if it is only a brief appearance at a soccer game or an inquiry about homework or the child's friends.

5. Be Aware of Your Own Feelings. Be aware of your own feelings and their expression in your behavior. As a parent of a dying child you may feel tired, frustrated, and angry. As a result, irritability and a short temper may be evident. You should recognize this and try not to misdirect these behaviors toward the healthy siblings. You also may be very concerned for the welfare of other children; nevertheless, you should attempt not to translate this concern into overprotective behavior or abstention from normal rules and regulations. Although such behaviors understandably stem from your fears of losing another child, they are often interpreted by the children as "just not caring anymore." Maintaining normal limits, therefore, is very important.

6. Have Siblings Help in Concrete Ways. Have the other children help out; this makes them feel useful and provides some order in their lives. You can not only have siblings help in household chores, but you can also let them share in the care of the ill child by bringing a glass of water, by playing games, or just by watching television together. Helping out can give you a break. Moreover, it allows the child to continue the sibling relationship with the ill brother or sister. It allows them to be actively involved. If children are allowed to choose their own helping tasks, they will often do so willingly and not be resentful of the extra expectations placed on them.

7. Keep Siblings Informed. Provide the well children with up-to-date and honest explanations about what is happening with the ill child. You should offer simple explanations, geared to the child's level of comprehension. Preschoolers, for example, are not likely to understand or remember detailed explanations. They need simple information that they can mull over and discuss frequently with you. Adolescents, on the other hand, need to be told everything. Regardless of their age, all children appreciate honesty and want to feel as though they are included in what is happening.

8. Reaffirm Siblings' Worth. Regularly reaffirm the worth of the well children. Children need repeated reminders from you that they are loved, and that you appreciate their help. You should not wait until the well children begin to misbehave before giving them attention. It is a good idea to plan a sit-down chat periodically to let them know how things are going, to see if they have any unanswered questions, and to reaffirm their worth and their contribution to the situation.

Suggestions for Professional Caregivers

Because parents have great difficulty in attending to the ill child and to the needs of other family members, personnel involved with the child and family can also play an important role in helping the well siblings cope during the time of illness.

1. Include siblings in family meetings with individual members of the medical, oncology, specialty team.
2. If siblings cannot attend meetings, inquire about the healthy siblings: Who is looking after them? What have they been told? What concerns do they have?
3. Allocate time to spend just with the siblings: Go for a walk, play a game (depending on sibling ages). This time gives opportunity to talk, to assess their understanding or concerns or both, and to allay fears and anxieties to the extent possible.
4. Solicit assistance from the siblings in caring for the ill child and encourage their active involvement in the child's care at home.
5. If siblings cannot come to the hospital, encourage their indirect involvement with the ill child via phone calls, letter writing, or photos. Polaroid photos are particularly good since they can be taken home to the siblings immediately.
6. Offer teaching sessions via slide shows, demonstrations, or puppet shows to convey disease-related information. Plan such sessions for evenings or weekends when siblings can attend.
7. Develop sibling groups where possible. Such groups provide siblings with information and support from others in similar situations. If a

group is not feasible, put siblings in touch with one another via a phone or pen-pal program.

8. Provide encouragement and positive reinforcement of children's coping behavior.
9. Facilitate open discussions between parents and their well children. Encourage the expression of thoughts and feelings.
10. Support the parents in meeting the needs of their well children.
11. Facilitate the healthy children's relationships with their peers. School and friends compose a major component of the lives of children; positive experiences with both are integral to optimal adjustment. The siblings' friends can be encouraged to visit and to participate in the ill child's care as well. They, too, should be given information about the illness, and about how they can help their friend. Open communication with the school nurse and the siblings' teachers should also be undertaken.

Helping the siblings in these ways also directly supports parents. For example, including the school-age siblings in the family meetings with the oncology specialty team means that everyone hears the information at the same time. This reduces the burden on the parents, since they do not have to repeat information. Instead, parents can direct their energies to reinforcing or clarifying what was said by the nurse or the physician.

By spending time with the healthy siblings, either alone or in sibling programs, hospice professionals can assess how the siblings are managing. That information can then be used either to reassure the parents that the siblings are doing okay or to identify ways in which parents can be helped to meet a well child's needs.

Finally, the nurse or physician can serve as a catalyst for open discussion between parents and children. Parents often feel concerned about how their other children are doing, but they may have difficulty initiating discussion or sharing "bad news" with the other children. By being open and honest in conversations with the parents and their children, hospice caregivers can model such discussions and thereby facilitate similar communication within families.

☐ Involving Siblings During the Dying Process

There are no rules for how to handle the siblings of a terminally ill child at the time of death. There is, however, one general principle that applies to the siblings during all phases of a pediatric hospice experience and particularly at the time of death: Brothers and sisters should not be excluded. The degree to which they are included varies with each situation and with each child. Most often it is the case that adults' first reaction is to protect the other children and to find alternative places for them to go. This automatically means that the children are excluded. It would be much better if, instead, adults considered "What can the children do here?" rather than, "Where can we send the children?"

Traditionally, health professionals have wanted to protect the parents and siblings from witnessing the rapidly changing physiological event, i.e., the dying process and the death event. However, with the hospice focus on the dying child, health professionals increasingly realize that the child needs the parents and may also want the siblings to be present as he or she is dying. Most parents and siblings, if informed about the physiological changes (e.g., Cheyne–Stokes respirations), can handle these changes emotionally and can concentrate on the child.

Some parents may hold the dying child in their arms, rock the child in a rocking chair, or sit by the bed holding the child's hand. Physical contact with the child is encouraged. Siblings often can provide some of the care such as bringing a glass of water, helping to feed, or giving gentle backrubs to their brother or sister.

When death is imminent, the siblings should be made aware of this fact and should be permitted to go to school or to stay at home (or at the hospital) with the ill child. The important thing is not to force a child to leave who would rather be present or to make a child feel guilty for leaving if that is what he or she prefers. The sibling should also be able to choose without guilt whether he or she wants to see the dead child. If siblings have not been present at the death, then telling them the bad news requires sensitivity. (See Chapter 3.)

☐ Involving Siblings in the Funeral

Attending the funeral is of great benefit to siblings. Funerals are for those left behind. Funerals provide opportunity to connect with family and friends, to offer love and support to one another, to cry together, and to remember. Funerals help siblings realize that their brother or sister is dead and will not be coming back. Siblings should not be denied the support that funerals can provide. Some siblings feels ambivalent about attending the funeral—they want to go and at the same time are afraid of going. In talking with siblings about the funeral, begin by explaining what will happen there. Adults should describe to siblings what will happen, who will be there, and that some people may cry. Tell them how long it will last, and outline the ritual, referring to such things as the minister, priest, or rabbi talking, the singing of hymns, and the saying of prayers. Tell siblings if the casket will be present, and if it is, if it will be open or closed. If siblings have not seen their brother's or sister's body, then tell the children what the body will look like—it will be very still. It may appear as if the child is sleeping but is not. The body will not be breathing and the color will be pale. Tell siblings they can touch the body, if they wish, and that it will feel cool and firm. Tell siblings that they can talk to their brother or sister and say good-bye one last time. They can verbally express their love, if they choose, or they can place a gift, such as a flower, a note, or a drawing, or something of their own choice, in the casket as a way of saying good-bye.

Many siblings voice concern over what they are supposed to do at the funeral. Ten-year-old Jake exclaimed,

> I wanted to be at the funeral, but I didn't know what to do. My mom was crying and my dad was crying, and everyone was crying. And, I didn't know if I could cry. And then people talked [to me], and I didn't know what to do.

Children often feel at a loss because they do not know what is expected of them. Prepare siblings by telling them what is expected of them, such as what to wear, and that it is okay to cry, or not. Warn them that they might even find something funny, and if they do, it is okay to laugh. Prepare siblings for the parents' potential distress, and give them things to do if their parents are very upset, such as offering tissues. It is often a good idea to identify a caring and trusted adult to pay attention to siblings. This person can be prepared to spend time with the siblings, offering reassurance and explaining what is going on. Tell siblings what to say when people at the funeral express their condolences—suggest they can simply say, "Thank you." Also, prepare siblings for the ride to the cemetery and for the rituals that will happen at the graveside. If siblings can be included in the planning of the various rituals, and can even participate in them (by reading a verse or a poem, by singing or playing a musical instrument), so much the better.

Never force siblings to attend the funeral if they are adamant about not going. But very few children say that they do not want to go. If children do refuse, spend some time talking about what it is that makes them not want to go. Ask what the scariest thing would be for them or what is the worst thing that could happen at the funeral. Once children have had a chance to express their fear of going, they often will want to go. Siblings who did not attend the funeral later wish that they had gone. They feel as if they missed something important by not going. As 18-year-old Sally said,

> I didn't want to go to the funeral.... I don't know why really—I was just scared. So I stayed at the neighbor's house. Then, when everyone came to our house afterwards, I felt left out—like they all knew something that I didn't. Even now [six years later], it's still on my mind. I wish I had gone.

Sally chose not to go the funeral and regretted her decision. But had someone talked with her and explained what to expect, her fears may have been alleviated and she might have gone. Other siblings had no choice about attending the funeral. They were simply not allowed to go. These siblings harbor long-lasting resentment about not being able to go. Siblings as young as 4 years can decide whether or not they want to attend the funeral. Once at the funeral, they must still be given choices—about how, and if, they want to say good-bye, about whether or not to place a gift or a note in the casket, about touching or kissing the child's body. Choice is central to children's mindful involvement.

When a child has died from a car accident, or a fire, suicide, or murder, the body may be damaged to such a degree that it cannot be made presentable. In such cases, it is helpful for siblings to see even a portion of the body, such as a leg or a hand. If this is not possible, then it is wise to have someone who siblings trust to identify the body and convey this information to siblings. This helps siblings accept the fact that their brother or sister has indeed died.

Although it is natural for adults to think of their children as needing protection from grief, siblings prefer to feel part of what is happening. They have no control over most situational variables—such as the cause of death or the duration of a life-threatening illness. They can, however, feel included in the events surrounding the illness and the death. Involving siblings is critical in helping them adjust to the death of their brother or sister. The degree to which they are involved depends in large part on environmental variables that are the subject of the next chapter.

7

CHAPTER

Environmental Variables Affecting Sibling Bereavement Responses

Environmental variables are those that contribute to the social-emotional atmosphere of the child's environment. Such variables are significant because coping and adaptive behavior cannot be studied apart from the context within which they occur. It is well established that social milieus have important psychological and health-related effects (Cobb, 1976; Kiritz & Moos, 1974; Nuckolls, Cassel, & Kaplan, 1972). It has also been established that the social environment has an influence on the behavior of children. Lewin's classic work (Lewin, 1950) of nearly half a century ago showed this to be true when, for example, different behaviors resulted among groups of boys when the social environments were characterized as authoritarian, democratic, and laissez faire. The effect of the environment on the aggressive behaviors of children has been well documented by Bandura (1969, 1977) and Bandura and Walters (1969).

Environmental variables have an enormous influence on children's response to loss (Furman, 1974; Bowlby, 1980). Children react more strongly than adults to these variables for several reasons, including their lack of life experience, their dependence on others for information, and their lack of alternatives to go elsewhere if their families are unsympathetic (Bowlby, 1980). Several authors have speculated on potential environmental factors that they say can influence the child's response to the transition of loss. Cain et al. (1964), for example, stated many years ago that:

> The determinants of children's response to the death of a sibling were found to include: the nature of the death; the age and characteristics of the child who died; the child's degree of actual involvement in his sibling's death; the child's pre-existing relationship to the dead sibling; the immediate impact of the death upon the parents; the parents' handling of the initial reactions of the surviving child; the reactions of the community; the impact of the death upon the family structure; the availability to the child and parents of various "substitutes"; the parents' enduring reactions to the child's death; major concurrent stresses upon the child and his family; and the developmental level of the surviving child at the time of death, including not only psychosexual development, but ego development with particular emphasis upon cognitive capacity to understand death. The effects upon the child obviously are not static, undergoing constant developmental transformation and evolution. (p. 750)

Cain et al., however, did not explore the nature of the relationship between any of the above factors and children's bereavement responses, nor have many others explored this relationship. In my own work, I have found two environmental factors instrumental in sibling bereavement response: the sibling relationship and family environment. A related factor, parental response to grief, is a significant aspect of family environment.

☐ Sibling Relationship

The nature of predeath relationships between spouses as a critical variable that influences bereavement outcome when the other dies has been a topic of adult-focused research (Parkes, 1972; Raphael, 1977). However, few studies of sibling bereavement have examined systematically the effect of the predeath relationship between siblings on bereavement outcome in the surviving siblings.

The concept of shared life space is a useful one for examining the predeath relationship between siblings and the degree to which the sibling relationship serves its functions for siblings. Life space as defined by Parkes (1972) consists of "those parts of the environment with which the self interacts and in relationship to which behavior is organized" (p. 103). Parkes proposed that the amount of stress that can be expected in bereavement seems to have a lot to do with how much of each other's life space the deceased person and the survivor occupied. The greater the shared life space, the greater is the potential for disruption and stress; the less the shared life space, the less is the potential for intense disruption during bereavement.

Western societies are characterized in part by small family units. Within this structure, dependent children and their parents occupy enormous sections of each other's life spaces. Similarly, siblings in these small families share with each other large proportions of their life spaces. Furthermore, children who fulfill several functions for each other occupy larger portions of each other's life space than do siblings whose relationship serves fewer functions. A sibling's death disrupts the surviving child's life space; the degree of disruption varies to the extent that the two siblings shared their life space prior to the death of one of the children.

This relationship was demonstrated in my study of 34 families that had experienced the death of a child from cancer 2 to 36 months prior to the time of data collection and who had at least one surviving child between the ages of 6 and 16 (Davies, 1983, 1988a). The primary analysis conducted in the original study focused on one child per family ($N = 34$) (Davies, 1983). The secondary analysis was computed on a sample composed of the total number ($N = 55$) of surviving siblings in the 34 families (Davies, 1988b).

Measuring Closeness

The closeness index represents an attempt to measure the concept of shared life space. The responses to six interview items focusing on aspects of the siblings' shared life space formed the basis for the measure. These items were (a) stated closeness, (b) shared activities, (c) shared time, (d) shared belongings, (e) confiding, and (e) defending. For the responses to the first four of these six items, a 3-point value label was assigned as follows: 1 = minimal, 2 = moderate, and 3 = maximal. For the other two items, the value labels were 1 = minimal, 2 = one-way, and 3 = mutual. The responses were coded with the appropriate value label according to the specified coding category descriptions (Table 7.1). Assigning a value to each item and totalling the values for all six items resulted in an ordinal index of closeness. A total score on closeness could range from 6 to 18 for any one child. The internal consistency of the index was assessed at 0.69 using Cronbach's alpha.

Descriptive data pertaining to the children's scores on the behavioral items of the closeness index are presented in Table 7.2. The majority (58.1%) of the children were rated as being very close to their sibling before the sibling's death. These children were described as "close" or "very close," or as being "closer to one another than to other siblings." Considerable variability was found on the three items that focused on the amount of sharing that occurred between the two children. For example, while 15 children were rated as "minimal" on shared activities, 25 and 23 children, respectively, received a "minimal" rating for shared time and shared belongings. Approximately one-fourth of the bereaved children confided in their siblings, and both utilized each other as sounding boards and shared secrets with

TABLE 7.1. Coding categories and description for closeness index item

Item	Coding Categories	Description
Stated closeness	(1) Minimal	When response states explicitly that the two children did not get along well together; that their relationship was not a smooth one; or states that DC or SC* was closer to another sib than to each other.
	(2) Moderate	When response states that DC and SC were close but is qualified in some way, e.g., because of a difference: "They were close considering the difference in their ages," or because of some external condition: "They were close because there were no other kids around."
	(3) Maximal	When response explicitly states that SC and DC were very close, they got along well, or thought of each other as "special" in some way; or response states that SC and DC were closer to each other than to other sibs in family.
Shared activities	(1) Minimal	When response states that SC and DC did not do many things together, that they did some things together but had their own friends, or that SC did more with another sibling than with DC.
	(2) Moderate	When response states that SC and DC did things together usually in a group setting, i.e., with other sibs, with family, or with friends.
	(3) Maximal	When response states that SC and DC did more things together than with the other sibs, or they were dependent on each other for playmates.
Shared time	(1) Minimal	When response states that DC and SC spent relatively little time together, or that SC spent more time with his/her friends or other siblings than with DC.
	(2) Moderate	When response states that SC and DC spent time together in the context of the whole family, with other sibs, or with mutual friends.
	(3) Maximal	When response states that SC and DC spent more time with each other than with other sibs or friends, or that SC and DC spent a lot of time together.

(*continued*)

TABLE 7.1. (*Continued*)

Item	Coding Categories	Description
Shared belongings	(1) Minimal	When the response states that SC and DC had their own rooms and own toys, and they did not share with each other, that they shared little, or that SC shared more with another sibling than with DC.
	(2) Moderate	When the response states that there was some sharing between SC and DC. They may have had their own rooms and own toys, but shared some toys, or their own rooms and shared most toys, or that they shared a room and had their own toys.
	(3) Maximal	When the response states that DC and SC shared most things, i.e., shared a room and toys; or that they shared a lot or shared well.
Confiding	(1) Minimal	When the response states that DC and SC did not confide in each other or that they confided some, not a lot, or not much.
	(2) One-way	When the response states that one child confided in the other but that the other child did not reciprocate the confiding or sharing of secrets.
	(3) Mutual	When the response states that SC and DC confided in each other and shared a lot with one another.
Defending	(1) Minimal	When the response states that SC and DC did not defend each other; that there was some other behavior that contraindicated defense of one another, e.g., tattled a lot, were happy with their rivalry; that SC and DC defended each other sometimes, and that they sort of defended one another, or that they sometimes stuck up for one another and at other times enjoyed the other's being scolded.
	(2) One-way	When the response states that one of the children defended the other but that it was not a reciprocal defense.
	(3) Maximal	When the response states that they defended each other or that they stuck up for each other.

*DC, deceased child; SC, surviving child.
Tables 7.1 through 7.6 originally appeared in Davies, B. (1988). Shared life space and sibling bereavement responses. *Cancer Nursing, 11*(6), 338–347, and are reprinted with permission.

TABLE 7.2. Descriptive data on closeness index

Index	Item	Category	*N*	%	Mean
Closeness	Stated closeness	Minimal	14	25.4	2.5
		Moderate	9	16.5	
		Maximal	32	58.1	
	Shared activities	Minimal	15	27.2	2.2
		Moderate	20	36.4	
		Maximal	20	36.4	
	Shared time	Minimal	25	45.3	2.3
		Moderate	10	18.2	
		Maximal	30	54.5	
	Shared belongings	Minimal	23	41.8	1.6
		Moderate	10	18.2	
		Maximal	13	23.6	
	Confiding	Minimal	31	56.4	1.7
		One-way	10	18.2	
		Mutual	14	25.4	
	Defending	Minimal	21	38.1	2.2
		One-way	14	25.5	
		Mutual	20	36.4	
	Total score	6–11	20	36.5	12.5
		12–18	35	63.6	

one another. Nearly equal numbers of children received either "minimal" (21) or "mutual" (20) ratings on the sixth item of the index, i.e., defending. The possible range of scores on the closeness index was 6–18.

Bereavement Outcome Related to Closeness

The relationship between bereavement outcome and shared life space was examined by calculating the correlations between behavior scores (previously discussed in Chapter 4) and the closeness index scores. There was a trend for siblings who had been closer to their deceased siblings to show more sadness and withdrawal (internalizing behavior) ($r = 0.31$, $p < 0.07$).

This relationship between internalizing behavior and closeness was examined further by comparing the closeness index scores of those children who had the highest internalizing scores ($N = 12$) with those who had the lowest internalizing scores ($N = 11$). Using the *t* test, the difference between the two groups was significant ($t = 2.5$, $r < 0.05$) (Table 7.3). That is, those children who had the highest internalizing scores also had the highest scores on the closeness index.

TABLE 7.3. *T* test between high and low scoring groups on internalizing behavior

	Closeness Index			
Group	*N*	Mean	SD	*t*
High scoring group	1211	13.7	3.6	2.5*
Low scoring group		10.3	2.9	

$^{*}p < 0.05$.

TABLE 7.4. Means, standard deviations, and *t* tests between poor–fair adjusters and very good–excellent adjusters

Adjustment Rating	Mean	Standard Deviation	Standard Error	*t*	*p*
Poor–fair	13.7	3.4	0.92	1.94	0.06
Very good–excellent	11.5	2.9	0.71		

The relationship between overall adjustment and shared life space also indicated that closeness between siblings affected bereavement outcome. During the interviews, mothers were asked to rate their children's overall adjustment as poor, fair, good, very good, or excellent. The majority of children were reported as having an overall adjustment rating of "good." Fourteen children were rated as having "poor" or "fair" adjustment and 18 children were rated at the other end of the continuum as having "very good" or "excellent" adjustment. A *t*-test comparison of the closeness index means between the "poor–fair" adjusters and the "very good–excellent" adjusters reflected a trend for the less well adjusted children to have been closer (Table 7.4).

Closeness as a Predictor

Given the relationship between closeness and internalizing behavior scores, these variables were identified as ones that may have predictive value in

TABLE 7.5. Regression analysis summary

Predictor	*F* to Enter or Remove	Multiple *R*	R^0	Overall *F*
Internalizing behavior*				
Closeness	3.46*	0.31	0.09	3.46*
Number of sibs	2.66	0.41	0.07	3.15
Elapsed time	1.67	0.46	0.04	2.7

*$p < 0.07$, **$p < 0.001$.
*Age difference did not meet minimal statistical criteria for inclusion in equation.

determining bereavement outcome. A stepwise multiple regression analysis was calculated with internalizing behavior as the dependent variable. Four predictor variables were entered to determine which of the four variables was the best predictor, the second best, and so on. The four predictor variables were (a) closeness in age between the surviving and deceased siblings as measured by the difference in months between the birth dates of each sibling pair; (b) shared life space as indicated by the children's scores on the closeness index; (c) elapsed time in months since the siblings' death to the time of data collection; and (d) number of surviving children. Shared life space or closeness between the siblings was shown to have the greatest predictive value for internalizing behavior (Table 7.5). That is, the closer the siblings were before the death, the greater the likelihood that the surviving sibling will experience sadness and withdrawal after the death of the other sibling.

Summary of Findings

Correlations between closeness and behavior scores suggested that bereaved siblings who were closer to their sibling before the death experienced more internalizing behavior problems after the death. Comparisons between the groups of children with the highest internalizing scores and those with the lowest scores also showed a significant difference between the groups—those with the highest scores had been closer to their now-deceased sibling. Furthermore, the regression analysis indicated a trend for closeness to predict internalizing behavior. These findings support the ideas of Bugen (1977) and Parkes (1972) who both proposed that the more central the lost person was to an individual's life, the more intense the bereavement response.

The foregoing analyses suggest a trend for greater closeness between siblings to be associated with more internalizing behavior in the surviving siblings following one sibling's death. The closeness index was composed primarily of items that reflected the amount of life space shared by the two siblings—shared activities, shared time, and shared belongings. Two items, confiding and defending, were chosen to measure the degree of mutuality in the relationship. These five items were intended to measure shared life space as represented by the functions the siblings fulfilled for one another. Qualitative analysis suggests that it may be desirable to further refine the measurement of closeness in future studies by considering two additional dimensions: the affective quality of the relationship and the meaning of the relationship for the survivor's life. These dimensions are inherent in the concept of centrality.

Centrality

In his model of human grief, Bugen (1977) presented the concept of centrality as a determinant in the intensity of grief. He discussed several criteria that help to define a central relationship. First, centrality refers to a person whose presence and importance is so profound that the mourner feels as though his or her life is meaningless or senseless without the loved one. The qualitative data in this study provided examples of such relationships: "Jonah was very close to his sister. They would do things together, spend time together. He seemed to worship her; he had such admiration for her," and: "Gillian and Joseph were inseparable.... They did everything together from the day that Joseph was born." At a lesser intensity, centrality may refer to a person whose love and nurturance were seen as having been a needed element or a vital source of support in the individual's life. Such a relationship was evident for Marie and her brother: "They had a somewhat stormy relationship, but she would ask him for help with her homework, Girl Scout things, and skiing—he was her major 'consultant,'" or "Janet used her brother more as a sounding board or as a confidant, rather than the other way around."

Third, centrality may also refer to a person to whom the survivor had become behaviorally committed through daily activities, as happened for two surviving sisters: "Mia would rock him and carry him and give him his bottle. She was his special babysitter," and in another family, "Karyn would babysit for her and would take her along and be responsible for her on errands and outings."

The qualitative data in this study provided examples of relationships in which the two siblings were described as being very close even though they had not shared many of the other aspects of shared life space. The closer two siblings were, the more difficulty the surviving child had after the death of the other. For example:

> In one family, there were three children who were 11, 13, and 15 years of age when their little sister, Jennifer, was born. The two oldest children were girls who had a close relationship and spent a lot of time together, thereby often excluding their 11-year-old brother, Cameron. Cameron was especially attached to the new baby when she was born and would spend hours caring for her and playing with her. When Jennifer became ill, Cameron was the one to read to her and encourage her to take her medicine. He even took her for rides on his motorcycle.... No one else was allowed to touch his bike, but his little sister rode in style. Cameron was 15 years old when 4-year-old Jennifer died. Because of their age and sex differences, Cameron and Jennifer had shared few belongings and they had spent relatively little time together. Cameron had sometimes come to the defense of his little sister, but he had, according to his mother, "opened up to his little sister more than to anyone." All family members agreed in the interview that Cameron had been Jennifer's closest sibling; they had shared a very special bond. He missed his little sister very much and was having many more problems than either of his surviving sisters. He was irritable, withdrawn, argumentative, and lonely.

In another family, 6-year-old Margaret was the only surviving child after her younger brother, Tommy, had died 12 months earlier at the age of 18 months:

> Because of their age differences, Margaret and Tommy did not share a room, toys, or other belongings and they did not confide in one another. Margaret had defended Tommy in a protective sense. Margaret was, however, very involved in caring for her baby brother—rocking him, feeding him, keeping him occupied. She was, her mother said, "very attached to her brother." After his death, Margaret was withdrawn, anxious, and fearful.

These two siblings, Cameron and Margaret, had been very close to their siblings, clearly demonstrating centrality in their sibling relationships. Both children had scored high on internalizing behavior, particularly on the subscale labelled either "uncommunicative or social withdrawal." Cameron's score on this subscale was at the 87th percentile and Margaret's was at the 90th.

According to these examples, emotional closeness between children seems to be of importance in sibling bereavement. Further investigation of emotional closeness as a component of the concept of shared life space is warranted, but the findings presented here emphasize that health care professionals need to be particularly sensitive to those bereaved children who shared a close relationship with their brother or sister.

Professionals must also be aware that the concept of "shared life space" as originally put forth does not necessarily refer only to positive relationships.

For example, there are cases where friends and acquaintances of adults whose spouse dies, wonder "Why is she so upset? Those two used to argue all the time. You would think she would be glad to be rid of him!" Aside from the fact that grief is an individual and personal experience, this widow shared a great portion of her life space with her husband, even though the interactions were primarily negative. As a result, his death may greatly affect how she lives her daily life. The same is true for siblings. Some children, particularly older ones, simply do not get along with one another—they spend a lot of time arguing or fighting with one another. Although not discussed in the literature, or elsewhere, there are cases of child abuse where the perpetrator is an older sibling. In these cases, the two siblings share significant portions of each other's life space, although in harmful ways. When one of them dies, the bereavement response of the surviving child must be considered in light of this relationship.

Interrelationship of Closeness and Involvement

Not only is there a need to investigate further and develop adequate tools for measuring closeness and involvement, there also is a need to explore the interaction between the two concepts. For example, for those children whose sibling's presence is so profound because of the meaning she or he gives to their lives, it could be especially crucial that these children be very much involved in their sibling's illness and death as a way of facilitating adjustment to the loss of the sibling. In support of this suggestion, the following example is of a child whose brother was very central to her life, whose involvement in his illness and death-related events was minimal, and whose adaptation to his death was at pathological levels for depressive behavior. Marla's story also emphasizes the significance of closeness between twins. Twins, sharing their life spaces from the moment of conception and beyond, are usually very closely bonded. When a twin dies, it is as if a part of the surviving twin has also died.

> Marla and Marcus were twins. They were always together, described by their mother as "almost too close." They played together and went everywhere together. Since their family lived in the country, there were no neighborhood playmates for the two children. Marcus became ill when he and his sister were 8 years old. During the four months of Marcus's illness, he and his mother were at the hospital and Marla was cared for at home by her father and grandmother. She went to visit Marcus at least once a week. When asked about the nature of family discussions during this time, the mother said, "We didn't hide anything, but we never had any real discussion including the children." When Marcus died, Marla was in the hospital playroom alone. She learned of her brother's death from her father who simply said, "Marcus had gone

to be with Jesus." Marla attended the memorial service with her parents but couldn't recall that she had participated in any special way. In her interview, Marla regretted not having been able to say good-bye to her brother alone, and she missed him "all the time."

Marla's brother was central to her life and had been since their birth; he was an integral part of the meaning of her life. During his illness, Marla was minimally involved, and at the time of his death and memorial service, Marla was present but did not seem to be "mindfully" involved. Marla's overall behavior problem score ranked at the 62nd percentile; however, her score for internalizing depressed behavior ranked at the 97th percentile. For children whose siblings are so meaningful to their lives, involvement is crucial for successful grieving.

☐ Family Environment

The family provides for its members the necessary relationships, both in quality and intensity, out of which normal growth and development may occur. It has been stated that the overall climate or total family atmosphere is the major influencing factor in children's development of a sense of identity; the family is more important than any other social group for formation of relationships and the self (Evans & McCandless, 1978; Gesell, Ilg, & Bates, 1974) and for development of resilience against stress and learning how to cope and adapt (Murphy, 1974).

Billings and Moos (1982) and others have investigated the role of the family in mediating children's development and adjustment. Relationships have been reported to exist between various dimensions of the family environment and child and adolescent behavior. An emphasis on independence and cohesion in families is related to the development of assertiveness and self-sufficiency in children; a strong emphasis on ethical and moral issues may be associated with children's proneness to guilt, insecurity, and symptoms of emotional and physical disfunction. Cohesive and expressive families with relatively little conflict tend to have children who show fewer behavioral and emotional problems. Finally, children in well-organized families tend to show better social and emotional adaptation but less self-control (Gottfried & Gottfried, 1983; Moos & Moos, 1981; Nihira, Mink, & Meyers, 1981). In clinical and empirical work, the family is portrayed as a dominant influence on bereavement resolution among children (Cain et al., 1964; Cobb, 1956, 1976; Krell & Rabkin, 1979). However, relatively little attention has been given to describing bereaved families and their effects on children.

The influence of the family is especially pertinent for children's adaptation because children are so dependent on their families. Bowlby (1980) explains that children react more strongly than adults to these variables for several reasons. Many differences arise from the fact that children are more dependent on their families than are adults for information and support. Whereas adults seek and are given prompt and detailed information about the death and related events, in most cases children are entirely dependent for their information on their parents. Furthermore, if adults wish to find additional understanding and comfort, they can do so by talking with friends, making appointments to see their clergy or a counsellor, or joining support groups. Children, especially younger ones, can seldom turn elsewhere if their family is unsympathetic to their needs for information and solace. The child's family, therefore, is critical in creating an environment that may positively affect the child's response to a sibling's death.

There are several aspects of the family environment that play a role in siblings' bereavement responses. One of the most significant is the degree of cohesiveness within the family and whether or not the children are made to feel that they are integral parts of the family. The family's capacity for interacting openly with one another and with others outside of the family and religious orientations are also significant.

Measuring Family Environment

The FES, developed by Moos and Moos (1981), was used to assess the social climates of families in which a child had died from cancer within the past 2–36 months (Davies, 1983, 1988a, 1988b). The FES is a 90-item true–false questionnaire focusing on the measurement and description of three aspects of family environment: interpersonal relationships among family members, the direction of personal growth that is emphasized in the family, and the basic organizational structure of the family. The FES consists of 10 subscales measuring these three domains. For each subscale, scores range from 0 to 9. Higher scores indicate a more positive social climate in a variety of families.

Significant relationships were found between five of the FES subscales and various behavior scores (Table 7.6). First, the relationship between cohesion and behavior scores indicates that the greater the degree of commitment, help, and support that family members provide for one another, the fewer the numbers of internalizing and externalizing behaviors among surviving children. Second, conflict correlated positively with externalizing behavior. In families with greater conflict, children tend to act out more frequently. Third, intellectual/cultural orientation correlated negatively with internalizing scores and externalizing scores. In families in which political, social, intellectual, and cultural activities are emphasized, bereaved children have fewer behavioral problems (both internalizing and externalizing) and are more socially competent. Similarly, in families with an emphasis on an

TABLE 7.6. Correlations between CBCL scores and FES subscales

	Total Behavior Problem Score	Internalizing Score	Externalizing Score	Social Competence Score
Cohesion	−.25	−.54***	−.45**	.01
Expressiveness	−.30	−.23	−.32	.07
Conflict	.15	.21	.34*	−.12
Independence	−.16	.05	.02	.28
Achievement orientation	−.01	.08	.08	.19
Intellectual/cultural orientation	−.29	−.43**	−.41**	−.44**
Active/recreational orientation	−.30	−.41**	−.23	.57***
Moral/religious emphasis	−.34*	−.44**	−.17	.17
Organization	.01	−.12	−.01	.07
Control	−.21	−.19	−.07	.24

*$p < .05$; **$p < .01$; ***$p < .001$.

active/recreational orientation, bereaved siblings show fewer internalizing behaviors and greater social competence. Finally, children in families with a stronger moral/religious emphasis demonstrate fewer internalizing behaviors as well. Several of these dimensions require additional discussion.

Bereavement Outcome and Cohesiveness

The significance of the concept of cohesiveness is attested to by the extent to which this concept is addressed by various disciplines in the family and mental health fields. Psychiatrists, family therapists, family sociologists, small-group theorists, and group therapists have all utilized the concept of cohesiveness in their work. To be cohesive means to be harmoniously united by common interests, by a sense of social membership, or by emotional ties. It is the "emotional bonding members feel toward one another" (Olson, Sprenkle, & Russell, 1979). Moos and Moos (1981) utilized the concept of cohesion as one dimension used to distinguish the social environment of the family. Cohesion, in the Moos' terms, refers to how close family members feel toward each other.

Findings indicate that families who are more cohesive and active and put a greater emphasis on religious aspects have children who demonstrate fewer behavioral problems up to 3 years after the death of a sibling from cancer. The relationship between cohesion and behavioral problems in the children supports the findings of other researchers who report an increase in behavioral problems in children in families characterized by a lack of cohesion. Stewart (1962), for example, in a long-term prospective study, suggested a negative correlation between psychosomatic symptoms in children and the degree of family cohesiveness. Fifteen years later, Christensen (1977), using the Moos FES, documented that fewer behavior problems led to delinquency in adolescents when family treatment focused on improving family cohesion. Conversely, Fowler's (1980) investigation of relationships between family environment and behavior problems among young children showed behavioral displays of aggression were associated with less cohesive family environments.

Bereavement Outcome and Social Involvement

Subscale scores in intellectual/cultural orientation, active/recreational orientation, and moral/religious emphasis were significantly related to lower internalizing behavior scores. An emphasis on these values may predispose the families to participate in recreational, cultural, social, and religious activities or events, thereby increasing the likelihood of social involvement, which in turn may promote adaptive behaviors in the children. This suggestion is supported by the relationships between the families' scores on the active/recreational orientation and intellectual/cultural orientation subscales and the children's social competence scores. The higher the family emphasis on these two dimensions, the greater the social competence demonstrated by the children.

The relationship between the families' emphasis on social involvement and the children's behavior requires further investigation with regard to the support received by both families and children as a result of such involvement. The role of social support in promoting the family's recovery from crisis has been indicated by several researchers (Caplan, 1987; Cobb, 1976). Parkes (1972) indicated that social support was critical to widows' adaptation following the stress of bereavement. It seems likely that social support may be influential to children's bereavement outcomes as well.

Although statistically significant, the association between social support and children's behavior is low in an absolute sense. Holahan and Moos (1983) note that this relationship is true of other research in this area, and they have suggested that this relationship might be strengthened by using measures of both qualitative and quantitative aspects of social support. In this study, qualitative interview data did provide an indication that the families' scores on the active/recreational orientation and the intellectual/cultural orientation subscales (both of which pertain to activities involving other people) were related to the number of friends and relatives and the type of support received from them. For example, the family with the lowest score (1) on the active/recreational orientation subscale also had a low score (2) on the intellectual/cultural orientation subscale. The situation in this family was as follows:

> Four years prior to the interview, Mr. and Mrs. Jones, with their two children, Sarah and Ben, had moved from the East Coast to a western city. At the time, Sarah was 12 years of age and Ben was 10. Ben died two years later. The family first lived in the upstairs of an old house; the owners lived downstairs, and although they "were very good to us when Ben first got sick," the Jones family had little contact with these people. Shortly after Ben's diagnosis, the family moved into a low-rent townhouse where "we don't have much to do with the folks here." The family had few friends. Their only visitor when Ben died was a minister they had called, by looking him up in the Yellow Pages, to come to help with the funeral. Neither the mother nor Sarah could recall that any of Sarah's friends had attended the funeral. Extended family members were minimal: "We don't have no family really—Sarah's half-brother moved out here when Ben died so he's all we got."

In another family with low scores on these two subscales, the mother reported, "No family came when Luke died. We have few friends and no one but us (the immediate family) was at the funeral. That's the way we wanted it." This family scored 4 on the active/recreational orientation subscale and 3 on the intellectual/cultural orientation subscale.

Furthermore, the behavior of the surviving children in each of these two families reflected difficulty in coping. Sarah had had many behavioral problems since her brother's death. In fact, she was the only child in the study who had dropped out of school. Sarah's total behavior problem score was at the 90th percentile and her social competence score ranked at a percentile of 1.5. The percentile ranking of the surviving child in the second family was not so extreme, with his total behavior problem score ranking at the 78th percentile and his social competence score at the 31st percentile. The boy's mother, however, expressed a deep concern for this child's behavior: "He's been having depressed moods since Luke died—he has no one to do things with. And he wanted to just quit school and get a job."

In contrast to these two families is the family who scored highest (9) on both the active/recreational orientation and the intellectual/cultural orientation subscales. The mother said:

> My nephew (aged 22) came as soon as Rhonda died. His own brother died last year so he really can help Ricky (one of two surviving children). He's so good—he helps cook and he built a new room for us in the basement. He's so good with Ricky—he really is good for us all. My aunt was here when Rhonda was sick and so was my best friend. My brother is a priest and he comes as much as he can—you know, since Rhonda has gone, we've been all alone only one night. My friends at school are good too—they knew Rhonda because I used her as a subject for a project at school—there were loads of people at the funeral—all of the boy's friends were there and so were their teachers.

The surviving child in this family had very few behavioral problems, was doing very well in school, and liked school. He maintained his participation in extracurricular activities and enjoyed being with his friends and extended family members. His total behavior problem and social competence scores ranked at the 19th and 88th percentiles, respectively. These examples suggest that social support gained by having a family emphasis on social, cultural, recreational, and religious events seems to serve as a protective function for children who have experienced the death of a sibling.

Bereavement Outcome and Moral Religious Emphasis

Families who scored highest on the FES subscale of moral/religious emphasis had children with fewer behavior problems. It seems that families who are actively engaged in religious activities are more likely to have stronger social support networks, and in this way religious activity was seen to help siblings. However, religious beliefs themselves were not necessarily helpful to grieving siblings. There was a difference in families who rigidly adhered to religious dogma and those who were open to exploring their religious beliefs. Some families could question God's role in this tragic event—they were angry at God and said so. They did not necessarily abandon their faith; in fact, many developed a stronger faith, but they were able to express their anger and frustration with God. They actively engaged in conversation with God, sharing the entire range of feelings with Him and showing an openness to self-exploration. In other families, individuals held back any anger at God, saying, "This was God's will, so we must accept it." These families felt that to express anger at all, but especially at God, was wrong. In such families, siblings were not free to express their doubts and anger either and suffered in silence.

Bereavement Outcome and Expressiveness

Expressiveness within the family is different from whether children talk or not. Parents are frequently concerned about the fact that their child is not talking and does not express or share his feelings and concerns. Several factors come into play. Temperament is discussed in an earlier chapter (Chapter 4) as an individual variable affecting sibling response. Some children are naturally more quiet than others; they tend to be more withdrawn and are less likely to talk about their feelings. These children may keep their thoughts and feelings to themselves, and talk about them only infrequently. Many times, children hesitate to mention anything related to the death for fear of upsetting their parents, and so this gives parents the impression that their children are not talking to anyone. Siblings often say that they are very concerned about their parents and purposely avoid topics that would add to their parents' distress. Parents indicated that adolescents in particular are less likely to talk to their parents. But, in talking with adolescents, many of these young people confirm that they do talk with others—with their friends or with the parents of their friends. Again, out of a desire to protect their parents or an inability to feel at ease talking about certain things with their own parents, these young people find others to talk with.

Aside from individual differences in siblings' tendency to talk, there is a general atmosphere in families which predisposes to the sharing of thoughts, feelings, and concerns with the family. Moos and Moos (1981) call this aspect, "Expressiveness." They define it as the degree to which the social climate encourages open expression of thoughts, feelings, and ideas. Research findings indicate that the relationship between this FES subscale and siblings' behavior scores is not statistically significant. This finding is of much interest, given the general assumption that talking facilitates healthy grieving. Kaplan et al. (1976), for example, provided an example of the value of an expressive environment in their prospective study of coping patterns of 50 leukemic families. They noted that effective coping is present when open communication is evident, and discrepant coping is present when communication is restricted. These authors suggested that open communication results in freely sharing feelings of grief, concerns, and fears. The mutual willingness to share thoughts and feelings provides a significant source of support; restricted communication limits support.

There is evidence to suggest that the bereaved appreciate the opportunity to express their feelings. Less than half the widows in a study by Glick, Weiss, and Parkes (1974) were able to express their grief freely with at least one other person; 67% reported that those individuals who allowed or encouraged such conversations were helpful. Over 88% of bereaved individuals in another study (Schoenberg, Carr, Peretz, Kutscher, & Cherico, 1975) felt that "expression rather than repression of feelings, and crying, should be encouraged at least sometimes" (p. 365). Maddison and Walker (1967) interviewed women approximately 13 months after the death of their spouses and found a relationship between a decline in physical and mental health and the occurrence of unhelpful interactions at the time of the loss. Women with the greatest number of health problems were those who had experienced a large number of interactions in which the free expression of negative feelings was directly or indirectly blocked. The authors concluded that the women who showed a poor outcome may have experienced a need to talk and freely express their affect but were faced with an environment that failed to provide an opportunity for doing so. Finally, in an experimental study with a group of widows, Raphael (1977) treated the women with "support for the expression of grieving affects such as sadness, anger, anxiety, helplessness, hopelessness and despair" (p. 1451). When assessed 13 months after their spouse's death, women who had been randomly assigned to the treatment group reported significantly better psychological and physical health than those assigned to a no-treatment control group.

The applicability to children of the relationship between opportunity for expressiveness and adaptation is also evident in the literature, but documentation does not exist to such an extensive degree as in the adult-related literature. With regard to the more general adjustment of children whose parents are divorced, limited data suggest that well-adjusted children come from homes where children are encouraged to discuss divorce-related concerns (Jacobson, 1978). In discussing the surviving siblings after the death of a child, Shrier (1980) concluded that major disturbances in functioning are particularly prominent in families where there is "a conspiracy of silence, where the death is not allowed to be discussed, and where there is avoidance of the intense feelings of grief, anger and guilt provoked by the loss" (p. 156).

If talking is so valuable, then why was expressiveness not significantly related to any behavior score? A possible explanation may be that the degree of expressiveness often differs according to the topic being discussed. The open expression of feelings and ideas may not be encouraged in situations pertaining to cancer and death. Cancer generally continues to be a stressful topic for discussion in our society, and few people are willing to discuss death-related issues openly and comfortably. So open expression may pertain to many topics and areas of concern to family members, but it may exclude the discussion of the fear or sadness of death. This exclusion may not necessarily be conscious—often it is communicated implicitly by the lack of willingness to experience and openly express painful emotions. In such families, questions can be asked and answers discussed as long as they focus on such things as treatment, medications, or pain control. Expression of fears or sadness is not so readily supported. In one family, for example,

> All the children were told exactly what the doctor had told us [parents]. We understood the meaning of what leukemia was, that is possibly death, but we didn't want to acknowledge it or talk about it because that meant giving up hope.

and in another,

> We never talked about the fact that he [ill child] might die. The thought of him dying was to deny our belief in God and faith in Him that He would make everything all right. I [mother] can't say I never thought about it, but when I did, I just pushed the thought down.

In these situations, the explicit discussion of impending death was not encouraged. And a pattern may have been set so that following the death, the open expression of grief may also be inhibited. This suggestion is supported by Birenbaum (1989) and Birenbaum et al. (1990) who studied the relationship between parent–sibling communication and siblings' coping prior to and after the death of a child with cancer. Prior to death, parent–sibling communication was positively related to social competence (interpersonal) and school functioning. However, this relationship was not found at any time after the death. Parent–sibling communication was inversely related to external behavior problems following the ill child's death at each point in time but not before the death. Findings suggest a complex relationship between parent–sibling communication and sibling coping. Similarly, open discussion about other illnesses, such as AIDS, or about death from causes that are often stigmatized, such as suicide, may be limited and impact on the siblings in those families.

Birenbaum (1989) suggests parent–sibling communication is "context specific." Before death, talking about the illness and death is context specific and thus has use for the sibling. Following the death, the situation changes. While open expression may pertain to many topics and areas of concern to family members, the discussion of the fear or sadness of death may be excluded. Similarly, the open expression of grief after the death may not be supported, even in the most expressive families. This observation puts into question earlier assumptions that parent–child communication during the illness positively affects the coping strategies of the child during treatment and sibling bereavement outcome. Disease-related communication is not necessarily the same as communication surrounding death, dying, and grief.

Parent–Child Communication

The importance of effective communication has been recognized as an essential element in facilitating individual and family coping with childhood chronic life-threatening illness. Some parents state explicitly that they perceive the significance of their role in facilitating expressiveness regarding the death: "The most difficult thing has been to try to get him to talk when he needs to and to keep my [mother] own mind open." Yet, how a family communicates about the illness can be indicative of general communication patterns (Adams-Greenly, 1984). Communication indicates not just telling of facts but the creation of a climate that allows and encourages expression of feelings. Lee, now 13, remembers that she, as a 4-year-old, had been told the facts—her brother had died. But there was no mention of any emotions or other reactions, and the environment was not conducive to asking questions: "I didn't really understand it. Everyone else was crying and I couldn't understand why everyone was crying and being sad. I mean, I knew something bad had happened, but I didn't know what.... Why was everyone crying?" She also remembered being confused at the funeral:

> The service was long. I couldn't understand what they were talking about. I just remember that. It wasn't sad because I didn't know what was happening.... I was more scared than sad because everyone else was crying and I didn't understand and I didn't know who to ask, or if could ask.... I don't think I even knew what to ask. But I remember just knowing that I wasn't supposed to ask or get in the way.

Parent–child communication about death and dying has been used as a predictor of coping in the ill child, the parents, and siblings. However, discrepant findings are reported that preclude definitive conclusions about the relationship between parent–child communication and sibling bereavement outcome. Townes and Wold (1977) reported in their study of 22 siblings of 8 leukemic patients that the siblings' evaluation of the patient's disease as life threatening was related to increased parental communication about the implications of the disease and about the experience of living with the illness in the family. Early in the illness, poor adjustment was not associated with communication but rather with age and sex; boys and older children had more problems (Townes & Wold, 1977). The value of providing a similar "safe" forum for healthy siblings and the effects of such discussion on subsequent bereavement response has received little attention.

However, available empirical evidence suggests that communication is a major factor influencing sibling adjustment and bereavement (McCown & Pratt, 1985). Factors influencing the extent and effectiveness of such communication among parents, dying children, and their siblings were investigated retrospectively with 77 mothers who were members of the Compassionate Friends Organization (Graham-Pole, Wass, Eyberg, Chu, & Olejnik, 1989). Mothers who talked more freely with dying children also did so with the siblings; communication was more open with older than with younger children. The researchers concluded that this dialogue was very helpful for both the dying children and their siblings if the former were mostly at home immediately before death, if there was extensive and specific discussion about death and dying when a parent was the major discussant (not significant for siblings), and if the family's religious faith was a significant source of support. However, following such discussions, the emotional state of the dying children and the siblings contrasted markedly. Mothers perceived the latter showed significantly more sadness, anger, denial, and fear. Noting this finding, the authors questioned whether siblings need a different kind of communication that focuses specifically on their own loss and distress. Children's imaginations are highly developed, and dealing with the realities of death in the family may be both kinder and easier for them to cope with than the ordeal of experience by fantasy (Bluebond-Langner, 1978; Dominica, 1987). Despite several methodological limitations of this study, findings indicate appropriate communication is at least as important for survivors as it is for the dying child.

In my research, many parents were concerned about the level of discussion about the death. Several mothers acknowledged the importance of open discussion and expression of feelings when they made comments such as: "The most difficult thing has been Larry's [surviving child] not wanting to talk about it." Yet they realized that discussions subsequent to the death seldom focused on fears or other feelings related to the death. In many families, discussion was primarily of a reminiscent nature: "She [surviving child] doesn't remember or talk much about the illness itself or the death, but mostly talks about 'remember when we used to.'" "Joe [surviving child] likes to remember all the things they used to do together."

In other families, expressiveness was valued, but perceptions of children's capacities to understand altered the encouragement of open discussion: "She [surviving child] had been told what the diagnosis was, but I [mother] felt she was too young to really understand what the diagnosis meant, and what the possible outcome might be."

Grieving siblings themselves recall what they were told and were not told. Liza, now 19 years old, recalls what she and her sister were told when their brother was dying nine years ago:

> I don't think anyone ever actually just sat us down and said what was happening.... I don't imagine that the doctors are going to waste their time explaining this to two little kids. Leave that to the parents. I think mom just figured we were better off either not knowing, or you already knew because there was constantly the hospital trips and they were going to try a bone marrow and they took blood out of all of us. It made my sister sick and they had to put her in the hospital room for a few hours. We saw an article in the paper that said, "Parents choose home care for son when he was dying." But, no, nobody ever told us. After he died, no one really talked to us about it.... We would sometimes remember things about him, but talking about what we were feeling wasn't really acceptable—it just seemed to make mom and dad really sad, and so we didn't talk about it.

Liza and her sister had never talked about their sadness with anyone, not even each other. Liza said it was an "unspoken family rule" not to talk about such things as feelings, especially sad or angry feelings. Liza and her sister both experienced considerable depression after their brother's death. Liza commented, "If only we could have talked about it, it would have helped, I think. But, talking about anything in our family is not easy to do.... There's just a general sense of 'keep quiet about anything that might be upsetting.'"

Parental Grief

Furman (1974) said that following a spouse's death, the surviving parent, caught up in his or her own needs and preoccupation, can easily overlook the needs of children for information, security, and participation in mourning. The same would be true for the parent following the death of a child, perhaps even more so, if as Gorer (1965) says the loss of a child is the most painful loss.

Parental grief is a critical factor in sibling adjustment and bereavement (McCown & Pratt, 1985). Yet there are few studies in the literature that explicitly examine the relationship between parental grief and sibling bereavement response.

Pettle Michael and Lansdown (1986) found that parents' and children's adjustment were not related in a study of families whose children died of cancer. In contrast, one of the other few available reports (Demi & Glibert,

1987) found that parents' emotional distress correlated with siblings' emotional distress, although parents' grief patterns were not correlated with siblings' grief patterns. Parents who are in touch with their own feelings communicate to their children, either overtly or covertly, that it is okay to feel emotional pain and to express this pain. Parents who report low emotional distress may be denying the impact of the loss, or they may have a lifelong pattern of suppressing emotions. This denial or inability to express emotions is learned by their children. Demi and Gilbert reported that parents and siblings use differing patterns of grief. Siblings tend to use avoidance, while parents tend to use intrusion to cope with grief. This finding makes sense when we realize that children most often express their grief through behaviors rather than through cognitive processes or emotional affect. As an example, when parents are highly distressed with intrusive thoughts about the deceased child, siblings use avoidance in an attempt to soothe and comfort the parent and to keep from being overwhelmed with intrusive thoughts themselves. As 12-year-old Jackie explained, "It was easier to not bring up any talk about Joannie [deceased sister], because mom would cry—it was easier not to get her upset." Further research might examine the relationship between parents' grief responses and their own ability to be expressive about the death and the influence of this relationship on the children's grief.

Implications for Caregivers

Most nurses, physicians, social workers, psychologists, clergy, counsellors, and teachers who work with children subscribe to the belief that children's behavior is a joint function of the child and the environment. Findings reported in this chapter substantiate this belief in that closeness between the siblings, and certain characteristics of the family environment were related to the children's behavioral response to a sibling's death.

Emotional closeness seems to be of importance in sibling bereavement. Further explorations into the relationship between closeness of relationship and bereavement outcome are warranted. However, findings to date serve to emphasize the need for adults who work with grieving children to be aware of the potential impact of the predeath relationship between the siblings on the surviving brother or sister. When assessing the relationship, it may be helpful for caregivers to refer to the descriptions of stated closeness that are described in Table 7.1.

Cohesion in families, as a dimension of the family social environment, was significantly related to lower behavioral problem scores in bereaved siblings. Health care professionals can use this information to reinforce positively the families of ill children who are cohesive—relaxing hospital rules so that all family members can visit the ill child, for example, and can stay comfortably at the hospital. Professionals must also develop methods of facilitating cohesion within those families who are less supportive of one another. Changing institutional practices is one example of what could be done to encourage family cohesion during the ill child's hospitalization and following his or her death. For example, having conferences with the whole family, including even the ill child when that is appropriate, as a supplement to conferences with parents may help to foster cohesion. The interactions among all family members may foster awareness of each others' needs for information and support. A group approach does not work for all families, nor can professional caregivers expect all family members to be present at all times. Family members need permission for "time out" to attend to their own needs and to participate in the ongoing day-to-day activities of life outside the hospital or hospice program. Opportunities to attend to these activities also contribute to family cohesion.

Family cohesion can be threatened by the intense emotions experienced by the parents and siblings of the dying or deceased child. The regulation of affect is a stressful task. Negative feelings may be modulated or suppressed so as to avoid additional stress; such feelings, however, may erupt in inappropriate ways, causing resentment that eventually erodes cohesiveness. Caregivers can predict and anticipate with families the emotional reactions that they may experience. Initiating discussions in which families can openly acknowledge and ventilate their feelings helps to normalize such reactions and provides family members with an opening to share their own emotions and reactions and with an opportunity to become closer to one another.

Findings also indicated that families with greater emphasis on social, cultural, recreational, and religious involvements tend to have children with fewer behavioral problems. Further research into the role of social support for families and children following the loss of a child is warranted. Meanwhile, health care professionals can be sensitive to the social support that families have by welcoming members of the family's extended network into the child's care. Where such support is lacking for families, professionals can encourage the development of some support by having available information about community-based support groups. Not all families choose such forms of support, and such wishes must also be respected. Knowing that siblings in such families may be at greater risk during bereavement is key to careful follow-up of siblings by health care professionals, teachers, clergy, or other adults familiar to the child.

The social avoidance that often accompanies terminal illness and death may inhibit family interactions with their social network. Many families report the loss of friends and sometimes family when their child dies—others may be just too uncomfortable to keep in touch, or they may tire of hearing about the sadness. In such situations, caregivers can explain how friends often may want to help but do not know how. Families can be assisted in specifying their needs and in being assertive in requesting help from friends or in letting go of unsatisfying relationships and finding new friends who are more supportive.

Family environments, interactions between siblings, and interactions between parents and siblings all differ considerably across families. Such differences impact on how families, and the siblings within those families, grieve the death of a child. Such patterns are well established before the death—those patterns also affect grieving siblings as is discussed in the next chapter.

Family Functioning: Impact on Siblings

When a child dies, the child's family is forever changed. How the family responds to and incorporates that change is critical for surviving siblings. Even before their child dies, families have characteristic ways of being in the world, ways of managing crises, ways of solving problems, ways of expressing views and sharing with one another, and ways of interacting with the outside world. When families experience stress, or face a crisis, these characteristic ways of coping are what the family uses to manage the situation. Families therefore respond to the death of a child in ways that reflect their usual pattern of managing life's events. These ways of coping are more or less functional. The degree of functionality in families impacts significantly on sibling bereavement response.

☐ Levels of Functioning

Several family theorists have attempted to delineate functional and dysfunctional coping strategies used by families following stressful events (Barnhill, 1979; Kantor & Lehr, 1975; Olson et al., 1979; McCubbin & Figley, 1983). McCubbin and Figley outline an inventory of generic coping strategies utilized by families in response to normative and catastrophic stress. Crosby and Jose (1983) use this framework to delineate general elements that contrast functional and dysfunctional coping of families in response to the death of a family member. They state that "individuals and families react to the demands induced by death in ways which either promote recovery (functional) or impede recovery (dysfunctional)" (p. 81). My colleagues and I also found this to be true in a study of families caring for a terminally ill adult member (Davies, Chekryn Reimer, & Martens, 1994; Davies, Chekryn Reimer, Brown, & Martens, 1995). We found that families caring for a terminally ill member experience the transition of "fading away" with greater or lesser difficulty, depending on their level of functioning. How families interact according to eight delineated dimensions of functioning contributes to their success or difficulty.

The Crosby and Figley framework (McCubbin & Figley, 1983) was tested using a pooled data source from three groups of families whose child died from cancer between two months and nine years prior to data collection (Davies, Spinetta, Martinson, McClowry, & Kulenkamp, 1986). The first group of 52 families resided in Minnesota and North and South Dakota, the second group (N = 25 families) in Southern California, and the third (N = 34 families) in Alberta, Canada, and Washington and Arizona. The total sample therefore was 111 families from six states and one Canadian province. The families were primarily Caucasian, and over half the parents had completed high school or one to two years of college. The age of the children at death ranged from one month to 19 years, and approximately two-thirds were male.

Twelve elements were delineated that characterized functional and dysfunctional coping (Davies et al., 1986). Subsequent analysis and findings from other studies (Davies et al., 1995) resulted in the condensing of some of the original categories, so that now eight dimensions are identified: communicating openly, dealing with feelings, defining roles, solving problems, utilizing resources, incorporating changes, considering others, and confronting beliefs. These dimensions occur along a continuum of functionality so that family interactions tend to vary along the continuum rather than being positive or negative, good or bad.

Communicating Openly

In families where communication is more closed than open, there is a lack of free expression. Instead of allowing each person to speak for himself or herself, another family member frequently responds to questions, speaking for others. For example, when 10-year-old Johnny was asked about his response to the death of his sister, his mother spoke for him, "Johnny has been really quiet about it—he usually doesn't say much."

Often in interviews with families characterized by less open communication there is considerable talk during the interview, but it is not focused on the issue to which the question being asked. Or, in response to the interviewer's question, the answer may be a simple "no" or "yes" without elaboration. Communication is limited or guarded instead of free-flowing and spontaneous. When interviewing individuals apart from the family group, information that had been shared in the group is corrected or explained. For example, when talking with 14-year-old Tammy about her sister's death, Tammy was insistent upon explaining a statement that her father had made during the family interview. He had hinted that there was some tension with regard to extended family, but nothing more had been said. In her individual interview, Tammy clarified that her father was upset with her mother because of the maternal grandparents' coming to visit after the death and "taking over" and "forgetting to go home." Tammy indicated that, "It's not something we talk about, but we all know what the problem is."

Open communication in families means that family members talk about anything with no fear of recrimination for their expression. In bereaved families, there is free discussion about the deceased child, the illness (if the child died from an illness), death, and the family's responses since the time of death. In such families, there is a sharing of information within the family. Parents provide siblings with age-appropriate versions of what they know; siblings tell parents what they know. There is a general sense of agreement about events, without any secrets. Each member of the family offers a similar version of the story, whether they are in the family group or being interviewed individually.

As discussed in the foregoing chapter, a family can be very open but not necessarily expressive. Some families are very open when relaying facts about events, but when it comes to sharing their feelings, especially those feelings typically thought of as negative (sadness, anger, resentment), these are not necessarily shared. Families who communicate openly, however, tend to express feelings as well as facts. For example, when families were asked to describe what had happened on the day of the funeral, open families not only described events but also discussed their feelings about these events. In addition to describing the location of and attendance at the funeral, they referred to their own emotions at the time, such as how difficult that day had been for them or how they had appreciated their friends on that day. Families who were less open, and less focused on process, focused their responses primarily on the events, such as describing where the funeral was held and who attended; there was little mention of the emotions associated with the day. Consequently, how families deal with feelings becomes a relevant dimension of functionality.

Dealing with Feelings

Some families focus primarily on a narrow range of feelings, with greater intensity associated with anger and hurt. They do not acknowledge their uncertainty or talk about the paradoxical feelings they experience. Grief is highly controlled; some members even appear to avoid feelings of grief. Instead, they shield themselves from the pain, often hinting that they do not express what they feel. As one father said, "I don't allow myself to cry. What good would that do? It only brings back all the pain.... It's better to just get on with our lives." Sadness is dismissed with such comments as, "I've seen enough tears now," by one father in response to his daughter's crying several days after the funeral. In such families, there are often reports of intense feelings being expressed later in response to another event, of seemingly much less magnitude. In Janna's family, for example, tears were discouraged. Fourteen-year-old Janna had missed her brother terribly and knew that she was not supposed to cry: "Dad told us not to cry—it wouldn't bring Skip back and so there was no point in crying. He said that he had seen enough tears to float a battleship, and he didn't want any of it. So, I didn't cry—none of us cried." Later in the interview, Janna described what had happened when Skip's dog died: "About a year and a half after Skip died, his dog got run over on the street in front of the house. When that dog died, I thought I would never stop crying. I don't know why ... I hadn't really liked that old dog very much, but I sure cried when he died."

These families seldom comment on having any good days at all—typically, they add no qualifying phrase to the response, "Yes, it's been pretty bad." They express guilt about feeling good without any recognition that feeling good is also an appropriate human emotion. They seldom choose to do anything that is fun; they feel that they should not get any pleasure from life because they do not deserve to have fun anymore: "After what's happened to us, how can we ever laugh again?" These families rigidly define their grieving role.

In contrast, other families express a range of feelings, from sadness and sorrow to anger, even to happiness and satisfaction. They recognize and tolerate the range of feelings associated with grief and express them freely. These families express their vulnerabilities and fears, as one father did: "It's been difficult.... The sadness is sometimes overwhelming—like we have been lost at sea and no one can find us." These families, however, usually go on to say, as this father did, "But, that seems normal when you lose a child.... Some days are better than others, and we hope for more good days than bad ones." These families are willing to admit their hurt but conscientiously work at not having "all bad days." Aware of their own humanity, they accept limitations as well as strengths. As a result, they give themselves permission to feel both good and bad, and they see the paradox of sometimes feeling happy and sad at the same time. "Yes," one adolescent said, "it is pretty bad, but we have our good days too. And we laugh sometimes too—though at first we felt guilty when we did. But, life is sad and funny, both at the same time sometimes."

Defining Roles

In some grieving families, roles are rigidly maintained. Family members not only narrowly perceive their grieving roles but also rigidly define their roles in the family as well. For example, in one family where the oldest child had died, the father said to the second child, "You are the oldest now and you are responsible for the little ones." Traditional gender roles are rigidly defined, as they were for the father who "maintained control and didn't cry" over his son's death and was proud of his surviving son who did not cry at his brother's funeral. Fathers in more role-flexible families are able to express their grief openly and cry in the presence of other family members.

Sometimes it is the child who imposes a new role on himself or herself. When this happens, and the situation is not attended to by the parents, the result is that the family condones the new behavior in the child, thereby reinforcing the child's perception that he is expected to fulfill this new role. For example, 13-year-old Helmut began to dress like his deceased older brother; he cut his hair the same way and enrolled in karate classes as his brother had done, even though Helmut's talents were more musical than athletic. His father's joking with Helmut and others about these new behaviors served to reinforce his surviving son's commitment to taking the place of his older brother. In some families, one or both parents expect that the surviving child will assume the characteristics or abilities of the deceased child. For example, a father whose son had died, and with whom he had enjoyed skiing, took his not-so-athletic daughter skiing. He became very annoyed when she was unable to keep up with him as his son had done. In families where there is greater role flexibility, there is an acknowledgment that one child is gone, but the other children are not expected to fill the empty space. They remain valued for who they are, and are made to feel special for their own characteristics, abilities, and ways of being. They are regarded as integral, actively involved members of the family.

Solving Problems

Some families approach problems by focusing more on why the problem occurred, and on who was at fault, rather than generating possible solutions.

All families describe special events as being especially difficult. They feel extremely sad when anticipating holiday occasions such as Christmas. In families where the focus is on blaming, rather than problem solving, families describe such occasions as "dreadful." In one family, for example, everyone acknowledged Christmas as having been exceptionally difficult. However, in advance of Christmas, they had not shared their anticipated feelings of sadness and had made no plans for how they might cope with the dreaded day. Consequently, they spent the day at home alone, each feeling miserable, having only soup for their Christmas dinner. The children blamed mother for the dreadful day because she had not felt like cooking; mother blamed her husband because he had not offered to take them out for dinner; and father blamed the children because they said they did not feel like going to out to eat.

The opposite is true for other families. These families identify problems or difficulties as they occur and openly exchange information. All members are involved in problem solving, and the contributions of each person are acknowledged and appreciated, resulting in a sense of mutual support and togetherness. They consider multiple options, are open to suggestions, and are creative in implementing alternative strategies. In preparation for special occasions, such as Christmas, these families discuss what changes they want to make to get through the holiday. One family decided to go on a Christmas skiing trip; another decided to invite special friends over to share the turkey dinner. Although such activities did not negate the families' sense of overall sadness, they represented their attempts to prepare in constructive ways for what they anticipated to be a difficult day.

Families who actively solve various problems perceived they have changed over time. In recalling all Christmases since their child had died, for example, they said such things as did the father in one family,

> Each one is hard.... There are always the memories of Mark, and we sometimes wish he could still be here. But we know that's not possible, and so we learn to go on with things. Each year gets a bit easier.... Joan is away at college now, and she comes home for Christmas. We all have new things to talk about.

In families with few problem-solving skills, there is little, if any, sense that any change is occurring. Every subsequent special day is just as difficult as that first Christmas had been for the family described above. It is as if the family had no power to change the situation. Another example occurred in a family where the oldest son, Peter, had died at age 12, three years prior to the interview. Peter's sister, Cathy, now 11 years old, was demonstrating several behavior problems. The mother stated, "Cathy always was resentful of Peter; it was just made worse by the illness. She still resents him, even now that he's not here." The theme of Cathy's resentment toward her brother was frequently heard throughout the interview. No mention was made about how either parent responded to this state of affairs, or about how it affected any of the children, or about how anyone had tried to intervene in the situation. Cathy's resentment was a fact of life that was to remain in the family—change seemed impossible.

Cathy's family illustrates those families who approach problems by focusing more on why the problem occurred and who was at fault than on generating potential solutions. They seem so caught up in the emotions associated with the situation that they cannot act on the problem. In addition, they seem to feel persecuted or singled out as the only family to suffer such distress:

> I don't think we will ever get over this. Why should our child have died? Can you imagine anything worse happening? I went to one of those talking [support] groups once, but it didn't help at all. No one understood what it was like for us to lose our son. They still don't. No one cares. It's just us against a world of people with children who are still alive.

This father's son had died suddenly of a brain aneurysm just as he was about to leave for college, after having won a scholarship to go. He would have been the first person in the family to have gone to college. The son died five years prior to the interview.

Some of these families commented about religion in ways that implied there was no need to attempt to cope actively with the experience: "God will take care of this" or "This is God's will." Such families perceive that acknowledging their grief or sadness, or questioning events, indicates a lack of faith on their part. They simply leave everything to God. In contrast, other families tend to ask, "How can we cope with this?" Many such families turn to their religious faith as a source of support, but they also acknowledge that they, too, have to do something to cope with the situation. Eventually, they perceive that some good, no matter how small for some, results from their experience. They are able to see both the good and the bad. Sometimes members in these families even said, as several mothers did, "I would never wish this experience on anyone else and I certainly wouldn't want to go through this again, but, you know, I've become a better person despite the pain."

Utilizing Resources

Families differ considerably in how they utilize resources. Some families use few resources. They describe fewer friends and acquaintances who offer assistance. These families seem unable to communicate what their needs are, or what they want, either as individuals to each other, or as a group to others outside of the immediate family. Any assistance they receive comes mostly from formal sources rather than from informal support networks. Moreover, when they receive assistance, they appear dissatisfied. One mother, during an interview nine years after the death, commented to the interviewer,

> You're the first one ... you're really the first one I ever talked to at all. We never went to the Candlelighters[4] program—we never went to any of it, because it's, to me, too much like hashing things over that are ... too final.

When their expectations are unfulfilled, they are angry. One mother complained, "No one in this family understands what it's like to lose your baby. They just get so impatient with my tears." When talking with the father, he commented that, "A father grieves all alone." And the two young school children felt like neither of their parents really understood what it was like for them to have lost their baby brother: "Mommy and Dad are so sad. They don't know we are sad too." The parents were unable to seek help for themselves or for their children. The change in the family was immobilizing.

In contrast, other families use a wide variety of resources, including friends, community agencies, support groups, and each other. These families feel free to ask for help or to reject unwanted offers from others. They receive considerable family support and identify many friends or acquaintances who offer help, particularly emotional support and empathy. They seem open to accepting this support and express satisfaction with the results. In addition, they seek suggestions on resources and take the initiative to locate other resources as needed.

Incorporating Change

Some families are resistant to reorganization; they seem static. They lament that they will never be the same again or attempt to continue to go on living as they had before, as if trying to ignore the impact of what has happened. These families are stuck at feeling sad, depressed, or angry. They sometimes seem driven and compulsive, not as a result of growth or change but rather as a result of not being able to move past their position of resentment or sadness. One mother sighed, "It doesn't get any easier. I just keep busy to try to forget." If they become involved in health-related issues or activities, it is primarily as an attempt to work through their feelings, rather than as the result of having worked them through.

---

[4]Candlelighters is a volunteer services organization that addresses issues of childhood cancer through various parent support groups. Its mandate is to enhance the quality of life of children and teens living with childhood cancer and their families.

They resent the loss of old friends who are unable to cope with the illness and death of the child. And these families are unable or unwilling to make new friends. One family, for example, felt deserted by friends, so they just "crossed them off their list" and had no further contact with them. Moreover, they were unwilling to develop any new friendships because, "What good does it do to have friends? Look what our so-called friends have done to us." Such families are not tolerant of their own reactions, the need to change, or of the reactions of others.

Other families are open, flexible, and adaptive in their reorganization to incorporate change. Describing the decentering that resulted from their loss, they explain how they feel the need to find a new center and a sense of getting on with life at some point. Mothers are able to go back to school or return to work if that is the new direction they want to follow. The same applies to fathers. Siblings are willing and encouraged to pursue their own interests. They find themselves wanting to get reinvolved with other families whose experience has been similar, such as other families of children with cancer, often in a way that helps them share their experience for the benefit of others. These families are able to drop old friends when they find that these people no longer understand their changed values in life. They are able to make new friends who share their new perspective. As one father explained,

> We have lots of friends, and most have been really good. But there are some who deserted us ... yes, that's how it felt ... deserted. They just couldn't handle what was happening. It probably scared them—made them realize their kid could die too. So we have just gone on without them. It still hurts. But at the same time, we have found new friends—people who understand and let us talk about Bill instead of turning deadly silent whenever we do.

These families seem to take stock of the changes, identify their needs, and put issues aside while retaining the lessons they have learned.

All families struggle with incorporating the past into the present. A vital member of the family is missing, and it takes considerable reorganizing of the family to incorporate this change. Some families regret what they had done or not done that may have contributed to their child's death. "If only" is a common phrase in their conversation: "If only we had taken him to the doctor earlier," "If only the treatment had worked." Other families also experience the "if onlys." They, however, are able to see them as part of a normal and expected grief response. Their comments reflected the view that, "We probably could have done some things differently, but we did the best we could." They can tolerate their own personal ambiguity, and can tolerate differences as well.

Some families have difficulty incorporating memories of their child's good and naughty behavior into their lives now. Memories of the deceased child are only positive and are, in fact, often saintly. There is failure to acknowledge that the child had been a normal child who misbehaved as any normal child would. In other families, memories of the deceased child include both good and bad behaviors that characterize all children. Families take great pleasure in remembering times when the deceased child had been mischievous, as well as the good things about the child.

Considering Others

In some families, the focus is on each person's individual grief and on his or her own style of grieving, without relating it to others in the family. Each person seems to carry the burden of grief all alone, without empathy or understanding of how the others in the family are grieving. In response to questions about how the family is doing now in relation to their grief, each person answers only in relation to himself or herself as if assuming that the feelings of the others were the same as his or her own. For example, a mother in such a family replied, "I'm doing fine—there's no problem." She made no mention of her husband's or children's responses unless the interviewer asked specifically about the other members and even then her responses of "Ummm, okay, I guess," indicated that she had thought little about their responses.

Even when asked directly about others' responses, individuals in these families responded about themselves. For example, a grieving father was asked about how his wife and daughter were adjusting to the death. Instead of describing their behavior, he replied weakly, "I just don't know about those two," portraying his own sense of helplessness. Individuals in these families also fail to show any awareness of or consideration for variation in coping styles among the other members. In one such family, the mother was asked who in the family was most affected by the death. She sighed, "I guess it was tough on all of us. I don't think . . . I really don't know." The father then added, "I don't know how you can judge. You can't really judge how people are feeling." Granted, one cannot judge another's feelings, but this father was not able even to describe how he thought other family members might be feeling. In another family, the father very matter-of-factly conducted his son's funeral and then proclaimed, "I don't what to hear anymore about this [the death] again." He perceived that his grief was over, and so it should be for the other members of the family as well. There was no appreciation for the feelings of the others.

In contrast, in other families, responses to the query about how the family is doing reflect an awareness of each person's grief and an acknowledgment and acceptance of individual variations in grief responses. For example, one mother said, "We're all doing better now, but when we feel sad we each have our own way of dealing with it. Jimmy goes for walks, Marsha likes to cry for a while, and I like to keep to myself." Family members show empathy and respect for the other members of the family. There is evidence of mutually meeting one another's needs. In these families, members show concern for one another and acknowledge the individual and varied responses in grief for each person. They express concern and compassion for one another.

Confronting Beliefs

After their loss, some families leave their beliefs unchallenged; others confront their beliefs. The former perceive that fate was responsible for the loss of their child, and they accept fate's hand without question. As a result, there is an absence of expressed emotion, particularly toward God. Some perceive God as all good and express no negative feelings about God's work. They proclaimed, "This is God's will and we must accept it; God would not want us to be sad." Others now saw God as all bad: "I had such faith in God before this happened, but how could a good God allow this to happen?" They reacted by turning completely away from religion. In contrast, other families frequently question God's role in the situation, but they still like God anyway. They often accept their child's death as fate, but they also acknowledge their feelings about what happened. There are able to express their dissatisfaction with fate. For example, they openly ventilate their anger at God.

Additionally, these families examine their beliefs about what is really important. They learn to appreciate the finiteness of life. In many cases, their perception of life changes from a quantity-of-life to a quality-of-life focus. For example, one father changed jobs to one of lesser pay so he had more time to devote to his volunteer activities for the local Ronald MacDonald House (a community project that provides accommodations for families while their child is hospitalized). Money and material values become less important to these families. They confront their old beliefs and as one adolescent boy stated, "person-related values are now more important than thing-related values." These families are better able to focus on their children's needs. They are better able to make their surviving children feel valued for themselves, better able to make the children feel special.

Helping Siblings Feel Special

Helping children to feel special is probably the most important contribution that families can make in aiding siblings to adapt to the death of another child in the family. The analysis from two studies supports the relationship between family functioning and bereavement outcome: (1) a study of self-concept in bereaved siblings (Martinson et al., 1987), and (2) a study focusing on the meaning of mementoes in families (Davies, 1987b). The relationship between family emotional environment and sibling bereavement response has been validated in additional family and sibling interviews since the original studies were completed.

The siblings for the initial analysis in the self-concept study were members of 59 Midwestern families who participated in a home care program for the dying child (Martinson, 1980). These families have been assessed at periodic intervals since the death of the child; the data for this analysis were from an assessment conducted at seven to nine years.

Two questions guided the study. First, what is the long-term effect, if any, on the self-concept of children whose sibling died from cancer? It was hoped that the research would clarify whether or not children who are bereaved due to the loss of a sibling reported self-concepts similar to those of "normal" children and adolescents, at seven to nine years after the death. The Piers–Harris Self-Concept Scale (Piers, 1976; Piers & Harris, 1969) was used to assess the self-concept of the participating siblings. Statistical analysis of the Piers–Harris scores indicated that bereaved siblings scored statistically higher in self-concept than the normative group of children. Additional discussion of these findings appears in Chapter 5.

The second question guiding the analysis was, Within the group of bereaved siblings, what factors may contribute to optimal levels of self-concept? Content analysis of siblings' and parents' interview data provided a response to this question.

The interviews of the six siblings with the highest and the six siblings with the lowest Piers–Harris scores and of their parents were content analyzed. It was thought that if there were any such factors, they would most clearly be identified in comparing these two groups.

One factor was clearly identified that influences the development of higher or lower levels of self-concept among bereaved siblings: the feeling of "I'm not enough" in children with the lower self-concept scores. This characteristic was consistently evident in the children with the lowest self-concept scores and was clearly absent in those who had the highest scores. This feeling occurs when children perceive that they do not compare favorably with the deceased sibling or when children feel displaced by the addition of new siblings to the family. These perceptions by siblings are more likely to occur in families who do not openly share their thoughts and feelings, rigidly maintain roles, have difficulty incorporating change into the family system, and disregard the feelings and responses of others.

"I'm Not Enough"

Implicit, and sometimes explicit, messages within the family are the source of siblings' perceptions about their own worth. Often these messages are present even before the deceased siblings died; the perceptions of "I'm not enough" are long-standing. Fifteen-year-old Susan, for example, was only 7 when her brother died. But, she remembers,

> Grandma always liked Marc more than me. Like on his birthday, she'd send him a birthday gift, and on my birthday she'd send me one but she'd also send him a gift. Then, when Marc got sick, she'd say, "Marc was a good boy; you should be like him," and stuff like that. I was upset because I could never figure out why she liked him more than she liked me.

Susan's father also had made comments that reinforced Susan's sense that she was not as good as her brother. She clearly perceived that her father did not think she was as good as a son would be to share activities:

> Marc's death was hardest for my dad because it was like having his only *son* die. It always seemed like . . . how do I say this? Like when our neighbors are out with their sons, and I can always see it in my dad's eyes that he wants to be out with his *son*, throwing the ball around.

In Susan's view, she can never be the child her grandmother adored, nor can she be the son her father desires. Susan can never be "enough" to make these people happy.

Seventeen-year-old Tom also perceived that, in his father's eyes, he did not compare favorably with his deceased brother. Tom's mother described the relationship between Tom and his father: "Tom and his dad [Dale] were never really quite as close as Dale and Bob [deceased son] were. When Bob was born, everybody used to say, 'Call him little Dale' because they looked so much alike. So I really think that Dale always felt a little closer to Bob and stuff." Pausing, she quickly reassured, "Though you never got the impression that Dale had wished it would have been Tom rather than Bob or anything like that."

In each of these families, the father's preferences for his deceased son were openly acknowledged by the parents in their interview. Susan's mother said, "I think that my husband would still like to have a son." Later in the interview, the father said, "Yeah, about what she said earlier, I'd like my son." The child's perceptions were accurate. Furthermore, the parents made comments that continued to reinforce the surviving child's feelings of not being as good as the deceased child and of not being enough. Although Tom was a well-accomplished boxer, his dad would comment, "I wonder what kind of boxer Bob would have been."

Parents of low self-concept children do not see their children as special in the way that the parents of high self-concept children do. In fact, they perceive them to be no different than other children despite their experience with serious illness and death. As a result, these children do not feel special. For example, Susan's mother remarked that a lot of the items on the questionnaire related to children's behavior problems applied to Susan, but "not because of her brother's death, but because she is 15 years old, and she's just like all kids her age." Tom's mother said of him, "He's always worrying ... but then I don't know if that's because of Bob or because of kids in general because they are all such worry-warts."

For some siblings, a factor contributing to their feeling of less worth than the child who died is the sibling's sense of responsibility for the death. This factor, as an individual factor, is discussed in Chapter 5. When parents, or other family members, reinforce the view that the death was the surviving child's fault in some way, this adds to the child's feeling of low self-worth.

In both Susan's and Tom's families, information was not shared openly and feelings were not expressed. Susan's father could have openly admitted to Susan that he missed his son, he could have shared his grief, but in ways that showed consideration for her feelings—with the reassurance that he still was glad that he had his daughter. Neither set of parents demonstrated functional problem-solving skills—there was some indication in both families that the parents were aware of their surviving child's perceptions or feelings, but there was no indication that the parents were actively developing strategies to change their child's perceptions. Roles were being rigidly defined—Susan's father wanted a son and could not see the value in his daughter because she did not like to engage in typically male activities. Tom's father persisted in comparing Tom with his deceased brother, instead of commending Tom for his boxing achievements. Both families had limited social networks, so neither Susan nor Tom had any other source of support. In Susan's case, her grandmother was in contact with the family, but she contributed in a major way to Susan's feelings of "I'm not enough."

Parents of children with high self-concepts give no indication that the surviving child is not as good as the one who had died, nor do they even hint at blaming the surviving child in any way. These parents indicate that they value their surviving children even more as a result of their other child's death. Micky's mother said, "We are much more aware of how special our children are and how blessed we are to have them. Like I said earlier, we think they're wonderful."

Parents of high self-concept children refer to pride in their children, not necessarily for their accomplishments but just because of who they are. They are also explicit about telling their children how much they are loved. As Kyle's mother described her daughter, "She is one well-adjusted child; she's a real sweet kid—a real joy." Barbara's mother said, "She's a special kid. We always tell her we love her." Barbara's father, referring to both Barbara and her other living sister, said, "They're great kids. I wouldn't take even a hundred million dollars for either of them." Comments such as these reflect parental attitudes that serve to make their children feel loved, valued, and, therefore, special in their parents' eyes. Feelings of being special are emphasized by the parents' understanding of their children's reactions to the sibling's death. Parents perceive their children as unique in comparison with most children. Paul's mother reflected about her son, "Paul is very sensitive, and because of the death he's more sensitive to people that have hurts or something like that. That was his personality before, but it's just made it significantly stronger."

Feeling Displaced

Feeling displaced by other children is the second factor contributing to siblings' feelings of "I'm not enough." This occurs when other children are added to the family, either through parents' remarriage, adoption, or the birth of new siblings. Nine-year-old Mona had very low self-concept scores. Given the events that followed her brother's death, it is easy to see why Mona would feel displaced:

> Mona was only 2 years of age when her brother died. Her parents were separated at the time and were divorced shortly thereafter. Mona's mother (Mrs. M.) remarried within a short time and subsequently gave birth to a second baby boy. At this time, Mrs. M. and her new husband became the managers of a group home for five retarded children who needed 24-hour attention. After two years at this job, Mrs. M. recognized that she was "burning out" and quit. However, she then cared for a foster child who was also retarded and who eventually required institutionalization. Meanwhile, Mona's father married a woman who had three children, and together they had two additional children. Mona therefore was displaced by several other children in both her parents' lives. In fact, Mrs. M. herself stated that, she "filled in her own life [after the death of her son] with other kids" and that Mona "may have felt replaced" as a result.

Parental divorce is not the critical factor in a sibling's feeling displaced. Rather, it is the addition of other children who are perceived by the sibling as substitutes for the one who died. The sibling then feels that the reason for having to add these other children is "I'm not enough." "Otherwise," the sibling thinks, "why do mom and dad need those other kids?" For example, Jim's parents adopted another son four years after the death of their oldest son. The adopted boy was six months older than Jim. On being informed about his parents' plan, Jim exclaimed, "But I don't want anybody to take Rob's place!" Jim perceived that there was no one who could take his brother's place, but it seemed to Jim that was what his parents were trying to do. To Jim, there was only one reason: he wasn't "enough" for them.

In summary, the differentiating characteristic between high and low self-concept children is the feeling of "I'm not enough" in children with the low self-concepts. This feeling is present when the child perceives that he or she does not compare favorably with the deceased sibling or when children feel displaced by other children or both. Consequently, surviving siblings may feel that they can never "be enough" to make their parents happy. This feeling is reinforced in situations where surviving children are believed to be in some way responsible for the death. Furthermore, parents of low self-concept siblings do not describe their children in ways that reflect perceptions of their children as special. Parents of children with highest self-concepts are complimentary about their children, referring to them as very special and valued for being themselves.

Manifestations of "I'm Not Enough"

The feeling of "I'm not enough" is manifested in two patterns of behavior. The first is overachieving; the second is parental caregiving. Tom's persistence at boxing is an example of how he overachieved in order to show his dad that he was tough and "good enough," despite his small body frame. In addition to practicing and travelling around the country to fight, Tom also attended school full time and had a job.

When Jim's adopted brother arrived, Jim, according to his dad, "became superkid . . . he just knocked himself out proving he could ride a bike better, he could throw a ball better." Rather than acknowledging either Tom's or Jim's accomplishments and skills, the parental behavior in both cases actually reinforced the boys' sense of inferiority. Tom's father continued to remind Tom about his brother by wondering what kind of boxer he would have been.

Parental caregiving is the second behavioral pattern seen in the children who have reason to feel as though they are "not enough." Many bereaved siblings are described by their parents as caring, thoughtful, and giving individuals; parents often indicated that these characteristics become more prevalent as a result of the death. However, the object of caregiving differs between siblings with high self-concepts and those with lower self-concepts.

Children with higher self-concepts direct their care to younger siblings or to peers. They demonstrate responsibility by being helpful in age-appropriate ways. Children with lower self-concepts direct their caregiving primarily to their parents. They take on an adult responsibility of caring for other adults. As Mona's mother said, "Mona was the one who was my total support; she was the one who looked after me. It must have been quite a burden for her."

Several other behaviors are evident in children with lower self-concepts that were not evident in children with higher self-concepts. Some do not do well in school. One child in the study had history of shoplifting, and two children were obsessive about cleanliness. One of these children showered at least four times a day, and the other rewashed every dish before eating. These were behaviors that had not been present before the death of the sibling. These children also lived in families who manifested lower levels of functioning. In contrast, siblings with higher self-concepts, or who were not having behavior problems, lived in families demonstrating higher levels of functioning.

Families who openly share information, allow and even encourage expression of feelings, actively engage in creative problem solving, flexibly redefine roles, utilize a wide range of resources, reorganize to incorporate change, are considerate of others, and confront their own beliefs create emotional environments that facilitate siblings' adaptation to the death of their brother or sister. In such families, siblings are well-informed of what is happening and are encouraged to express their own thoughts and feelings. They feel they are an integral part of the family because their perspectives are considered; they feel part of the solution instead of the problem. They are exposed to other people—friends and extended family—which increases the likelihood that they can find someone to relate to, even during those times when their parents are too distressed or simply too tired to give them the attention the children desire. They learn to be adaptive—that life goes on, and that exploring one's own beliefs is conducive to coming to terms with those beliefs. They learn that they can be themselves—that they are loved for who they are and they do not need to become the child or adolescent their deceased sibling was in order to be a valued member of the family.

☐ Sharing Meanings within Families

The second study that offers data to validate the importance of family functioning to bereavement outcome is one that focused on how families handle the belongings of their deceased child (Davies, 1987b). This study described what 34 families did with their child's clothes, room, and mementoes. Conceptual analysis of the data resulted in a theoretic scheme, which hypothesizes that the deceased child's belongings may serve as memories with meanings, that these meanings may vary among family members, and that discrepant meanings may influence bereavement outcome within the family and among the siblings.

Individuals' private meanings of mementoes of the deceased child may vary, and there may be discrepancies between the mutually held family meaning associated with a memento or belonging and the private meanings attributed by individual family members to the memory. Families attached mutual meanings to some belongings—the deceased child's bicycle brings back memories of how fast Johnny could ride and the delight and excitement his antics brought to everyone. Family members also had discrepant meanings: To Johnny's younger brother, Paul, that bike was also a source of resentment because he had never had as colorful a bike; now, Paul secretly hopes that maybe he can have Johnny's bike. To Johnny's dad, the bike brings some comfort. He remembers teaching Johnny how to ride it, and wants to polish it up and keep it in the garage next to his workbench as a reminder of the good times with his older son. When families do not openly share information or freely express their feelings, or show consideration for how other family members might feel, there is greater likelihood of discrepant meanings. In the Jones family, for example, a collection of artwork hung on the wall of the dining room:

> The pictures had been drawn by Mary when she was a child in her early grades at school. Mary died two years ago when she was 8. After Mary's death, Mrs. Jones framed Mary's drawings and created the display. Mr. and Mrs. Jones and their son, Peter, now 8 years old, shared the mutual meaning of this wall as a "memorial wall." The individuals' private meanings however were very different. To Mr. Jones, the wall was an artifact of his wife's grieving, and he simply tolerated it. To Mrs. Jones, the wall had great depth of personal meaning—it represented her way of keeping alive a part of her only daughter who had died. To Peter, the wall also had deep personal meaning. He had asked his mother if he could put some of his pictures on the wall too. But his mother had replied, "No, the wall is a special wall because Mary can't make any more pictures for me. You can make mommy a lot more pictures."

To Peter, the wall was a constant reminder that his older sister was very special—much more special than he since he was still alive, so his pictures were not as valuable, nor was he.

Another example comes from the Smith family, where the mother had used memorial money for the deceased child to commission a painting of her children:

> In the foreground of the large, two-by-three-foot painting, which hung on the living room wall, were her two surviving children: Sam, age 8, holding on

> his lap his 2 1/2 year old sister, who had been born the day his older sister had died. In the background was the portrait of her deceased daughter. To Mrs. Smith, this painting was her "pride and joy"—it represented to her the "three most important people in the world." To her husband, it had much less significance. He had not had a part in having it painted nor in deciding where it would be hung. Further, he felt rejected since he was not included as one of the "three most important people" in his wife's view. Finally, to young Sam, the painting served as a constant reminder of the sister he no longer had. She, in fact, had become a "presence" in his life, constantly watching over his shoulder, while he had to help look after the imposter who had come to take his first sister' s place.

The painting, beautiful and creative as it was, had discrepant private meanings for the members of this family. The greater the discrepancy between the mutually held family meanings and the individuals' private meanings associated with a belonging or memento, the greater the potential for unhealthy grieving within the family and among its members. Both the Jones and the Smith families indicated that they were experiencing great difficulty in adapting to their daughter's death. Both surviving boys scored within the highest percentiles (90th and 87th) on the Achenbach CBCL, a standardized measure of behavior problems in children and adolescents (Achenbach & Edelbrock, 1981). If the private meanings could have been shared within each of these families, the parents may have appreciated their son's different perspectives. The parents would have had opportunities to reaffirm their love for their surviving children and to let them know that they, too, were special. Mrs. Jones may have permitted, or even encouraged, Peter to add his pictures to the collection on the wall. Mrs. Smith may have chosen to move the memorial painting to a less visible location, or even may have taken it down, or had a smaller photo made of the large painting so that she could keep it in a place special to her.

In contrast, in the Evans family, an event occurred that clarified the various meanings associated with the deceased child's (Mary's) room:

> Mary's room had been the one closest to the main living area of the family's trailer home. Joey's, the 8-year-old surviving sibling, room was at the far end of the trailer. After Mary's death, Mr. and Mrs. Evans decided that it would be better to give Joey the closer room in an attempt to help him "feel less far away from the action" and "less lonely." They selected wallpaper and accessories adorned with Smurfs, Joey's favorite cartoon characters, and the father redecorated the room as a surprise for his son. Upon completion of the room, Mr. Evans proudly showed the new room to Joey, but Joey was not nearly as excited as his dad had anticipated. In exasperation, the father exclaimed, "I spent $60 fixing up this room just for you!" Knowing that money was very scarce in his family , the young child realized the significance of his dad's spending that sum of money. In awe, Joey turned to his mother, gasping,

> "Dad spent all that money just for *me*?" Both parents were then able to tell Joey how special he was to them and it was for this reason that they had spent the money on the room.

From this point on, the newly decorated room took on new meaning for all members of the Evans family. It no longer was just Mary's old room, redecorated; it was a new room redecorated at great cost especially for Joey. Without this interaction between Joey and his parents, the room would have kept its mutually held meaning of "the newly decorated room," but Joey's private meaning would have been discrepant from his parents' private meanings. Instead, the brief conversation enabled Joey to see the room in a new light, and the discrepancy was cleared. Thus, when the mutually held meanings and the private meanings attached to any specific belonging or memento are shared openly and understood by everyone in the family, there is greater opportunity for healthy grieving to occur. When meanings are not shared, the potential exists for misunderstanding among the family members, and the process of integrating the death is hampered.

Actions Speak Louder than Words

Words are not the only medium for expressing to surviving children that they are special—nonverbal actions sometimes speak just as loudly. In the process of conducting interviews with families, they are often eager to show me a picture of their deceased child. I have learned that the way in which the photos are displayed delivers clear messages to the surviving children. In some families, a photograph of the deceased child is the only one hanging on the wall or sitting on a cabinet. In other families, the deceased child's photograph is one of several photos of all children in the family. In the first case, the message is, "This is our child who died. He is special." In the second case, the message is, "These are our children.... They are all special." When asked about their responses to the photographs of the deceased child, few siblings object to the photos. They understand their parent's or parents' desire to have the photo on display. But they are very much aware of the message conveyed by the photos on display. When only one photo is up, siblings will comment, "That's my brother—my mom likes to have his picture up." When photos of all children are displayed, siblings often comment, "That one is my brother.... Mom and dad like to still include him in the family."

Most parents do not intend to convey messages of preference or favoritism in how they display photos. Parents will often exclaim, "But that's not what I intended!" I have not met any parents who consciously do things that would make their other children feel as if they are not special. The word, "consciously," is the critical factor. Parenthood focuses on *consciously* thinking about one's actions and the potential impact of those actions on children. To *not* think about one's actions with regard to their effect on the children is the problem. Parents do not usually go out of their way to make their children feel bad about themselves, but those parents who make a conscientious, concerted effort to think about their actions in terms of their effects on their children are the ones who make their children feel special.

Implications for Caregivers

A family-focused perspective is prerequisite to working with grieving siblings. Children and adolescents must be placed within the context of their family's emotional environment. Therefore, those who work with grieving siblings must assess the level of family functioning.

As they carry out family assessments, practitioners must recognize that some families are more difficult than others to assess and to work with. Some families may be reluctant to share differing viewpoints in the presence of one another. The practitioner needs to obtain information from more than one family member and to gather data over time, as some families may reveal critical information only when they have developed trust. Negative perceptions of past experiences may leave some families hypersensitive to interactions with the health care, social, or other systems. These families do not easily tolerate any change or unforeseen circumstance that interrupts plans.

Part of understanding a family includes having family members tell their stories. In some families, the stories tend to be repeated and feelings associated with them resurface. Practitioners need to spend considerable time listening and acknowledging these feelings.

Professionals who work with families tend to offer a variety of options to families so that they may choose what suits them best. This may work well in families where discussion is open and spontaneous, where the input of all members is considered, where creative problem solving is seen as a challenge. However, this approach may be less successful in families where there is little consensus about the problem, reluctance to seek or accept help, rigidity in beliefs, and inflexibility in roles and relationships. Resources may need to be offered slowly to these families, perhaps one at a time, and considerable attention must be given to the degree of disruption associated with each suggested change. Practitioners need to make an extra effort to ensure the best possible fit between the resource and the family. A family that receives unsuitable services may decline the entire concept and perceive the experience as yet another example of failure of the health care or other system to meet its needs.

Parents are instrumental in creating optimal environments for their children. It is critical that health care professionals support attempts to improve parent–child relations in general, and also specifically during and after the death of a child in the family. Health care professionals must recognize that parents in such situations feel overwhelmed. At the same time, professionals must devise ways of helping parents see each child as special. Doing so is integral to creating environments that promote the optimal development of all children and particularly those who have lost a sibling. Encourage parents to examine their own behavior with their children: Do they favor one child over the others? Ask them to identify the special attributes of their surviving children and encourage them to share these perceptions with their children.

Professional caregivers can encourage families to be aware of the subtle meanings that may be associated with various belongings or mementoes. The visible mementoes that families have within their homes can portray clear, although implicit, meanings. It is also important to encourage families to share openly their private meanings. When families are not aware of the private meanings of particular memories, difficulties may ensue. It must be emphasized that the suggestion should not be interpreted to mean that all family members should attach identical meanings to various mementoes. Rather, professionals must help families develop the awareness that each person may not attach the same meaning to any one memento, and that these private meanings may be different from the mutually held meanings attached to the memory. In the Jones and Smith families, for example, the problem was not just that mutually held and private meanings existed, but that no one discussed or was aware of the discrepant meanings. If they had been, it is more likely that some action that took into account the husbands' and the children's individual meanings could have been taken. Instead, the mother in each case assumed that her private meaning was in fact the same as the family's mutually held meaning and was therefore shared by her husband and son. Helping families to share their mutually held meanings and their private meanings helps them recognize that each family member may perceive and feel differently in response to the death. Helping families gain such awareness through encouraging the sharing of information creates opportunities for healthier grieving among all family members and increases the likelihood that siblings will be made to feel special. How siblings are supported in their grief has far-reaching implications. These are discussed in the next chapter about the long-term effects of sibling bereavement in childhood.

Long-Term Effects of Sibling Bereavement in Childhood

For many years, prevailing descriptions of bereavement suggested that grief is a time-limited process, beginning with the death and ending when the grieving person has "relinquished ties to" (Freud, 1957) or has become "emancipated from" the person who died (Lindemann, 1944). More recent theorists also supported this view (Bowlby, 1980; Raphael, 1983; Parkes, 1986). It was assumed for many years that the grieving process should be complete within a year or two at the most. This view originated in Lindemann's classic work (1944), where he indicated that grieving individuals are "back to normal" within less than a year, and sometimes within as little as six weeks following the death. Evidence of distress after the first year or two is most often interpreted negatively, sometimes even as evidence of pathological grieving. Such individuals are perceived as not "letting go" and are criticized for hanging on to the past and for not getting on with their lives. But few studies of bereavement have extended beyond the first year or two following the death.

At the time of completing my first investigation into sibling bereavement (Davies, 1983), there were no reports in the literature about the longer-term effects of bereavement on adults or children. My research findings indicated that sibling responses change over time and, in fact, suggested that some children demonstrated more internalizing behavior problems with the passing of time. Consequently, I welcomed the opportunity to continue my work as a postdoctoral fellow under the supervision of Dr. Ida Martinson, then at the University of California, San Francisco. Dr. Martinson is one of the few investigators who systematically followed families for longer than the first year or two after a death (study funded by the California Division, American Cancer Society grant 2-120-PR-14). I participated in her study of families who were interviewed seven to nine years following the death of a child from cancer, and we have continued with additional exploration of these families' experiences (Davies et al., 1986; Martinson et al., 1987; Martinson, Davies, & McClowry, 1991; Martinson, McClowry, Davies, & Kulenkamp, 1994; McClowry, Davies, May, Kulenkamp, & Martinson, 1987). My particular focus, however, was on the siblings' responses. To continue exploration of the long-term effects of sibling bereavement in childhood, I more recently interviewed adults who, in their childhood, experienced the death of a sibling (Davies, 1995a, 1996).

Findings from these studies indicate that sibling grief is an individual journey that should not be expected to follow time limits and a specific path. Instead of completing their grief in a year or two, siblings continue to feel bouts of sadness and feelings of pain and loss years later. They describe how their sibling remains with them always: Brian, now 22, asserts, "I don't think you ever get back to normal.... Things change. It's always with you.... He's [brother] always with me." Carol, now 33, makes the point succinctly: "My sister's illness and death are part of my life, and always will be." Rather than saying things that suggest letting go of their loved one, siblings describe something different.

After a period of time, siblings are able to get on with their own lives. They learn, play, go to school, graduate from high school, attend college or get jobs, marry, and have children of their own. They pay their taxes, attend family reunions, celebrate special occasions, and suffer subsequent losses. Their own children leave home; they retire from work. They age. And, through it all, they experience the lifelong impacts of having had a sibling die—shadows in the sun.

☐ Sibling Responses

Bereaved siblings, seven to nine years after the death, and adults who in their childhood experienced the death of a sibling recall that their responses at the time of the death were like the bereavement responses described in earlier chapters. They recall having difficulties with eating, sleeping (either because of bad dreams or nightmares or being afraid of the dark), lowered concentration, and increased fears of the dark and of being alone. Many siblings remember how their experience made them "feel different" from their childhood peers, how they withdrew into themselves, or how they lashed out in anger against the world.

Some siblings look back on their responses at the time of the death and experience retroactive guilt—feeling guilty for how they reacted. Brian, now 15, was only 7 when his brother died:

> I wasn't really old enough to realize how sick he was. I was here, I knew, but I never really noticed how badly he was sick. I could see all the pain he was in, but I didn't really take anything serious sometimes and that's what . . . I didn't see it like I do now. I look back and I . . . I ask myself, "Geez, how couldn't I have noticed that? Couldn't I have just pushed myself a little bit to . . . just to notice what was happening?" . . . I just wanted to go outside and play in the sandbox and run around, play ball, you know.

Bereaved siblings need reassurance that what they did at the time was normal for a child of that age. Other siblings, particularly those who were very young when the death occurred, do not remember their brother or sister and wish that they did. Some express guilt over not being able to remember their sibling and the events surrounding the death. Jody, now 18, was 10 when her brother died:

> I feel bad because I don't remember anything that happened. Ooh, I'm getting all choked up. I just wish I remembered more about it . . . and about him . . . because I don't. My dad told us what was happening . . . but I just thought that it was something that could be taken care of.

Many siblings also describe the ongoing presence of other responses that they attribute to the death of their brother or sister. These responses include sensitivity to reaching the same age as their brother or sister was at the time of death, recurring sadness, loneliness, fearful of recurrence, and curiosity. In addition, siblings attribute features of their outlook on life, themselves, and others to their bereavement experience.

Sensitive to Being the Age at which the Sibling Died

In the early years following the death, siblings who were younger than the age at which the child who died are very much aware of their age in relation to their deceased sibling. They often experience considerable difficulty as they themselves approach the age at which their brother or sister died. For some, like 19-year-old Leroy, it was because he did not feel that he was as able as his brother had been when he died at 19 years of age:

> It bothers me to be the same age as he was. I think back and I am not prepared at all for death like he was. Not at all. I only hope that I can be prepared like he was. He was ready . . . accepted it. He knew what was happening. He had religion behind him to give him the strength, and when I saw that in him, I envied it and said, "Gosh, I wish I could be like that." But I haven't accomplished that yet, though that's my goal.

The behavior of others often reinforced siblings' fearfulness and unease. Zoeann, now 25, recalls her experience as she approached age 18. Both of Zoeann's older brothers died, three years apart, just before their 18th birthdays:

> I got cards, letters from people—even from my folks' friends, people I wouldn't get stuff from ordinarily—to the point that they scared me. It was like all these people didn't think I was going to make it. It was just kind of scary, I guess.... I didn't do anything on my birthday. It was the first year that I stayed at home and I didn't do anything. I just went to bed. I just thought, "I wasn't going to blow it now." I was afraid that something could happen to me on that day. I wasn't going to be in a car where something could happen, and it was odd because up until that point, I didn't slow down, but come my birthday, I just shut down.

Some other siblings are increasingly aware of approaching the age at which their brother or sister died because of the overprotectiveness of their parents. After losing one child, parents are typically more protective of their other children—they want to do all they can to avoid losing another child. Parents' protective nature increases even more as the surviving children reach the age of the child who died. Martha's mother, for example, refused to allow Martha, now 14, to attend her girlfriend's birthday party aboard her uncle's yacht. Martha's sister had drowned in a boating accident at age 14.

Some siblings, now much older, recalled that when they reached the age of their deceased sibling they became involved in or interested in death-related issues. But they were not always aware of the links between their interest, their age, and the age of their deceased sibling. When Mary was 10, her 17-year-old brother died. Seven years later, Mary chose "Dealing with terminal illness" as the topic for three major school projects. As Mary reflected,

> At the time, I had a burning need to do those projects. My teachers tried to convince me to change topics, but I was so stubborn, and I didn't know why. If I'd made the connections then, I believe I would have gained even more from doing those projects.

Some siblings feel that they do not really begin to live their own lives until after they have passed the age at which their sibling died. Only then do they feel as if they can "relax" and just be themselves: "I dreaded turning 18—I was sure that something bad would happen to me, just like it did to my brothers [who both died in their 18th years]." As the years go by, many surviving siblings, as they reach other marker birthdays, remember their deceased brother or sister: "I recently celebrated my 60th birthday ... and you know what I thought? That, if my brother were still here, he would be 65, and we could really have a whopper of a celebration ... two old coots!"

Recurring Sadness

Siblings' grief resurfaces periodically—less often as time goes by, but it still recurs. Recalling the story and its many aspects even many years after the death often stimulates waves of tearful sadness and even sobbing for some siblings. It is not "unresolved grief" but a long-lasting sadness over having lost someone very special. Remembering the experience sometimes brings forth a resurgence of sadness.

Episodes of acute sadness are most often triggered by selected events—seeing a movie about siblings or death, hearing a favorite song of the deceased, hearing a song that was played at the funeral, or seeing someone that looks like the deceased:

> There'll be times when ... I'll be watching a movie ... and it'll remind me ... at those little times you feel that way.... Just the other week, there was a movie on TV called "Alex." It was so good, and I cried so hard. Times like that ... you feel it all over again. (Nick, age 29)

Attending another funeral, particularly for the first time after the sibling's funeral, often triggers acute sadness:

> Grandma's was the first funeral I had been to after Tiffany's. It was very traumatic for the whole family. We walked in and it was like, "Oh my gosh ... Tiffany!" It was like, "We can remember Tiffany so well now." It all just came back. (Mary, age 24)

In addition to the periodic acute sadness, many siblings experience a more pervasive, ongoing sadness because they simply miss their brother or sister: "When I think of Seth, it's not always a crying sad ... it's more like 'too bad Seth's not here,' or 'I wish Seth could be here now.' " The sibling's death creates an empty space that remains forever. Nine years after his sister's death, 22-year-old Mark said,

> I miss my sister.... We were real close. I miss her for the things we did together as children ... like watching cartoons together on Saturday mornings. I remember I would come down to do that after she died, but it just wasn't the same. The things that I do now, the things that we used to do together—they just aren't the same anymore. It's like an empty part of me, of *my life* that is always there.

The empty space is particularly evident to siblings at times when the family group is together—special occasions, holidays, family photo sessions, where they feel there is "always someone missing."

Siblings frequently miss their brother or sister during times of major transition in their own lives—when they are graduating from school or college, getting married, having children of their own, or facing troublesome times when they long for their brother or sister's advice. Even as siblings get older and experience life's later transitions, such as having grandchildren or retiring, they still sometimes miss what they imagine their relationship with their sibling would have been. Feelings of loneliness persist for many, particularly those whose only brother or sister died or those who were especially close to the deceased sibling. Missing the deceased person is an ongoing feeling, not always in the forefront of siblings' minds but more, as Leroy (quoted earlier) said, "down in the basement where you can go and look at it once in a while."

For some siblings, the feeling of sadness is itself a trigger for thoughts about the deceased sibling. Some bereaved siblings become aware of a recurring or persistent sadness that they cannot explain. With increasing self-awareness, the sadness triggers thoughts and memories of their sibling, deceased long ago. After hearing my conference presentation about the long-term effects of sibling bereavement, a woman approached me with tears in her eyes:

> I came to your talk to hear about what I could do to help my son because my daughter died last year. But, as I listened to you, I felt that you were talking to me, *about me*.... I have felt so many of the things that you described and have wondered why. I have just realized that I think it has to do with my twin sister ... she died when we were just babies. I have never talked about it or even wanted to. I just crossed it off.... My mother, no one in the family, ever talks about her. But hearing what you said about the long-term effects today has me all choked up.... There is a connection there still.

Such siblings sense that something is not quite right with their lives but have no idea of what it might be. Then while in therapy or while attending a presentation about the topic, they experience "a light going on" as they gain new insight. "You carry the feelings with you, and that's a burden you carry through your life and you don't know why.... You sort of figure it out and you think, 'Wow, that's a breakthrough!' " (Paula, age 48). Paula continued,

> If my mother were still alive, I'd have a lot of questions for her. Even before I heard your program, I'd sit in this family room, because I do have mood swings—one day, I was sitting here, feeling really down. I said to my husband, "I don't belong. I've got shallow roots. Here I am in a nice house, why aren't I really happy?" And then I thought, "I don't really feel close to my own family, my sisters and my own dad." I started to think back, and I thought, "I wonder if it has something to do with S. [sister], with that death in the family." Because it was a really traumatic thing for me. It's only been recently that I've really thought about the experience. I didn't talk about it before because I never even thought that her death was significant in my life.

For some siblings, their new insight triggers tearing or even uncontrollable sobbing. As Malcolm (51 years) explained,

> My wife encouraged me to come to this conference. I sat stunned as I realized what you were describing was *my* life. I couldn't breathe, and I felt so much like crying. It was as if you had thrown cold water on me. All these years, and I only now realize the impact of my brother's death on that young boy I used to be.

Some siblings recall feeling overwhelmed with emotion whenever they talked about the death (if they did talk about it) but did not know why.

> When I talked about his death, which isn't often, I had a lot of emotion. I never knew why; I never really knew why I felt so upset. It was just something I totally repressed . . . and now that I have been able to talk about it, and the effect it had on me, about how angry I was at my mother for leaving me at home alone with him when I was only a child myself . . . I can see that so much of what I was feeling came from that experience. Now, knowing that, I feel so much better. I still cry sometimes, but it's like I know why I am crying and I am sad. Before when I cried, I was sad *and* scared because I didn't have any idea where those tears were coming from.

Others have gone through therapy, but the therapist has not asked any questions about the deceased sibling or about whether there had been any deaths in the person's life.

> It was absolutely amazing to me when I went to your talk that day. I could not believe what I was feeling because I don't talk about this, I've never talked about it, and I've done a lot of therapy, and it's intriguing to me to realize that neither one of my therapists has ever asked . . . when you were up there talking about those little critters, and it was like somebody gave me permission to go back and look at who that person was, who I was when I was young, and I was so young to go through all that stuff. . . . I had grieved the childhood I didn't have from other postures, but this was like a whole layer that I hadn't weighed because there's no way you could expect a kid of 9 to go through all that stuff without affecting the way she looks at the world.

Another woman realized the impact of her sister's death while filling out a family history questionnaire prior to entering a therapy group.

> You had to write your life on paper and tell why you thought you needed the group. I can remember going to the beach to write it down, thinking that if I wanted to get into the program, I would have to do this. Suddenly, I got to my sister, and I started crying and crying, and I thought, "I'm sitting here in the middle of this beach and I'm sitting here crying, they'll think I'm weird." So I got in the car and got home and I couldn't stop crying. That's when I realized that stuff about my sister was still there and that was reason enough to qualify for the group.

For some siblings, recurrent disturbing dreams cease when they recognize the impact of the death. Many siblings continue to dream about their brother or sister for many years following the death; for some, their dreams are frightening. Paula said,

> I had dreams for a long time ... but they were more like nightmares. There was always a young child in my dream, and it's following me and I can't get rid of it. I used to have this repeating dream for years, right through my twenties and thirties. The only way you could tell whether this child was alive or dead was to put a mirror under its nose to see if it was breathing. And there was no breath, and I was terrified. I was just trying to get away.

Paula didn't talk to anyone about her dreams or about her deceased sister because she "never thought that Sophie's death was significant in my life." Only later, after realizing that her sister's death had a profound impact on her, did Paula's terrible dream cease.

Fear of Recurrence

Siblings continued to fear, throughout their lives, a repetition of the same fate for themselves or for other loved ones. Siblings whose brother or sister died from cancer express continuing concerns about the recurrence of the illness, in themselves or in other family members. Even younger siblings such as Amy, now 14, who was only 6 when her brother died from cancer, confesses:

> I still worry about getting sick.... I cannot stand to go to the doctor. I'll probably get sick before I go ... I worry so much. My ... nerves are very bad. I get nervous a lot, easily, for anything. And I'd worry about getting sick, worried that you're going to hear that you have cancer too.

Another 14-year-old worried that her younger brother and sister also had cancer: "I thought that maybe Sam and Yolanda could get the same thing, that they might have even been born with it." Ann, now 17, said, "I worry about getting sick.... I still think ... to this day, I still think that it's in my blood too ... and I worry about it. I get worried when other people are sick."

Lana, now 24, shares similar concerns:

> I'm always worrying about getting sick. Any little thing I get. I'm getting paranoid ... I'm going to the doctor. After seeing what takes place with cancer, with both dad and Lana, I don't think I could handle it if I ever got it. I worry about everybody close to me. And, if I get a little lump, I'm afraid it's cancer.

Memories of their sibling's illness experience remain vivid in siblings' minds and strongly influence their current responses to health care problems of their own. Many adult siblings attribute their intense dislike for hospitals to their early experience with an ill sibling who died. Gary, now

27 years, whose brother died nearly 10 years ago from cancer, tells about his reaction to a diagnostic test:

> I didn't think I was too concerned, but during the test, I almost passed out. I think it was nerves or something. Because I got real dizzy, real faint-looking and ... I don't know if it was just standing, but ... I kept on thinking a little bit about Ronnie, and his scanner and he was laying down through that thing and going back and forth. I think trying to stay perfectly still got me really nervous.... I damned near passed out. Sweat was running down all over the place. I don't know what it was but I didn't feel good, and I kept remembering what it was like for Ronnie.

As young adults, when bereaved siblings have their own children, the normal parental worries about an ill child are magnified. Candace, now 33, talks about her "constant" fear of illness in her loved ones:

> I have a constant fear of illness in my family ... you know, every time he [child] gets even a little symptom, I am petrified. He had a ... bad fever this summer. They took a blood count and his white count was high. Immediately, I'm going, "Are you going to do more tests? You have got to do more tests!" Our pediatrician is saying, "Candace, this is normal. What's your problem?" I said, "Well, I had a sister with leukemia and that was one of the first signs and because of that ... I'm really hyper." And I think I tend to be ... well, I ... but I tend to be a little bit more catastrophic [negative] about every little detail.

As older adults, bereaved siblings' fears continue: Beth, now 62, confesses:

> You'd think I would learn! I worried about my own kids getting cancer like Babs [sister] did, and now I worry about my grandchildren. Babs is still with me ... every time I get a fever, or one of my kids, especially when they were small, and now it's Suzi [granddaughter] ... it's the same fear coming back ... could it be leukemia? But I remember how sick Babs was—she had such terrible pain and had seizures all the time. I don't want to ever see that again!

Siblings whose brother or sister died from trauma, whether it be accidental, homicide, or suicide, continue also to fear a similar event occurring again. Thirty-five-year-old Marsha talked about her brother's traumatic death due to a farm accident:

> I'm not afraid of death itself. I do believe in some sort of after life, but I am afraid that it might be a violent kind of thing like it was for him. I worry too about my own kids—I didn't want any of them to ever even visit a farm—I know it may sound silly, but I still worry that it could happen again. It happened once—why not again?

The ongoing fear of recurrence is not always conscious until an event occurs that reminds the sibling of their early experience. Dick recalls,

> We were on a vacation, and my son, after playing lacrosse, yelled to me, "Hey, Dad, watch me!" And he just runs and jumps into the pool. I didn't know he had learned to swim.... And just for that instant, I was really afraid. I didn't know he could swim. He had learned to swim at a friend's house, and there he was, "Look what I can do, Dad." So, that's scary. I guess I was just frightened fast. Overly frightened because it was a small pool ... you really couldn't drown in it and there were a half dozen adults around. But, I was scared ... the memories just came back in a flash and I could see it happening all over again.

Curiosity

Siblings wonder about what their brother or sister would be like now if he or she were still alive: "I miss him still. I always wonder, if he was here, what would he be doing now ... and how it would make our life different—if he'd be married and have a kid and I'd be an aunt, or something like that" (Jody, 18 years). Gary, age 27, shared similar thoughts about his brother: "If only he were here ... to see what he would be like. How tall would he be, how he'd be making a living, what girls would he have been with, and who would he have married, would he have a kid already?" Siblings are often curious about themselves in relation to their deceased sibling: "I wonder what it would be like to have an older brother now. He could do things that I couldn't do ... he was always bigger than me, and I always wanted to be like him. Would he still be bigger than me ... could I do all the things that he could?" (Jay, age 21)

As siblings get older, they sometimes reflect on their own thoughts as Carol, age 33, does:

> I think that one of the things that is increasingly harder is that as we get older, my sister always stays young. You realize that she won't ever be able to do so many things.... One of my cousins who got married this summer was the same age as Camille.... It was interesting, sort of weird, to think that's the age Camille would have been. You know, she's sort of frozen in time. It made me sad because Camille wouldn't have that opportunity. I always think of her as a little girl, but I wonder what she would be like now.

Most bereaved siblings wonder about how their lives would be different today if the death had not occurred. For example, many wonder if their sibling were still alive, how their family composition would be different: parents may not have divorced, later-born children may not have been conceived. Siblings perceive that their own position in the family would have been different: "Losing an older sister has made me the one to put mom and dad through the dating stage and all that kind of stuff.... I've had to be the first one and I was the youngest child."

Outlook on Life, Self, and Others

Outlook on Life. Siblings reflect on the ongoing effect of their experience on their ways of looking at the world, their approach to life. Many siblings feel as if the experience taught them to appreciate life more, to live each day to the fullest because they know from firsthand experience that life is limited: "You appreciate the beautiful days. I tell my kids that when they are feeling blue—nobody got sick today, nobody got hurt. We are all here together" (Mary, 32 years). Gary, age 27, reflects:

> It gave me the feeling like, "What the hell . . . life's too short. It might be my turn tomorrow—might as well enjoy life a little." But it made me have a different attitude on life, especially at that age, 19. . . . I buckled down. When I was 21, I already had my own farm. I had my shit together more than any of the other kids I knew at my age.

Adult siblings say they learned to appreciate one another more: "Realize that tomorrow the people you love might not be there." Many are confident in talking with others who have life-threatening illness and respect those who are very ill, even though they may look unusual or sometimes act inappropriately:

> Jill's sickness . . . Jill, being my sister . . . having been born, Jill being sick, going through the chemotherapy process, and Jill dying . . . has made me . . . respect other people for what they are and not just what they look like. At times, Jill was not a very pretty sight, but she was the same person. Deep down, everybody has a heart and feelings and so it's easier for me to deal with people in the outside world because I remember that, "Hey, looks aren't everything."

Many adult siblings reflect on what they learned and about comforting others who are grieving. They do not shy away from the discomfort of grief but instead are often the first to visit or provide assistance when someone has died.

Many siblings attribute critical life choices to their experience with death. Three siblings chose not to have children of their own for fear that they might die. These siblings felt that they could not go through what they had seen their parents suffer. Moreover, they did not want again to experience the agony of losing someone they loved so much. Several siblings chose health-related careers, particularly nursing, since they perceived that this was a profession where they could help others who were experiencing losses of many types. Some went into teaching or other fields where they could work with children. Other siblings indicated that they had chosen work far removed from illness and death, such as accounting, specifically to avoid encounters with reminders of what they had been through. Still others felt that there was no connection between their choice of work and their sibling's death. Some siblings felt unable to pursue their preferred career choice because of other events related to the death. Two women, for example, who wanted to go into nursing, did not because doing so would have meant leaving home, and they felt that their mothers could not have tolerated the "loss" of another child.

Outlook on Self. Had the child not died, most adult siblings perceive that a personal aspect of themselves would be different in some way: "I would not be as outgoing as I am," said 21-year-old Marnie. She continued, "When my brother died, I learned that life is very short, and that you have to make the most of it while you can. So I have tried to meet people and get to know them, and that way, get the most out of my own life." Fourteen-year-old Mathew felt the opposite: "If my sister were still here, somehow my personality would be changed.... I'd be more outgoing ... because the sadness got in the way."

Some siblings felt they grew up faster than they would have otherwise: "I grew up a lot ... real quick ... because my whole life changed." Growing up faster occurred especially in situations where one of the child's parents was incapacitated by grief. When Maggie's sister drowned, her mother became severely depressed and withdrew behind the closed bedroom door and then was institutionalized for several months for depression. Maggie—at 9 years of age—assumed responsibility for managing the family home. Thirty years later, she sighed, "I didn't only lose my brother, and my best friend—he was my best friend too—I lost my childhood."

Siblings commonly attribute current attitudes and behaviors to the experience of having lost their brother or sister. Forty-year-old Martha, for example, indicated that she is aware that she still uses illness as an "escape" when life gets a little exasperating. She indicated that she and her remaining siblings learned to "be sick at the drop of a hat if we wanted a little more attention from our mother." One fellow felt that he was more restless; he took more chances with his own life. Another sibling felt that her sister's death enhanced her commitment to healthy living:

> I don't smoke; I don't take any drugs ... unless I have to for a medical reason. Who knows what I could have gotten into in high school? But, I just didn't.... My sister didn't want to take drugs, and she had to so she could live, and she did for another 2 1/2 years, but I saw what those drugs did to her body. She didn't want to take them, but she had to, and I wasn't going to be stupid enough to take them when I didn't have to.

Outlook toward Others. When bereaved siblings grow up and have children of their own, they become much more aware of what the impact must have been on their own parents to have lost a child. Some siblings who participated in the research projects had themselves experienced the death of one of their own children. This experience brought forth memories of their sibling's death and made them even more aware of their parents' grief. Interestingly, very few siblings had shared their perceptions with their parents. They had both endured the tragedy of losing a child, yet they seldom talked together about their experience. When Bill was 9 years old, his only brother had drowned. Two years before the interview, Bill's son had died from suicide. Now, at 56 years of age, Bill said,

> The death of my own son was, in my recollection, just a terrible, traumatic, emotional, anger-filled, guilt-ridden situation. I did think about my brother and I compared the two.... They were both tragic, and traumatic, and both sudden. And I thought about how my mother must have felt ... some similar type of feelings when my brother died.... I talked to her about my son, but my brother never came up in the conversation. I knew how badly she was feeling for me through the whole situation, but we never talked about the earlier death.

As parents, bereaved siblings sometimes are jealous of the sibling relationships among their own children. For example, when the eldest of Bob's three sons died, Bob confided that he sometimes feels jealous of his other sons for still having brothers—something he no longer had after his brother died. Molly, 10 years old when her only sister died, has four daughters. She admits to sometimes feeling jealous of the close sisterly relationship they enjoy—just going shopping together, or planning family get togethers, and being able to talk about the ups and downs of their lives. Both Bob and Molly judge their jealousy as "improper" or "unacceptable." Neither of them had allowed themselves to admit to such feelings before. Both were considerably relieved to learn that others shared similar feelings, and that they weren't "bad" people for feeling jealous.

Many adults, through their experience, became very sensitive to the needs of young children. They themselves know they remember; they know that what they were told or not told greatly impacted on their formative minds. These adults realize other bereaved children may have similar experiences. As Maggie described,

> It makes me very, very angry when adults look at children as [if] they don't know anything ... when adults think they have the market on pain, when adults think they have the market on wisdom. I have trouble when adults look at age instead of experience. Like one gentleman told me, "If you're 4 years old and you've faced death, you are older than I."

Adults' sensitivity to young children, however, is sometimes limited by their own experience, if that experience has not been as well managed as it might have been.

Over the years, siblings grow, develop, and change. They remember their deceased siblings and their shared childhood experiences. Sometimes, however, the images may remain frozen in those early years. Some siblings become stuck in behavior or interactional patterns that are then re-created in subsequent situations, without ever realizing the sibling origin. These "frozen images" (Bank & Kahn, 1982) may carry over into subsequent relationships, interactions, and even employment options, as indicated above. These images may also carry over into parenting practices when the bereaved siblings have children of their own.

Images surrounding the death are more likely to become frozen when children are not allowed, or encouraged, to express emotions or ask questions. Interviews with the offspring of four of the participating adults, bereaved in childhood, suggest that these frozen images impact on the next generation as well. Ruth, now 55, described her experience with her brother, Samuel's, death. Her mother had been incapacitated with grief, and Ruth had been given much responsibility for the household following her brother's accidental death. She lamented that, "No one really paid much attention to us kids. I cried a lot, but mostly by myself." Her father had been too busy to spend much time with her, and her other siblings were all younger than she, so she did not confide in them. Instead, she said she learned to manage her grief by "swallowing" it: "If I cried, or asked too many questions, or even mentioned Samuel's name, Mother would start to cry and get annoyed with me for making her sad again." Sam, Ruth's 25-year-old son, recalled:

> Uncle Samuel died when he was 16. Mom was 11 at the time. Uncle Samuel was thrown off a horse and trampled while they were at a family picnic. As kids, we always knew about Uncle Samuel—in fact, he was really like a part of the family even though he died long before we ever came on the scene, but we knew about him and about how he died. We also knew that thinking about him made mom and grandma [maternal] really sad, and they would cry sometimes, just talking about him. It had quite an effect on mom, and the effect is still there, though it's toned down a bit. Mom never liked for us to go on picnics—the only ones we ever had as kids were in the back yard. Mom hates picnics—always has. She says it's because she doesn't like eating with the flies, but we all know it's because of memories of Uncle Samuel. When we were all kids, we would never go to a park or anywhere. Mom was always afraid that something bad might happen, just like with Uncle Samuel.
>
> I was the first one to come along, and I got named after Uncle Samuel. And, you know, it may sound weird to you, but I always felt like I was being compared to him in some ways—like he was a real adventuring type, loved to ride horses and really put out in sports. I am like that too, but no matter what I do, it's always "just like his Uncle Samuel!" I never learned how to ride horses though. . . . Mom wouldn't even hear of it. One time, I was invited to go on a sleigh ride, pulled by horses, and mom nearly had a fit—I had to

> promise that I wouldn't ride the horses. As if you could do that on a sleigh ride anyway! It's only as I have gotten older that I've realized the effect Uncle Samuel had on my life—and it's all because of the effect his death had on mom. She was only a little girl at the time, and it must have been pretty hard on her.

Sam's story is similar to that of the other offspring of the adults bereaved as children. When their parents' grief was not managed as well as it might have, their early memories of the experience were frozen in their parents' minds, and strongly, though subtly, influenced the lives of the children of the next generation.

Insights through the Rear-View Mirror

Years after the experience with death, many siblings are able to reflect on their experience and identify those factors that they believe influenced their immediate responses and that still influence ongoing responses. They talk about gender differences, closeness to the one who died, involvement, and talking as having an impact on their responses. In addition, some adult siblings identified the nature of interactions with their parents, which resulted in siblings feeling as if they "weren't enough," as influencing their immediate and ongoing responses.

Gender Differences. Adult siblings describe some gender differences in how they cope and how these differences affected their responses as grieving children. Peter (age 54), for example, says that men "have a different way of processing information. They don't talk the same way as women do, they don't ask questions in the same way." He says,

> My wife is more verbal than I am. If somebody calls to say someone is very sick in the hospital, or that so and so has died, she'll ask them all sorts of questions . . . what day, what time, what did they have, how did it happen, who was there, and she goes on and on. If I take the phone call and somebody tells me that, I say "thank you very much." If it was a death, I will ask where the funeral is going to be, and I get off the phone. My wife will ask me all those questions, and I never asked them.

Peter continues,

> I have learned that men and women are different . . . and so are boys and girls. So, when my brother died, and I acted out, and wouldn't talk to anyone about it, that seems pretty normal for a 9-year-old boy. My sister, on the other hand, cried and though I don't think she talked a lot either, she did handle it differently than I did.

Other adult siblings remember how gender affected their response: "As an 11-year-old boy, I wasn't supposed to cry. Even my little brother, who was only 5 when our sister died . . . we were told, 'Be brave. Big boys don't cry.' It's taken me 20 years to learn that it's okay to cry, and I still can't do it easily."

Closeness of Relationship. When adults recall a close relationship with their sibling before he or she died, they describe feelings of persistent loneliness. Bob explains: "I still feel at times a loneliness about not having a brother or a sister, and I look at other people who have a brother or a sister and when they complain, I say, 'How lucky you are to have a brother or a sister!'" Deaths of other loved ones do not necessarily compare. Bob's sister and father had also died, but it is his brother who occupies his thoughts when, for example, prayers for the dead are being said during a mass. Adults frequently differentiate their own responses from the responses of their other surviving brothers and sisters on the basis of closeness. Siblings who felt very close to the one who died are most affected by the death.

Involvement. Some adults do not remember much of the grieving they did as children, but they are aware of the subsequent effects: "I did a very good job of repressing as much as I could." This is particularly true for children who were not involved in what happened. When they had no opportunity to express their grief, or ask questions, their grief went underground, welling up periodically (and seemingly inappropriately) until they were old enough, or ready, to let it surface so it could be dealt with. Most siblings remembered their involvement in events related to their sibling's death, or illness if that was the cause of death. Having been forced to participate against their own choice left hurtful memories: "They made me kiss my sister—and I was scared to—I can still feel the cool sensation of her cheek on my lips and it makes me shudder." Choice is a critical feature. Other adults remember with fondness being allowed to touch or kiss their deceased sibling good-bye.

Talking. Siblings recount how talking about the death, their feelings, fears, and questions was critical to how they managed the death. Those who did not have opportunities to talk also say that had they been able to share with others, they would have been better off. Paula says it best:

> I didn't have anyone to help me. . . . It's so important to have an adult who could talk to you or help you. . . . Letting children get their feelings out . . . that's so important. If you could just have a way of finding out that you are not alone in these feelings, in the dreams. Being alone is the difficult part. I was lonely because I missed my sister, but more because nobody understood.

Not expressing grief until later in life may have to do with finding a language to express it. Children grieve wordlessly but often very loudly. It takes time; they need to find a language before they can talk about their experience. This is reassuring to parents who are concerned that their children will not "open up." Even when parents do all the things they are supposed to do, children will not necessarily, and sometimes cannot, talk about it at the time. Even in households where "children have been marinated with lots of talking about lots of things," children may not discuss their reactions. However, in families who are sensitive to feelings, the chances of eventually talking about the death and associated feelings are markedly increased. Even though children do not express themselves verbally, they still express their feelings through their behavior. They still are sensitive to the ways in which their parents and other adults react to them. It is this sense of being understood, of belonging, that is more important than actually talking about their feelings and reactions.

I'm Not Enough. Some siblings perceive that their parents' preference for or favoritism toward the deceased child continues for a life time. As one adult daughter remarked, "My mother still has a more intense relationship with this child who died as a baby than with those of us who've been around for over 40 years." It is not the death itself that traumatizes children but the child's reactions to what happens and how the child is helped. If the child somehow feels inadequate, excluded, isolated, and alone, then those feelings are what cause trouble for the grieving child. If parents in their vulnerability feel inadequate, and cannot share their own feelings with their children, and cannot reassure the children of the parents' ongoing love, then children are set on a difficult path. It is the way of coping, the way of expressing or not, the sense of inadequacy that children learn. This learning influences their development more than the event of their sibling's death.

☐ Maintaining Connections

Thinking about the Deceased Sibling

All siblings who participated in this research report that they continue to think about their brother or sister, some as often as every day: "He is always in the back of my mind, and often in the middle of my thoughts." Some siblings express guilt for not thinking of their brother or sister as often as they might: "Sometimes I don't think of him enough." Some, although very few, siblings reported that they thought about their brother or sister only on special occasions, such as Christmas or birthdays. Most (70%) thought of their sibling at least once or twice a month; 20% thought of their deceased sibling at least once or twice a week; and 10% had thoughts about their brother or sister every day. Ann, now 17, was 10 when her brother died seven years before: "I would say that he comes into my mind probably once a day at least. For the most part, I keep it . . . just keep it to myself . . . just a little memory of Steve. I talk about him much less than I think about him." Ann is typical of many siblings. She seldom shares her thoughts about her deceased sibling with anyone.

Leroy's (now 19) brother had died nine years before:

> I think about him often. . . . It's around . . . I work up at A&W and that's right by the cemetery, which is where he is buried. So . . . I think about it a lot . . . but not all the time, you know, because if I think about it all the time, I'll probably get bitter about it or people will get tired of listening to it so I just . . . I keep it in the back of the mind, where you keep all the things that you don't want to see all the time. You know, it's like putting things in the basement: you go through it once in a while and then you . . . you know, maybe you'll throw it out some day but probably not. But, you know, like I say, I guess you could say I keep it and face it and I go down there once in a while.

Thoughts about the deceased sibling are triggered by a variety of events or activities. Reminders are either external (events, activities occurring outside of the individual) or internal (stemming from inner thoughts and feelings). External reminders include such triggers as seeing movies or hearing songs that rekindle memories of the deceased sibling. Michael said, "I'd be driving down the road in my car and they'd play 'Dust in the Wind' . . . 'all we are is dust in the wind' . . . I would just start to cry."

Seeing objects that belonged to the deceased sibling is another external reminder. "I think about her maybe twice a week. . . . We got a music box for Tammy right before she died . . . whenever I see that, I think of her." Seeing photographs of the child or seeing someone who resembles the child were other external reminders. Attending other funerals always brought back memories and often a resurgence of grief: "When I go to a funeral . . . I can remember the scene of the whole thing. I relive it," said 35-year-old Matthew. Similarly, anniversaries of the sibling's birthday or death also trigger memories. Thirty-year-old Kate, who was 9 when her sister died just prior to Christmas, said,

> I still, up to this day, have an anniversary reaction. I can't say when it will happen. I think it might have been Christmas Eve this past Christmas when it hit me . . . where I'll find myself as that 9-year-old girl, those emotions will come back, and it will just hit me, and I'll be alone and I can't communicate that with anyone . . . a sense of tremendous alienation.

Internal reminders stem from siblings' thoughts about events in their own lives. Life events associated with growing older frequently serve as internal reminders, triggering comparisons between the sibling and the deceased child. Eighteen-year-old Laura comments:

> As I watch myself get older, and things that I did when I reached puberty or when I started wearing makeup and stated dating, I look back and say, "Gosh, Mary never . . . ever got to experience anything like this." And that kind of got to me . . . her life was very different. She never got to do the things that I did . . . and what I'm doing now. She never got to be a regular teenager.

For young adults, getting married and having babies of their own triggers thoughts about their deceased siblings. "If Sue were here, I wouldn't have to worry about who to choose for my bridesmaid," sighed Marie (28 years) as her eyes filled with tears. Her only sister had died 14 years earlier. When anticipating the birth of their own offspring, many siblings consider naming their child after their deceased brother or sister. Several follow through and give their offspring the same name. The pattern of missing their sibling continues in older adults when they experience life's developmental transitions. Kate, now 57, recalls how she missed her brother at her own daughter's wedding: "If he'd still been with us, he'd have given the toast to the bride." Kate's daughter recently had her first child, and Kate thinks of her brother again: "I'm a grandma now—hard for me to believe, but I am. I'd love to be able to get old with Kip [brother]. He'd be the baby's great uncle." Kate's husband died two years ago, and she often feels very lonely. Loneliness often triggers or accompanies thoughts about deceased siblings. Another woman, Beth (62 years), also a widow, was looking for someone to accompany her on a holiday cruise: "If Babs [sister] were here, maybe we'd go together. Sometimes I think of her now that Jack [husband] is gone. She should be here. She was eight years younger than me. I still feel like she shouldn't have died. . . . She would be here now. And we could go together."

Sharing Memories about Deceased Siblings

Most siblings do not often talk about their sibling or their memories, and when they do, they are selective about with whom they share their thoughts. They sense that others are uncomfortable with the topic, avoid it, or need to have too much explained: "I don't talk about it much. . . . If you do, then you have to explain the whole thing, and I don't want them to feel sorry for me. So we talk in the family mostly" (Mary, 24 years). Siblings find it easiest to talk with others who have experienced similar losses or who can identify with the experience in some way. Leroy, for example, talks only about his brother with an older man at work whose son had been killed in an auto accident: "We get to talking about people dying and stuff up there [at work] because he lost a son to a drunk driver. Others don't really talk about it. . . . Every once in a while, someone will say, 'Well, how long has he been dead?' or something like that, but we don't get in any conversations. A question here or there, but that's about it."

Jody, aged 18, talks "a bit with my mom and dad, but mostly with my friends . . . a guy at work—he's the same age as I am and he has a brother the same age as Jay [Jody's deceased brother]. He said he never knew what happened, but that I had a brother who died . . . and we sat down and talked."

Some siblings talk freely about their loss and welcome opportunities to do so: Peter, now 24, says, "I talk about him a lot . . . about once every other week . . . at least, which is a lot, I think. I've got a picture of him in my wallet. Somebody will say, 'Who's that?' . . . so it comes up that way too." A few siblings talk freely even to those who seem uncomfortable. Aware of their listeners' discomfort, they feel the need to talk anyway: "Like my mom, I've learned to talk about her [deceased sister] a lot and it doesn't bother me. It bothers other people, but it doesn't bother me."

Some siblings talk freely in their families about the deceased child: "It's fun to get together and talk about the old times, when Wanda was with us . . . and we always do that. You know we can just be sitting here, and all of a sudden, somebody will say something and we're discussing old times. We enjoy doing that." In other families, the conversation is more restricted. Some siblings avoid the topic to protect other family members, most often one of their parents who becomes very upset or angry when the topic is introduced into the conversation: "I think of her often, but I don't express it. It seems like less of a pain for them [mom and dad] if you don't say anything about it." Some siblings recount how the death still is not a topic of conversation. Forty-four years after her sister's death, one 48-year-old woman described her 78-year-old father: "To this day my dad won't talk about my sister because he sees it as negative—you never talk about the dead." Sometimes siblings avoided talking about the death in order to protect themselves:

> I don't think it's [the death] has been brought up with the family in seven years [since the death]. Once in a while, mom brings it up. I never mentioned it in front of mom . . . because I . . . I'd hate to get into some tearful recollection. I'm not a very emotional person; I am a stone.

Nearly all siblings, even those who choose to remain silent about their loss, appreciate the value of talking as a means of expressing the emotion: "I still break down and cry really hard. . . . I remember the summer after she died, I cried myself to sleep every night. I think part of it is . . . ummm . . . I don't talk about my feelings very often and keep it all inside and crying is how I let it out" (Mary, age 24). Some siblings talk not to other people but to their pets, and that too serves a therapeutic effect: "I especially like riding through the fields.... That's my quiet time. That's my down time.... I don't talk except to my horse. My horse is like a friend to me" (Jack, age 19).

Keeping in Touch

As they get older, siblings continue to maintain connections with their deceased brother or sister. Many siblings engage in specific actions that serve to keep them "in touch" with their deceased brother or sister. One young man, now 24, carries his brother's picture in his wallet to look at and talk to. Nineteen-year-old Rod, whose brother died when Rod was 10, says, "I think about him a lot. I've got a picture of him by my bed ... and we've got pictures of him all over this [parents'] house, so it's ... like he's still here. He moved with us to [new state] just like we did." Janice, now 21, and who was 12 when her sister died, says, "I think about her a lot. Her stuffed animals are all over my room, and so are her pictures. Even at night ... many times, I'll go to bed and I'll say my prayers and it's always, you know, 'Jackie, watch over me or take care of me.'"

Other siblings purposefully include the deceased sibling in the activities of their ongoing lives, often by incorporating some favorite memento into everyday life or into major events. For example, peach colored roses had special significance for Candace:

> When she was ill, I'd brought a lot of them to her, like a single rose to the hospital. She liked them. She'd smell those roses a lot.... She hated the stark smells of alcohol or betadine and would smell the roses instead. We used peach roses for her funeral. And for my wedding, we used peach roses ... three years later. It was just a real sense of having her there with us.

Similarly, Donna, now 21, as she prepares for her wedding, remembers her sister, Jill, who died at age 4, nine years before: "Like now, with the wedding, we always do something special for Jill. We put a pink rose alongside the altar for Jill so ... she would be there and we say a few prayers for her. Because she's part of the family even though she's not here, that's our one thing to remind us.... We wish she was here in body as well as in spirit." Members of Donna's family frequently mention Jill in everyday conversation ("I wish Jill could see us now!"). A new daughter-in-law to the family spoke: "I've noticed them talking a lot about it all the time. She's ... she's still here, you know ... still part of their lives. I didn't ever meet her, but I feel as if I know her."

Many siblings keep in touch with their sibling through conversations with the deceased or by offering prayers to the deceased, particularly for protection or guidance during difficult times: "Please come with me on this trip—I am scared and don't want to go alone." Sometimes siblings keep their connections to the deceased private because they are embarrassed to share them or because talking about the deceased is not encouraged. Older adults often wish that they had a memento of their deceased brother or sister, even years after the death, as a tangible reminder of the connection they still feel. In fact, siblings sometimes feel that their wish to stay connected, or to reconnect in some cases, is even stronger as they grow older.

The process of grief in families where a child had died from cancer is characterized by the empty space phenomenon (McClowry et al., 1987). Seven to nine years following the child's death, families described three patterns of grieving in response to their loss: "getting over it," "filling the emptiness," and "keeping the connection." Those who kept the connection reported vivid memories and stories that they did not want to forget. They cherished their recollections. They eventually found new interests, not to replace the loss of the child or to fill the emptiness, but to stimulate interest in the present. Similarly, the long-term effects of a child's death on siblings indicate that many of them also keep the connection with their deceased brother or sister.

Other authors have since described a similar phenomenon occurring in children following a parent's death. Silverman and Nickman (1996) report how children construct connections to their deceased parents whereby they maintain memories, feelings, and behaviors that allow them to remain in relationship with the deceased. The quality of this relationship changed over time as the children matured and the intensity of their grief diminished. Additional qualitative analysis of interviews with children whose parent had died indicated that the children's relationship with their deceased parent was sustained over the first two years following the death of their mother or father, and the relationship changed over this period of time (Normand, Silverman, & Nickman, 1996). It remains to be seen how the bereaved children's connection to his or her deceased parent changes beyond the first two years following the death, but siblings' experience indicates that the connection is one that remains forever. Such conclusions are in line with clinical experience that indicates that for many bereaved individuals, resolution does not occur within a predetermined time limit. Indeed, as Osterweis et al. (1984) state, for some individuals the pain of loss may continue for a lifetime even when there is successful adaptation. In fact, the concept of resolution, which advocates the need to divest oneself of the emotional energy invested in the relationship with the deceased, is put into question by these findings. The process of maintaining an ongoing connection is an integral component of grieving. These findings are consistent with those of other researchers working with bereaved adult populations (Klass, 1988; Rubin, 1985, Shuchter, 1986) and are consistent with Attig's (1987, 1996) view that grief is an active process requiring relearning the world, including one's relationship with the deceased. Although this sometimes involves disentangling from destructive aspects of relationships, it most often involves making a transition from loving in presence to loving in absence. When siblings die, living brothers and sisters still care about what their sibling cared about, cherish their memories, and allow their sibling's influences to shape their lives and characters. Many brothers and sisters garner strength, courage, and comfort from the behavior of their deceased siblings. For these siblings, shadows in the sun are softened considerably. The following and final chapter elaborates on the concept of shadows in the sun by integrating the ideas in the previous chapters into a comprehensive conceptualization of sibling bereavement.

10 CHAPTER

Putting Sibling Bereavement into Perspective

I began this book by describing how my professional interest in exploring the phenomenon of sibling bereavement arose from my encounter with Juan, the little boy whose older brother and mother were killed in a car accident and whose father was critically injured. Juan and his younger brother and sister had minor injuries. Juan visibly swallowed his pain and anguish, squared his fragile 8-year-old shoulders and bravely took on the responsibility of being the "oldest" in his family in response to the well-intentioned but misguided directive of his elderly parish priest. That little boy's life changed in that moment, and I often wondered what became of him. As I learned more about the often poignant experiences of numerous other bereaved siblings, it became clear that the death of a child does indeed leave its mark on surviving brothers and sisters. The death of a sibling is not something children simply "get over." Rather, their stories indicate that the impact lasts a lifetime—as shadows in the sun—perpetually influencing their ways of being in the world. Therefore, the death of a sibling in the lives of children is an event worthy of attention from all adults who have responsibility for, or interest in, the well-being of children. I hope that the findings presented in the foregoing chapters offer convincing support for this conclusion.

A question, however, still remains to be answered: How do all of these variables fit together into a meaningful whole? I have described various sibling bereavement responses and the many variables that influence those responses. I have emphasized that no one variable alone will predict or explain siblings' responses; rather, a combination of factors impacts on the experience of sibling bereavement. Looking more closely at the conceptual relationships among the variables and siblings' responses provides a more comprehensive description and has implications for those who care for bereaved children.

☐ A Paradigm Model of Sibling Bereavement

Originally intended for teaching students how to do grounded theory analysis, the paradigm model, as outlined by Strauss and Corbin (1990) also has utility for those interested in new ways of thinking about phenomena. Use of the paradigm model facilitates the linking of concepts denoting precipitating conditions, phenomena, context, intervening conditions, action strategies, and consequences (p. 99). There is no one right or definitive manner of fitting the components together. The goal is to use the model as a tool for exploring ways in which the various components create a meaningful whole. The paradigm model enables qualitative researchers to think systematically about data and to relate them in very complex ways. These authors suggest that our most common model of thinking about relationships among data is according to models of cause and effect. Whenever we encounter life situations, we tend to rely on a causal model where we perceive that something has happened because of a particular cause or condition to explain to ourselves and others why it may have occurred. The paradigm model is more complicated but more accurate in portraying relationships and in explaining various phenomena, extending beyond simple cause and effect.

Using a causal model has been a way of thinking for so long that it permeates the study or exploration of most phenomena. This is particularly evident in clinical fields where solutions are sought for relieving problems. In fact, many health professionals often believe that it is necessary to find the cause of a problem before a cure can be found. The predominant method of devising ways of helping others has been to investigate various sources or causes of an identified problem, determine which is the most likely cause, and alleviate the problem by eliminating or altering the causative condition. This approach works well in many situations, such as in determining which antibiotic is the most effective in curing an infection or in ascertaining which treatment is the most effective in healing a wound. The search for causal models is an effective way of making sense of things, of gaining control over what initially seems uncontrollable. It is logical, then, that the same approach is used in trying to explain other events as well, such as those that incorporate psychosocial, emotional, and spiritual realms—events such as sibling bereavement.

As the literature review in Chapter 2 indicates, there has been an ever-expanding effort during recent decades to learn more about sibling bereavement. For the most part, researchers adopted the causal model approach by selecting one or two variables to study in order to determine those factors that most strongly affect siblings' grief, with the underlying purpose of reducing as much as possible the potentially deleterious effects of their loss experience. Studies have focused on age, gender, suddenness of the death, self-esteem, attendance at funerals, and family environment, to name only a few variables that have been thought to influence the outcome of sibling grief. Outcome has been measured primarily in terms of behavior and emotional problems, although some studies refer to competencies and personal growth. Each study has contributed to our understanding of sibling bereavement. Yet findings have often been contradictory or inconclusive in identifying which variables are the most influential in predicting sibling bereavement outcome. This is not surprising, however, because there is no simple cause and effect relationship between any of the variables and the outcomes of sibling bereavement. The degree to which the experience allows personal growth in children, or the degrees to which children experience ongoing sadness, aggressive behavior, or fears of subsequent losses, depends on many factors, all of which interact in unique ways for each bereaved child. The paradigm model offers a way of viewing the relationships among these variables, showing that they all play a role in determining the nature of the child's bereavement experience. Using the paradigm model to assist in conceptualizing relationships among data must not be interpreted as forcing the data to fit into a predetermined structure. To do so would be an inappropriate use of the model and in harsh violation of the underlying principles of qualitative research. But, with the data from several projects already analyzed, the model has proven useful in portraying a comprehensive model that incorporates all of the findings and underscores the complexity of sibling bereavement (Figure 10.1).

Precipitating Event: A Child's Death

The death of a child marks the beginning of the experience of bereavement for brothers and sisters. As such, the death is the precipitating event, or the antecedent condition, for sibling bereavement. Circumstances of the death, described as situational factors in Chapter 6, influence siblings' experiences. When a death occurs without warning, whether accidental, homi-

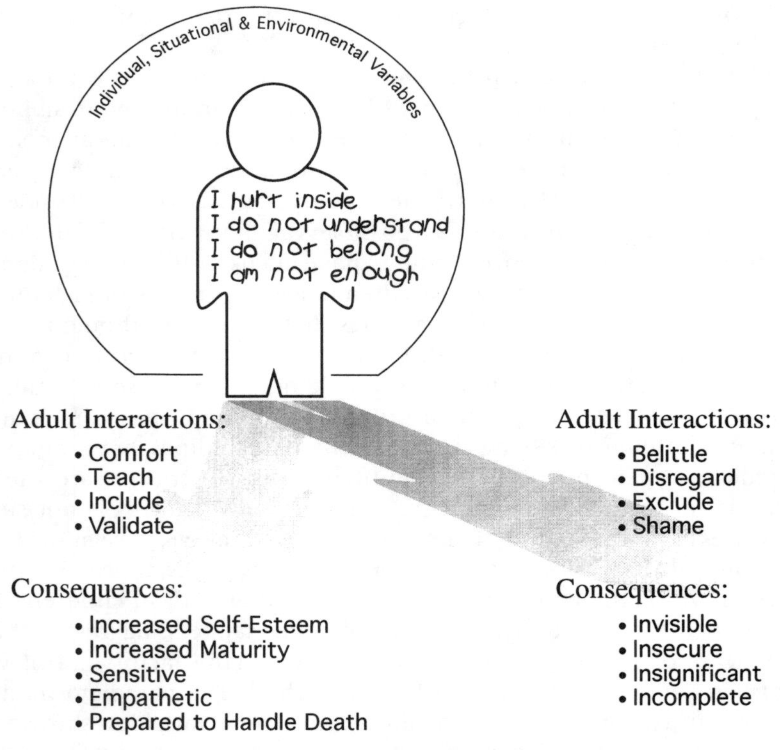

FIGURE 10.1. A paradigm model of sibling bereavement.

cidal, or suicidal, no chance exists for children to prepare for the event. They are caught off guard without having had any opportunity to prepare or to say their final good-byes. When a child's death follows a long illness, then chances are greater that well siblings have had occasion to at least consider the possibility that their brother or sister might die, although it cannot be assumed that long-term illness means children have been prepared for the death. Circumstances surrounding the death also impact greatly on the ability of others in the child's world to respond appropriately to the child. When a child dies without warning, parents are devastated and, understandably, often become nonfunctional. Their capacities to tend to the needs of their surviving children are severely limited by their own penetrating and pervasive grief. But simply knowing that a child has died, even if we know about the circumstances of the death, will not tell us much about how individual siblings will respond, although we do know that most siblings respond with many feelings normally associated with grief.

The Phenomenon: Sibling Responses

The central phenomenon in the paradigm of sibling bereavement is the sibling responses. The impact of a child's death on the surviving siblings is manifested in four general responses, best characterized in the words of siblings themselves. Two responses, "I hurt inside" and "I don't understand" are similar to those described in most literature about sibling bereavement and indeed about childhood bereavement in general. Such descriptions focus on the emotional/behavioral reactions of children and the cognitive responses that result from children's developing understanding about death. Looking beyond the more immediate, the long-term effects of sibling bereavement in childhood brought to light two additional responses: "I don't belong" and "I'm not enough." Not all children who have had a brother or sister die experience all responses; on the other hand, most children demonstrate all responses to varying degrees.

"I Hurt Inside." This response includes all the emotions typically associated with grief. The hurt that siblings feel includes sadness, anger, frustration, loneliness, fear, irritability, guilt, restlessness, and a host of other emotions that characterize bereavement, as described in Chapter 4. These responses are common to all who grieve, and children are no exception. To be human, to love is to feel many of these emotions when the one we love dies. Unlike adults who may more readily describe their emotions, children manifest their feelings in various ways since they are unable, or inexperienced, at identifying what they are feeling, let alone talking about their feelings. They may cry, withdraw, seek attention, misbehave, complain, pick fights easily, argue, have nightmares, fear going to bed at night, lose their appetites, or overeat.

Bereaved siblings' hurt stems from the vulnerability of being human, of feeling love for others, of becoming attached to others so that when they are gone siblings miss them. The other three sibling bereavement responses are rooted in a different kind of vulnerability—the kind that arises from children's dependence on the adults in their lives. Children rely on adults, in particular their parents, and in some cases on older siblings, for information, inclusion, and validation. Therefore, how parents and other adults respond to siblings' hurt contributes to the degree to which grieving siblings experience "I don't understand," "I don't belong," and "I'm not enough."

"I Don't Understand." Children's difficulty in understanding death is greatly influenced by their level of cognitive development as described in Chapter 3. However, once children know about death, their worlds are forever altered. Children growing up today are all too aware of the reality of death, but their awareness only compounds their confusion if they are not helped to understand and, in their own way, make sense of death and related events. When a child dies and when siblings do not understand what has happened, is happening, or is going to happen, they become more anxious in a situation where they already feel overwhelmed by unfamiliar sights and sounds. Their own feelings are also confusing to them; it is puzzling and frightening, for example, to feel very sad because one's brother has died and, at the same time, feel very angry with him for leaving.

"I Don't Belong." A death in the family tears apart the normal day-to-day ways of carrying out the tasks and activities of daily living. Parents are overwhelmed with their grief, with making arrangements, with caring for their other children. Surviving children are overwhelmed by the flurry of activity and the heaviness of emotion that surrounds them. They often feel that they do not know what to do. They may want to help but either do not know how or, if they try, their efforts are not acknowledged. Children begin to feel as if they are not part of what is happening. When children's unique ways of responding are not tolerated—such as when children ask questions when everyone else is silent, or when children prefer silence when the family norm is verbalizing, they feel even more as if they don't belong in their family.

In the aftermath of death, relationships in the family undergo major realignments and roles are reallocated (McGoldrick & Walsh, 1983). When the deceased child has played a central role in the family, realignment and role reallocation are more vital and usually more difficult (Vess, Moreland, & Schwebel, 1985). This reorganization may cause siblings to feel that there is no place for them any longer. They feel as if they don't belong in still other ways. Moreover, children who have experienced the death of a sibling often feel different from others, especially from their peers. As a result, they feel as if they no longer belong with their friends as they once did (Davies, 1995a).

"I'm Not Enough." This response is described in detail in Chapter 8. Children may feel as though the child who died was their parents' favorite child and they, as surviving children, are not enough to make their parents happy ever again. Some siblings, in attempting to explain why they were not the ones to die, strive to be good at all they do, always endeavoring to do more, trying to prove that they are enough, that they are worthy enough to live.

Responses in Context

As stated previously, the responses that characterize sibling bereavement do not occur in isolation but within the context established by many interrelated and overlapping factors. No one category of factors, nor any one isolated factor, accounts for the total experience of any individual child. The factors overlap and interplay with one another to create a complex array of circumstances that set the stage for children's bereavement experiences. Together, these factors create the context within which sibling bereavement responses occur.

In addition to situational factors (circumstances of the death), individual characteristics of surviving siblings, such as age, gender, temperament, coping style, and level of dependency, as discussed in Chapter 5, all play a part in setting the stage for how bereaved siblings respond. Environmental variables contribute to context setting as well. The predeath relationship between siblings also influences sibling bereavement (Chapter 7), as do the social climate and level of functioning within the family (Chapter 8). Families do not live in social vacuums, so their culture and community values and priorities also contribute to the context, along with those of the larger society in which they live.

Contextual variables are those that exist such as they are when the precipitating event (the death) occurs. For example, once a death has occurred, one cannot change the way in which the death happened, where it occurred, or how. These are givens. Similarly, variables that characterize the grieving child cannot be changed, such as the gender of the bereaved child, his age at the time of the death, or even the predeath relationship he had with his now-deceased sibling. Even environmental variables, as they exist at the time of death, cannot be altered because change is not retroactive. At the time of a child's death, families are characterized by their established patterns of communicating with one another, of expressing thoughts and feelings, of interacting with the larger community. This is not to say that these patterns cannot or will not change in the future, but whatever they are at the time of death contributes to the context in which newly bereaved siblings find themselves. These are all contextual conditions that bereaved siblings "come with." They are factors that help caregivers better understand the bereaved sibling's situation, but they alone do not fully account for how siblings deal with the death of a brother or sister. In addition, the interactions that children have with the significant adults in their lives play a critical role.

Intervening Conditions: Adult Interactions with Children

Intervening conditions act to either facilitate or constrain the strategies used to deal with a particular phenomenon. The strategies that children use to manage their responses are strongly influenced by how significant adults, particularly parents, interact with them. Considerable variability exists in how adults respond to grieving children.

In response to "I hurt inside," some parents and other adults allow, and even encourage, the expression of the hurt that grieving siblings are feeling. These adults endeavor to share their own feelings and thoughts with their children, thereby instilling a sense of being in this together and of hope for feeling better in the future. These adults understand that grief may take many forms and they are tolerant of children's various reactions. They are patient in allowing children to express their feelings and thoughts in their own time, recognizing that grief manifests in many ways over many months and even years. Such interactions comfort children in their grief, allowing them to express their thoughts and feelings in ways that work best for them. These children will still feel sad, angry, or irritable, but they learn that such feelings are acceptable and normal.

On the other hand, children learn that there is something wrong with such feelings when the adults in their lives limit expression of feelings. Children learn that it is not acceptable to express their feelings when adults do not share their own grieving with children or when adults ignore children's responses. Children learn to stifle their feelings when adults belittle or make fun of their reactions, when adults are impatient with children and force them to get on with things before the children are ready.

Parents and other adults are also instrumental in how children manage the response of "I don't understand." When adults have a solid grasp of levels of cognitive development in children and other aspects of development, they tend to respond more appropriately to grieving children. They provide honest information in ways that children can understand. They offer explanations of events so that children are better prepared for what to expect, which, in turn, minimizes distress. Caregivers who are open to questions from children give them license to ask any questions or to express any concerns, no matter how "silly" they may seem. Such caregivers also offer explanations of feelings, not just of events. Also, they help children interpret their own feelings and reactions. Children with whom adults interact in these ways learn that it is okay to ask questions, and they begin to understand death even though they learn that some questions have no answers.

Caregivers' behaviors can serve to inhibit children's understanding and reinforce their feelings of "I don't understand." When caregivers dismiss or avoid children's questions or comments, when they provide misleading, inaccurate, or platitude-filled "explanations," or when information is not provided in a timely way, then children do not learn, they do not have their questions answered, and their feelings of "I don't understand" are reinforced. When children are confused and do not feel as if they can seek help, they tend to assume responsibility for their confusion and think of themselves as stupid. Children then devise their own ways of dealing with their lack of understanding and confusion. They may make up their own explanations for events ("My brother died because he didn't do what dad said") or they themselves may assume responsibility for events ("Mommy is crying because I can't make her happy any more"). Some children, especially as they get older, will actively seek answers to their questions through asking individuals other than their parents or through choosing topics related to death for school assignments.

Caregivers' behaviors also influence the sibling response of "I don't belong." When children are included in what is happening, when they are an integral component of plans and activities, when they are prepared in advance for what to expect and what their roles and responsibilities might be, they can often manage very well. They feel as if they are part of the family, as if they have something unique to contribute, as if they have something worthwhile to offer. On the other hand, when children are excluded from events, from participating in the day-to-day planning and activities, or from being told what is going on and why, their feelings of "I don't belong" are enhanced. Such children may take risks, act out, avoid home in search for a place to belong, or escape through withdrawing into themselves or interacting with an imaginary friend. Lack of opportunity to be actively involved also restricts opportunities for enhancing children's understanding.

When children hurt inside, feel as if they are stupid because they don't, or can't, understand what has happened, or perceive they don't belong, feelings of "I'm not enough" are heightened. Adults can prevent or alleviate this response when they reassure children, both verbally and nonverbally, of their love for them. When caregivers, parents in particular, ensure that their children feel special and that their lives are very important to their parents, children are less likely to feel as if they are "not enough." They then feel loved, appreciated, and valued. As described in Chapter 8, the sibling response of "I'm not enough" results when parents and other caregivers unfavorably compare surviving children with the deceased child, when children feel displaced by the addition of new children to the family, when they do not feel special in their parents' eyes, or when children are not reassured of their parents' love. Feelings of "I'm not enough" also may result when bereaved siblings are given excessive responsibilities—such as Juan was given when he was told he had to be the "man of the family." When children are expected to behave in ways that are beyond their years, they cannot succeed, try as they might. They persist in trying harder to eventually "be enough" to fulfill the expectations of significant adults. Children who feel as if they are "not enough" may deal with their feelings of inadequacy and inferiority by overachieving, taking on the identity or various characteristics of their deceased sibling, excelling at meeting the needs of others, or becoming unrealistically good.

Consequences: Lifelong Effects

Siblings who are comforted, taught, included, and validated feel they learned from their experience; they feel as if they are much better people, more mature than their peers, more sensitive and empathetic to others in need, or better prepared to handle death in the future. Siblings who were belittled, disregarded, left out, and shamed live within darker shadows where they feel as if nothing good came of their experience. They end up feeling invisible, insecure, insignificant, and incomplete. Siblings' perceptions, whether affirming or diminishing of their self-esteem and capabilities, like shadows stretching across the land at day's end, may extend far into the future for siblings.

□ Implications for Caregiving Adults

Overall Goal of Intervention

One primary implication of the paradigm model of sibling bereavement has to do with the overall goal of helping bereaved siblings. What is often difficult for adults is the expectation that somehow children will achieve what they themselves find nearly impossible: a complete resolution and healing from the pain of loss. The consequence of experiencing the death of a brother or sister in childhood is that surviving siblings live forever with shadows in the sun. Bereaved siblings learn that life and death, living and dying are integral components of being mortal humans. The goal of helping bereaved siblings, therefore, is not to prevent the shadows, to "fix" them, or to make them disappear. The goal is to soften and shorten the shadows—to help bereaved siblings integrate their losses in ways that are regenerative rather than degenerative in the continual unfolding of their lives.

Interpersonal Focus of Interventions

A second major implication stems from the influence of adult interactions with bereaved siblings. Adult–child interactions are the vehicle for helping bereaved siblings. This implies that the focus of efforts to help grieving siblings needs to be directed toward the interpersonal level.

Most interventions for bereaved siblings focus primarily on the individual child. This is to be expected since grief has traditionally been studied primarily as an intrapsychic process. The foundation for this approach was clearly established by the well-known and respected psychiatrists and psychologists who pioneered the study of grief. This focus has been true for the study of sibling bereavement as well (see Chapter 2). As a result, many interventions for bereaved children have derived from traditional psychoanalytic treatment approaches as evidenced by Furman's (1974) pioneering work and even by more recent guidelines such as those that emphasize psychoanalytic approaches to loss (Baker, Sedney, & Gross, 1992). In addition, developmentally specific attributes, such as cognitive status, have provided guidance for interventions for bereaved children.

The paradigm for sibling bereavement implies that sibling responses extend beyond the intrapsychic realm. Although intrapsychic responses and cognitive understanding are significant in the paradigm, adult interactions with bereaved siblings are the conditions that intervene to determine bereavement outcome. Parent–child interactions are especially significant. In addition, professional caregivers—health care professionals, educators, clergy, and those who work with children in the community—can significantly alter the experience of grieving children through their interactions with them.

The journey that bereaved siblings follow is one that entails personal struggle and persistence. It is a journey that is made somewhat easier by the presence of faithful companions. As caregivers accompany grieving siblings on this path, however, they do so not as silent, passive companions. Just as siblings' processes are active ones (Attig, 1996), so too are those of caregivers who must actively support siblings in their struggle. Caregivers must let siblings know that they understand their journey is a long one, requiring a lot of energy, both physical and emotional. Caregivers must offer their own presence, patience, concern, and empathy, and do so with consistency and constancy.

To help grieving siblings with their struggle means that caregivers too must face their own selves, as part of their own inner journeys. They must reflect on what they believe about children—that grieving children have the capacity within themselves to heal, to grow, and to flourish or that grieving children have problems that cannot be fixed without expert or professional assistance. Sometimes caregivers, although well intentioned, misdirect their assistance when they believe that there is a "right" way to help, and they search for the correct procedure or technique. In fact, caregivers must alter their perceptions so that the help they offer each bereaved sibling is an adventure, a shared journey filled with unknowns for both travellers. If caregivers accept that each child is truly unique, then many standardized techniques will not really help as much as attending to the situation as a whole and to what the child, within that context, needs at that particular time.

Caregivers also must cultivate enough self-awareness so they can recognize honestly when they have difficulty meeting the challenges inherent in working with bereaved children. Caregivers must not shrink away from acknowledging when they feel stuck and must be willing to seek help themselves. Caregivers must reflect on their own skills and abilities, their own likes and dislikes. What types of children do they feel most comfortable with? What behaviors do they find the most challenging? The answers may tell more about the caregivers than about the children. Caring for bereaved siblings requires a continual process of self-learning and self-examination of how one is parenting, nursing, doctoring, teaching, or counselling. The process provides insight into how caregivers' own fears, frustrations, histories, expectations, and beliefs influence how they relate to children and, in particular, to grieving children.

Adult Comfort Level

The importance of personal interactions as the basis for relating to and helping bereaved siblings implies that adults who interact with bereaved children must be comfortable in relating to children and relating to them specifically about death. This has implications for what adults believe about children and for what they believe about how to relate to children. To develop solid relationships with children means that adults must not think of children as objects, but rather as fellow human beings, and relate to them not as experts, but as fellow travellers on a journey. Adults must think of bereaved siblings as persons, with their own spiritual, emotional, behavioral, and cognitive dimensions. This means caregivers must pay attention to each child's individuality and must recognize the potentially far-reaching impact of a brother's or sister's death on the child's life.

Family Level Interventions

The most significant adult–child interactions are those that occur between parents and their bereaved siblings. The paradigm suggests that family environment is a critical contextual variable for sibling bereavement—bereaved siblings do not exist in isolation but are clearly influenced by the family systems in which they live. Whether families are biological, adoptive, blended, or foster, they are key to children's experience of sibling bereavement. Another implication of the paradigm, therefore, is that system level interventions are also required and are of benefit.

The relevance of considering the family's bereavement experience is based on the view that the family is an open system of interdependent individuals with patterns of mutual interaction and exchange (as discussed in Chapters 7 and 8). Factors affecting one individual affect all others in the system. Traditionally, the family is seen as the first resource for grieving children, but the entire family may be in crisis when one of its members dies. Family therapists have long recognized that families seeking treatment for a troubled child, however, may unwittingly be merely presenting the symptom bearer of larger family dysfunction (Minuchin, 1974). It is appropriate, therefore, to view the family unit as the focus for bereavement care. However, although the importance of a family systems framework is often articulated by child care professionals in bereavement, it seems that few actually employ family systems approaches when assisting bereaved children (Rosen, 1996).

Family systems approaches mean that professional caregivers meet not just with the bereaved children but with the entire family unit. Family level interventions must focus on getting to know the family, discovering members' beliefs, asking questions that may enable them to explore their own ways of doing things and alternatives, and focusing questions on issues of relationship within the family. For example, when a child is acting out at home, the counsellor may ask how family members respond to his behavior, who is most and least supportive or tolerant of his behavior, whether there was a time when he did not feel like he had to behave as he is doing now, and what is different now than at that time. A systematic description of interactions between family members focuses on solutions and provides alternatives for intervention.

For some families, the stress of dealing with a child's death coupled with their decreased level of family functioning makes the situation almost overwhelming. The expectation that they will "pull together" to cope may be unrealistic. It is essential that professionals not judge such a family but appreciate that the family is coping as best it can under the most trying circumstances. For this reason, professionals need to work with the family as it is, rather than imposing expectations about what the family "should" be and how it "should" cope. These families need support and affirmation for their existing coping strategies, not judgmental criticisms. Moreover, alternative suggestions for coping can only be effective when family members perceive that their present coping strategies are compounding their stress rather than relieving it, and they are ready to change their existing patterns of functioning. The challenge for child care professionals is to use their knowledge, skills and support, affirmation and patience to assist the family through the crisis in a manner that supports the integrity of the family as much as possible. Important first steps are to find out what family members believe about the death situation and grief, what they expect of grieving children and of themselves, and how they have managed in previous times of crisis.

Parent Level Interventions

Most parents are willing and eager to do what is best for their children, but it is important to remember that parents too are greatly affected by the death of one of their children. We cannot assume that they will be responsible, understanding, patient, and, at all times, reasonable. They need to realize this, too. And children can learn much from parents who turn out to be human, rather than magically in control at all times. Some parents will do better than others. Explore with parents what they think is best and how they would like to fulfill their own expectations and desires in handling their children. No hard and fast rules guide what to say to children and how. Instead, parents ought to be encouraged, when deemed appropriate, to use their instincts and the knowledge of their own children in deciding what to say. It is also important, however, to help parents realize that talking with children about death is a skill that can be learned and enhanced with practice. Parents must know that there is no prescription or procedure, but with practice they can become more comfortable and skilled. Offering role-playing opportunities, for example, may help parents learn and practice ways of answering their children's questions and responding to their feelings. Parents need to be reassured that the specific words used to discuss death are much less important than is their talking about their own feelings, experiences, and fears. Children learn more from adults' behavior than from their words, and are very quick to pick up contradictions between what adults say and what they do.

Parent support groups are particularly helpful for some parents as they provide opportunities to share stories, experiences, strategies, challenges, and lessons learned. The parents who do not attend groups, however, are often the ones who feel most alone and are hesitant about using resources or seeking help. For such individuals, community groups, churches and public media presentations can serve a helpful purpose through articles in the newspaper or programs on public television about families, grief, and how to help bereaved children.

Above all, the relationship between professionals and bereaved siblings must support the relationship between parents and children. A strong relationship between caregivers and children may seem helpful in some ways, but the nature of help thus offered is lessened if it threatens or weakens the relationship between children and their parents. Professional caregivers must avoid replacing or overengaging with bereaved children at the expense of the relationship between parents and their children. Teachers, nurses, physicians, social workers, chaplains, and counselors must work cooperatively with one another, and together with parents, for the benefit of children. Collaborative efforts are required to prevent working at cross purposes and to prevent divisiveness.

Consider the Larger Context

The paradigm of sibling bereavement suggests that contextual variables play a role in influencing sibling bereavement. Families, as the most influential context for bereaved siblings, also exist within the larger context of culture, community, and society. A resulting implication of the paradigm is that child care professionals must also attend to these levels as ways of indirectly assisting bereaved siblings.

Child care professionals can strive to better understand cultural variations, rituals, beliefs, and practices. No profile of sibling bereavement is complete without some understanding of ethnic identity. To truly understand families when a child has died, their history must be acknowledged, their beliefs explored, and their rituals understood. Ethnic groups differ from each other in what they believe and in how they behave. For example, the value of children, particularly the value of female compared with male children, may vary considerably among different ethnic groups. A child's death then results in varying responses on the part of survivors. Gender differences may also affect how parents express their grief, which in turn, influences surviving children.

Child care professionals must use caution against their tendency to make assumptions based on superficial evidence, such as skin color or surname, since these visible signs of ethnicity can be misleading. They must also realize that families differ in the degree to which they reflect their ethnic heritage, but even families who may claim not to identify with the traditions of their ancestors are often still subtly influenced by their ethnic heritage. Beliefs about how one behaves during grief also must be taken into account when considering the role that ethnicity plays for bereaved siblings. The Japanese, for example, consider the public display of individual feelings improper, so encouraging open expression of feelings among Japanese children may not be useful advice. Many Chinese people believe that open discussion about death and grief is unacceptable. Eight-year-old Mary, for example, was a young Chinese girl whose family had lived in Canada for over a decade:

> When Mary's brother died suddenly in a biking accident, Mary's mother brought her to a children's bereavement support group. Mary was very quiet in the group but said that she enjoyed coming and playing with the other children. After only four sessions, Mary stopped coming. Her mother explained that both she and her daughter were finding it too difficult to withstand the persistent criticism of their large extended Chinese family where the belief was that death and grief should not be discussed openly, especially with strangers. Moreover, seeking assistance from outsiders was seen by Mary's grandmother as humiliating—a blot on the family's honor.

Understanding the customs of other cultures assists child care professionals to avoid causing needless offense and to devise more appropriate ways of helping bereaved siblings.[5]

Child care professionals can also help bereaved children in general ways by advocating for discussion about death and dying in schools, churches, and children's organizations as one way of helping children understand that death is part of life, preparing children for the losses they will encounter in life, and learning how to help those who are grieving the death of a loved one. They can support the use of, or provide, intervention programs in schools and other child communities for when a death or a related crisis affects the school community. Finally, they can support postvention programs that provide for follow-up and continued support of members of the school or other children's community. Fundamental to the success of all such programs, however, is communication and collaboration with parents to ensure that differing beliefs are considered. A statement titled, *"Children, Adolescents and Death: Myths, Realities and Challenges"* was recently developed by the Work Group on Palliative Care for Children of the International Work Group on Death, Dying and Bereavement (in press). This document puts forth myths, realities, and challenges to be addressed in relation to death education for children and adolescents. It strongly advocates for all adults, parents, and child care professionals to work together in assisting children and adolescents with grief.

Shadows across Generations

The paradigm of sibling bereavement describes the effects of the experience as long-lasting. In fact, the shadows may extend far into the future. The

---

[5]A useful reference for those wanting to learn more about cultural differences is a book titled, *Ethnic Variations in Dying, Death and Grief: Diversity in Universality* (Irish, D. P., Lundquist, K. F., & Nelson , V. J. (Eds.), Washington, DC: Taylor & Francis, 1993). This is a collection of articles that focus on beliefs and practices that differ from the predominant patterns in the United States and Canada.

TABLE 10.1. Specific goals for caregivers of bereaved siblings

Bereaved Siblings' Response	Goal of Adults' Interaction with Sibling
I hurt inside	To comfort and console
I don't understand	To explain and interpret
I don't belong	To include and involve
I'm not enough	To reassure and validate worth

consequences of shadows in the sun set the stage for when bereaved siblings themselves become parents; the shadows become contextual variables for the next generation. The shadows become especially dark if bereaved siblings experience the death of one of their own children. The observations of many family counselors reinforce the family systems notion that rather than grief ever being fully resolved, a loss is best conceived as a constantly evolving dimension of the family across three generations (Rosen, 1996). The sixth implication arises here: due to the cyclical nature of the paradigm, interventions with bereaved siblings and their families are critical to shortening the shadows in the sun. Moreover, when assessing children and families, it is helpful to review the history of deaths in the family for clues about earlier shadows that may linger.

Interventions According to Siblings' Major Responses

The paradigm model delineates four major responses which characterize sibling bereavement experience; it implies that it would be fitting to use these responses as the organizers for caregivers' interactions with bereaved siblings and to think in terms of the specific goals of interactions with bereaved siblings. (See Table 10.1.) Discussions in previous chapters include suggestions for how to achieve these goals. However, given the importance of adult–child interactions in helping bereaved siblings who "hurt inside," the following additional suggestions are offered for how to deal with this response. Briefer suggestions are provided for interactions focusing on the other three responses.

"I Hurt Inside." The most important thing that caregivers can do for children who are "hurting inside" is to comfort and support, to soothe, console, and sustain them. The objective is to help children accept whatever emotions they feel and to manage those emotions in appropriate ways. This sounds like such a simple task and yet is surprisingly difficult for many adults and particularly for parents who themselves are also grieving.

Helping children to deal with hurt is sensitively helping them to understand the reality of death and the feelings that arise. In order to do this, caregivers have to listen very carefully, mostly with their heart since children often cannot recognize what is happening in themselves, and they frequently cannot verbalize what they are feeling. Listening with one's heart, therefore, means recognizing children's needs before they are verbalized by observing children's behavior and noting changes in patterns of behavior (specific actions for dealing with many sibling behaviors are described in Chapter 5). Listening with one's heart means paying attention to children's behavior, to younger children's play and drawings, and to older children's music, poetry, stories, and artwork. It means looking at these various modes of expression without judging the colors, content, or character, but by simply accepting what children express. For example, this means responding to a child's drawing of a frowning face with, "You have drawn a frown," rather than judging or jumping to conclusions with, "You are feeling very sad."

Interactions are two-way processes whereby adults talk *with* children, not *at* them, which Rosen (1996) aptly refers to as "childspeak." When adults, and parents in particular, share their own thoughts and feelings and describe their own behaviors and reactions, children learn to label what they are feeling and through doing so begin to accept their feelings as normal and manageable. This kind of dialogue fosters shared knowledge of the reality of the death and the accompanying emotions as well as a sense of hope for personal survival. When adults do not know for sure what children are feeling, then providing opportunities for children to acknowledge or put words to their feelings is sometimes valuable. For example, saying something like, "Some days, I feel so sad about Johnny. . . . Do you feel that way too?" may offer a child an opportunity to agree or not. Even if he does not, putting words to the feelings makes them seem normal and ensures the child that feelings can be talked about. Effective dialogue also means that adults should take caution against talking too much, filling in awkward silences, and overwhelming children with too much information.

Comforting children is best done by someone that they trust and respect. Someone whom children know will honor their feelings, listen carefully, and take them seriously. To comfort children means that one does not lecture, give minisermons, judge, quote platitudes, name-call, tease, advise, interrogate, or jump to conclusions. Children trust more readily when they can expect consistent responses from caregivers. This does not mean, for example, that caregivers must always be "under control" themselves. Rather, consistency refers to responding to children in predictable ways that make them feel safe. It means responding to children honestly, sincerely, and with care. Honesty does not mean candor necessarily, but giving trustworthy information (Corr & Corr, 1995). Honesty also means adults must be honest about their own feelings. It may sometimes mean having so say, "I can see that you are wanting to talk, Susan, but I am feeling so sad right now, it's hard for me to talk with you." Such words acknowledge the child's concerns and the caregiver's current distress. Such words allow the child to learn that how she feels sometimes is also shared by adults and it helps to "normalize" what the child is experiencing. Such words teach the child how to put words into what they might be feeling and thereby allow the child to learn ways of coping with unsettling feelings. When such words are followed with, "but I will talk with you in a little while," the child also is reassured that she has been heard and will not be forgotten.

To comfort means to listen, to empathize with the child, to try to understand, to console through reflecting on children's expression of their feelings. Reflection is the basic principle of interacting with children who attend bereavement support groups at Canuck Place. Canuck Place, North America's first free-standing hospice for children, opened in November 1995. It provides respite care for families of children with progressive, life-threatening illness, palliative care for children in the terminal phase of illness, and bereavement care for children who have experienced the death of a sibling or parent. I am fortunate to have been involved in the development of Canuck Place and, in particular, in the bereavement program. I now volunteer as one of several facilitators for the children's bereavement group. The design of the bereavement program is based on the model used at the Dougy Center for Grieving Children in Portland, Oregon.

We have learned that offering comfort and support through reflection is acknowledging and accepting what children say and feel. It is identifying with children's energy and entering into a synchronous rhythm with them. Reflection is based on an attitude of supportive presence, an attitude that conveys messages of "Tell me more about you," or "Teach me more." Reflection means meeting children at their level, hearing what they are expressing, and allowing them to integrate their thoughts and feelings in their own way, in their own time. Reflection has less to do with the words one uses than with conveying an attitude that encourages children to express their own feelings, questions, and concerns. Comforting grieving children is not something that you *do to* them; it is a way of *being with* them.

"I Don't Understand." Suggestions for talking with bereaved siblings about death are discussed in Chapter 3; however, a few additional points might be emphasized here. To help bereaved siblings with their sense of confusion and lack of understanding about what has happened, adults need to build on those suggestions for comforting children who are hurting inside. Confusion and ignorance are additional forms of hurting, and, in response, adults need to continue to offer comfort and support. When adults have a solid grasp of levels of cognitive development in children, and other aspects of development as well, they tend to respond more appropriately to grieving children. They provide honest information in ways that the children can understand. They offer explanations of events so that children are better prepared for what to expect, which, in turn, minimizes distress. Caregivers who are open to questions from the children give license to children to ask any questions or to express any concerns, no matter how "silly" they may seem.

When encountering bereaved siblings for the first time, it is important to assess what they do understand. This can be done through asking if the children had an opportunity to ask questions about the death of their brother or sister, finding out how the children's questions were answered, and asking if there are any remaining questions that need to be addressed. Often, story books written specifically for children can be useful in explaining death to children and in letting them know that their reactions, feelings, and questions are normal.

Helping children to understand refers not only to providing facts or information about events, although this is very important. It is equally important to provide information about the feelings or sensations that children might expect. For example, the mother of 10-year-old Marsha prepared her for an award ceremony being held at her school in her sister's memory. She told Marsha why the ceremony had been planned, who would be attending and said,

> You may feel sad during the ceremony, or it may bring back happy memories of your sister. If you feel like crying, that's okay. We will tuck a tissue in your sleeve in case you need it. Afterwards, some of the kids may also feel sad and they may say so, but they may not know what to say and so they will just leave. Let's see how it goes.... You can stay beside me, or you can go with your friends if you decide that's what you would rather do.

When Marsha's classmates all left immediately after the ceremony without speaking to her, she was saddened but understood what their reasons might be from what her mother had told her.

The greatest barrier that adults experience in attempting to explain death and grief to children is a misguided concern for children. Assuming that children are too vulnerable to discuss the topic, or out of a desire to protect children ("They will have to face death soon enough.... Why worry them with it now?"), adults do a great disservice to children. Not talking about death arouses more concerns, questions, and confusion than honest and open discussion. In fact, the widest incidence of difficulty in adjustment is found in families where children are deemed incapable of understanding loss or too vulnerable to manage it (Rosen, 1996). Many books that focus on helping children with grief include helpful hints on how to talk with children about death (Fitzgerald, 1992; Grollman 1990, 1995; Wolfelt, 1983) and provide useful resources. In addition, books written for children about death provide excellent resources.[6]

"I Don't Belong." The advantages of involving children in the events surrounding death are discussed in detail in Chapter 6. I only want to emphasize here that encouraging children to participate in some way in the rituals surrounding death is reasonable when individual choices are also respected. Children must be given opportunities to participate, and opportunities to decline to do so. However, children almost always take their lead from significant adults. When children are hesitant, for example, to attend a funeral or take part in some other ritual, they are often responding to a subtle message from an adult who doubts his or her own ability to manage the emotions that might be stirred up by the experience. Again, this emphasizes the importance of adults carefully examining their own motives, behaviors, and reactions.

One of the most effective ways of helping children feel as if they belong is through bereavement support groups. In our groups in the Canuck Place program, we have found that children frequently assess the group's greatest value as helping them feel as if they are not alone; the group enables children to see that there are others who have had a similar experience and share similar responses. As 9-year-old Jennie said, "I learned that other kids had the same thing happen to them. . . . I don't feel so weird anymore."

"I'm Not Enough." Guidelines for helping children to feel as if they are valued, loved, and considered special by the adults in their lives, particularly their parents, are discussed in Chapter 8 and are only briefly summarized here. Children need reassurance about their importance, their significance, and that they are loved for what they are. Parents can give their children no gift more valuable than the feeling that they are loved, wanted, and cherished. If adults interact with bereaved siblings in ways that comfort their hurt, clarify their confusion, and involve them in what is happening, it is unlikely that children will feel as if they are "not enough." As described earlier, the sibling response of "I'm not enough" results when parents and other caregivers unfavorably compare surviving children with the deceased child, when children feel displaced by the addition of new children to

---

[6]One of the most recent compilations of books written for children about death and grief is by C. A. Corr (1995): *A sampler of literature for young readers: Death, dying and bereavement.* In K. Doka (Ed.), Children mourning, mourning children (pp. 163–171). Washington, DC: Hospice Foundation of America. In addition, a wide variety of books for children about death are available. One useful source is Compassion Books, 477 Hannah Road, Burnsville, NC 28714, (704) 675-5090.

the family, when they do not feel special in their parents' eyes, when children are not reassured of their parents' love, and when children are expected to assume responsibilities beyond their developmental capabilities. Unfortunately, some grieving parents experience considerable difficulty in feeling good about their surviving children and, as a result, ignore these children. It is critical for child care professionals to assist such parents in acknowledging their feelings and seeking assistance in dealing with them so that parents can do their best to nurture and comfort, reassure and validate their surviving children.

Siblings who experience the death of a sibling will indeed experience shadows in the sun. The shadows will vary in intensity and length. They will be influenced by a variety of factors but particularly by how adults interact with bereaved siblings. Because bereaved siblings, and the members of their families, are thinking, feeling, behaving, socially interacting, and experiencing beings with histories and stories of their own, we cannot predict the exact nature of the shadows that will result. Similarly, the effects of caregivers' interventions on the shadows cannot be foretold with certainty. What we do know is that comforting, explaining, including, and validating siblings' worth will go far to softening the shadows in the sun.

☐ Shadows in the Sun

Imagine the open countryside, green fields extending far into the distance. You focus in a little closer—you see a child running among wildflower carpets. She runs with the breeze, as she chases the bunnies who scamper between the trees. The child's gentle laughter tickles the air. The warmth of the sunlight surrounds her. Suddenly, seemingly from nowhere, a mysterious wind blows through, rippling the grass, bending the flowers, scaring the rabbits. The wind catches the child by surprise, and she shivers with cold.

At the same moment, the child becomes aware of a shadow over her shoulder. It is something she has not felt before. She is not sure what is there, but she knows that something, something dreadful is making that shadow. She is frightened: What is it? What could it be? She races to the picnic spot where her parents are enjoying the last of their strawberry pie, seeking the comfort of their embrace. But they, too, feel the presence of the shadow. The girl sees that they are frightened also. She has never before seen her parents look this way. With tremulous voices, they tell the child not to worry—the shadow will go away. But the girl is not convinced. She knows her parents are not telling her the truth; she knows her parents are scared. But they do not admit to it. So she thinks that perhaps it is somehow wrong to feel scared or at least to let her parents know that she is.

She wonders why they do not talk to her about the shadow. Maybe she caused the shadow. . . . After all, she did run off to play on her own. She was chasing the bunnies, and she did step on some of the flowers in the field. Maybe that is what made the shadow. Maybe if she sits quietly, without chasing any more bunnies or trampling any more wildflowers, the shadow will leave. Maybe she is adding to her parents' fear of the shadow and that is why they will not talk about it. Perhaps if she does not ask any more questions, or talk about being scared, her parents will not be scared anymore, and they will laugh and play with her once again.

The girl hears her parents' mumbled voices as they talk quietly together. She sees that they begin a dance, a dance she has never seen before. She wonders if it is a dance to make the shadow disappear. Her parents repeat the same steps over and over, and as they do so, their shadows begin to fade slightly. Then, to her surprise, the girl sees her grandparents, aunts, uncles, cousins, and many familiar people come to the field. She notices that they too are in the shadow. They join her parents' dance, and she sees that their shadows begin to soften, although the shadows never disappear entirely. But, as the girl sits quietly by herself and watches the others dance, she feels that her shadow is becoming darker.

Many days go by, and the girl's shadow remains a menacing presence. The only time the shadow seems a little less scary is when she plays with her imaginary friend. Together, they pretend to run in the field of flowers. The girl wants very much to return to the field where she used to run and play. Perhaps if she could get rid of her parents' shadows, then maybe they would take her on another picnic, and she could once again chase the bunnies and laugh with the wind. She tries and tries again to brush off her mother's shadow, but her mother only scolds her. "Nothing," her mother exclaims, "will take away the shadow." And all that results is that the girl's shadow grows even darker.

The girl cannot get rid of the shadow, no matter how hard she tries. She ignores it as best she can. She works very hard at school. She makes her bed everyday. She does what she is told. And for a time she forgets the shadow. But, just when she thinks it has disappeared, she sees a field of flowers and remembers that it was when she was in the field that the shadow first came.

Then, one day, something very strange happens. The girl made a new friend. Her new friend was not just an ordinary boy, he was a boy with a shadow! She could not believe it. She thought she was the only one with a shadow! His shadow was different than hers though—it was not as dark, and it was not as big, and he seemed to like his shadow. This puzzled her greatly. Why was his shadow so different?

The boy explained, "Shadows are normal, but if no one tells you about them, then you don't know that." He went on, "Everyone eventually has a shadow. Some people are very young when they first get a shadow, but others don't get theirs until they are older. Shadows can be scary," he admitted, "but if you have a friend to share your shadow with, then you won't be scared. And that's not all," he continued. "If you talk about your shadows—especially with your mom and dad, and with people like me who have shadows too—then the shadows become friendlier. Sharing the shadows softens them, and you learn that it's not so bad to have shadows in the sun."

Children have a natural propensity to grow and develop, as they often valiantly struggle to find the sun even in the darkest of circumstances. Like a single flower that stretches toward the sunshine while in the shadow of the rocks from which it seems to grow, so too children stretch toward the sun and seek growth. But children, some sooner than others, learn that life is not all sunshine. Life is also clouds and rain, wind and storms. Life is both sunshine and shadows. Experiencing the death of a brother or sister nearly always impacts on surviving siblings, although with varying intensity, and creates shadows in the sunshine of their lives. Like shadows, the effects of sibling bereavement lengthen and shorten, darken and fade, come and go.

Shadows are a naturally occurring phenomenon, not to be avoided or feared. Shadows cannot hurt you; the danger lies in what causes the shadows. Shadows happen—they just are. They cannot be prevented or avoided. And so it is with sibling grief. It naturally occurs after a beloved brother or sister dies. Grief just is. To try to prevent the pain and suffering that siblings feel is as impossible as trying to prevent shadows from forming during the course of the day. How much better to help children get to know the shadows and learn ways of living with them, rather than trying to ignore them or hiding from them, especially since, paradoxically, the harder we try to eliminate or avoid shadows, the larger and darker they become.

Shadows darken, linger, and threaten. A journey in the shadows can be a lonely, frightening venture. But with gentle and understanding companions, shadows soften, languish and comfort, and the journey is made easier. When adults, and particularly siblings' parents, walk alongside grieving children and offer solace for the hurt, menacing shadows begin to sway gently and their ominous shapes are transformed. When adults provide opportunities for conversation and explanation, and answer siblings' questions, the extremes of black and white soften to shades of gray. When adults include grieving siblings in activities, events, and decisionmaking, they are empowered to face the eerie shadows that form barriers around grieving children. When adults reassure bereaved siblings that they are special, that they are loved, that they are valued for just being, siblings are made to feel confident and may befriend the shadows. When adults share their own shadows with grieving children, children gain the courage to stare the shadows in the eye, reassured that they will not be swallowed by the darkness. When adults do not comfort children who are fearful of the shadows, when adults do not explain what shadows are about, when adults do not include children in events and rituals that help shadows fade, and when they do not reassure children that they are loved no matter how dark the shadows, bereaved siblings feel sad and lonely, confused, alone, and deficient.

To accompany children in the shadows, adults must walk beside them, not leading them from in front, pushing them from behind, or stifling them from above. Sometimes having shadows of their own may make adults more experienced travellers, but unless they have made friends with their own shadows, they may simply lead their young companions astray. Adults must realize that the goal of the journey is not to escape the shadows but to learn to travel with them. They must know that shadows need not be menacing or destructive but that they can become companions. In learning to live with shadows, we often come to appreciate them, even to find solace in them. Think of the cool respite the shade of an old oak tree offers on a hot summer's day. In the same way, happy memories and enduring connections to deceased siblings bring comfort and replenishment to surviving brothers and sisters while they struggle with the stress of ongoing daily life.

Shadows vary by season, by time of day, brightness of the sun, the presence of clouds, the composition of the object casting the shadow, the nature of the substance upon which they fall—shadows that fall upon the soft ground are gentler than those that fall upon a solid surface. The shadows of the early morning sun are longer than those at midday, and then, as evening approaches, the shadows again lengthen, extending into the far reaches of the horizon. So it is with sibling bereavement. Grief at the time of a child's death may cast long shadows, shortening as siblings enter young adulthood and beyond, but returning again and again as events spark memories and longings and as old age approaches. Shadows may extend even beyond old age, far into the future, influencing subsequent generations of children who are born into the shadows.

Initially unwanted and despised, and disguised as unwelcome fellow travellers, shadows persist in joining siblings' life caravans for the entire journey, and beyond—into lands yet unknown. Even in the brightest sunlight, shadows do not fade completely away. But, with the help of loving companions who are willing to share the shadows, who are willing to share the journey, we realize that it is not the light, but the warmth, that softens shadows in the sun.

APPENDIX 1

Summaries of Anecdotal and Scholarly Articles in the Literature

AUTHOR/TITLE/SOURCE	TYPE	SUMMARY/FOCUS
Balk, D. E. (1991). Death and adolescent bereavement: Current research and future directions. *Journal of Adolescent Research, 6*, 7–27.	Literature review	Reviews research of the 1980s pertaining to death and adolescent bereavement. Concludes that adolescent bereavement research focuses on death of a parent, a sibling, and one's own impending death. Defines need for research: (a) longitudinal investigations to study the trajectory of adolescent bereavement, (b) development of theoretical models to explain adolescent bereavement, and (c) integration with the traditional areas of adolescent inquiry, such as cognitive development, moral reasoning, gender socialization, and identity formation.
Blinder, B. J. (1972). Sibling death in childhood. *Child Psychiatry and Human Development, 2*, 169–175.	Case report	Presents three case histories that illustrate some of the clinical manifestations following the death of a sibling in childhood.
Castiglia, P. (1988). Death of a sibling. *Journal of Pediatric Health Care, 2*, 211–213.	Literature review	Summarizes several articles about sibling bereavement. Lists factors influencing siblings' responses. Concludes that sibling grief diminishes over time. However, grief is individual and affected by how various factors are managed during and after the death.
Coffel, D. (1989). The tiger in my life. *Issues in Comprehensive Pediatric Nursing, 12*, 309–310.	Anecdotal	Describes the effect of a brother's death on a sibling who was 9 years old when his 2-year-old brother was killed.
Davids, J. (1993). The reaction of an early latency boy to the sudden death of his baby brother. *Psychoanalytic Study of the Child, 48*.	Case study	Describes the psychotherapy of a boy (during ages 8 to10) who lost his brother to SIDS, highlighting six theories the boy has identified as causing the death. Emphasizes the value of the sibling relationship and the narcissistic needs fulfilled by this relationship.
Davies, B. (1997). Commentary on Van Riper's article on sibling bereavement. *Pediatric Nursing, 23*, 594–595.	Commentary	Based on Van Riper's account, provides guidelines for nurses to help bereaved siblings.

Gibbons, M. B. (1992). A child dies, a child survives: The impact of sibling loss. *Journal of Pediatric Health Care, 6*, 65–72.	Literature review	Summarizes factors influencing sibling bereavement (parents' responses, age-related conceptualization of death, the sibling relationship, communicating the loss, children at risk, survivor guilt, replacement children, and adaptation to the loss). Offers guidelines for nurse practitioners to use in assessing families and developing appropriate interventions.
Grogan, L. B. (1990). Grief of an adolescent when a sibling dies. *Maternal Child Nursing, 15*, 21–24.	Case study	Two brothers who lost their sister during their adolescent years nine years earlier discuss grief and adolescent tasks, such as autonomy and control and grieving the loss of childhood. Implications for nursing practice are addressed, with short- and long-term interventions.
Heiney, S. P. (1991). Sibling grief: A case report. *Archives of Psychiatric Nursing, V*, 121–127.	Case study	Describes one child's perceptions of the loss of a brother and provides clinical material for understanding typical sibling responses. Description of therapy sessions provides a model for working with siblings and demonstrates the value of art as a therapeutic medium. These strategies are useful for professionals who work with grieving siblings and may be applicable to other situations in which children experience a significant loss.
Krell, R., & Rabkin, L. (1979). The effects of sibling death on the surviving child: A family perspective. *Family Process, 18*, 471–477.	Literature review	Emphasizes that the death of a child invariably affects the family. Surviving siblings frequently become the focus of maneuvers unconsciously designed to alleviate guilt and control fate. Describes three types of clinically identifiable family patterns: (1) Families that emphasize silence and focus on guilt, (2) families in which the child becomes incomparably precious, and (3) families in which substitution and replacement predominate.
Lattanzi, M. E. (1989). Bereavement care for siblings. *Journal of the Association of Pediatric Oncology Nurses, 6*, 32.	Review	Discusses emotions and needs of siblings around the illness and death of a sibling, suggesting that the siblings of dying children may suffer just as much and perhaps more than the ill children.

(*continued*)

AUTHOR/TITLE/SOURCE	TYPE	SUMMARY/FOCUS
Mandell, F., Dirks-Smith, T., & Smith, M. (1988). The surviving child in the SIDS family. *Pediatrician, 15,* 217–221.	Case study	Describes impact of SIDS through the personal experiences of two of the authors. Both women describe how they felt at the time of their sibling's death and how SIDS affected their lives growing up and as adults.
Mufson, T. (1985). Issues surrounding sibling death during adolescence. *Child and Adolescent Social Work Journal, 2,* 204–218.	Case study/ Literature review	Focuses on three adolescents (age 13, 15, and 16) several years after the death of their sibling and the difficulties they had expressing their emotions surrounding the situation. Two of the deaths occurred 10 years previously, and the other, only two years before the interviews took place. Combines descriptive personal accounts with reviews of current literature.
Parkman, S. E. (1992). Helping families say good-bye. *American Journal of Maternal Child Nursing, 7,* 14–17.	Case study	This article focuses on literature and tools for pediatric intensive care nurses to use when helping parents and families through their crisis. The concept of an unexpected death in a family can bring about many fears and emotions. The article discusses the concepts of loss, untimely death, and grief, in general and relating to the case presented of a 10-year-old who was hit by a truck while riding his bicycle to school.
Pollock, G. H. (1986). Childhood sibling loss: A family tragedy. *Pediatric Annals, 15,* 851–855.	Case study	Discusses relevant research in the area of bereavement and presents a case study on childhood sibling loss. Sibling loss can occur through chronic illness (emotional, medical, surgical, long-term hospitalization), birth injuries, disability, chronic illness, ongoing need for medication, and restriction of diet and activities. Acute stressors of childhood loss can lead to later adversity unless the social context in which life and death events occur is recognized.

Romond, J. L. (1990). "It's sad and you hurt a lot": Letters from bereaved brothers and sisters. *Journal of Christian Nursing, Fall*, 4–8.	Anecdotal	Children's letters describe their hurt after a sibling's death and what helped them to survive the experience. After the death of the author's own son, she collected stories from children in other families who had lost a child.
Van Riper, M. (1997). Death of a sibling: Five sisters, five stories. *Pediatric Nursing, 23*, 587–593.	Anecdotal	Stories from five sisters demonstrate how children's responses to a sibling's death can vary greatly, even within the same family.
Walker, C. L. (1993). Sibling bereavement and grief responses. *Journal of Pediatric Nursing, 8*, 325–334.	Literature review	Reviews literature on sibling bereavement and grief obtained from a Medline computer search. Focuses on how early studies (1950–1985) identified pathological grief responses and later studies (1985–1992) identified emotional difficulties and increased maturity as responses to sibling bereavement.
Weston, D. L., & Irwin, R. C. (1963). Preschool child's response to death of infant sibling. *American Journal of Diseases of Children, 106*, 564–567.	Anecdotal	Offers pediatricians a better understanding of how preschool children respond to the experience of infant sibling loss. Presents common feelings and questions children of this age group may have and practical ways of helping or answering them.
Zelauskas, B. (1981). Siblings: The forgotten grievers. *Issues in Comprehensive Pediatric Nursing, 5*, 45–52.	Literature review	Includes a brief review of studies with a focus on children's behavioral patterns and reactions to the death of a sibling. Suggestions are given for what parents can do through play therapy.

Summaries of Research Reports in the Literature

AUTHOR, TITLE, & REFERENCE SOURCE	CHARACTERISTICS OF SAMPLE	SOURCE OF SAMPLE/ DATA	CAUSE OF DEATH	TIME ELAPSED SINCE DEATH	METHODS	FINDINGS
Applebaum, D. R., & Burns, G. L. (1991). Unexpected childhood death: Post-traumatic stress disorder in surviving siblings and parents. *Journal of Clinical Child Psychology, 20,* 114–120.	$n = 20$ families. 11 females, 9 males Ages 3–23 years	*Sample*: Family Bereavement Center of Wayne County, MI ($n = 2$); Compassionate Friends and Parents of Murdered Children in WA & MI ($n = 18$). *Data*: Questionnaire-through structured interview with parents and siblings.	Accidental ($n = 10$), homicide ($n = 10$)	4–77 months	The childhood post-traumatic stress disorder (PTSD)–parents' questionnaire was administered to the parent to obtain their perception of the child's PTSD response to a traumatic event (Pynoos & Nader, 1987)	All the siblings reported PTSD symptomatology; however, their parents were not necessarily aware of their child's symptoms. The surviving siblings in the accident and murder groups did not differ significantly in PTSD severity. Parents of murdered children did report more PTSD symptoms than parents of children who suffered accidental death. Higher levels of parental PTSD were also associated with higher levels of PTSD in the surviving sibling.
Atuel, T. M., Williams, P. D., & Camar, M. T. (1988). Determinants of Filipino children's responses to the death of a sibling. *Maternal Child Nursing Journal, 17,* 115–134.	$n = 73$ well school-age children, Roman Catholic. Ages 6–12 (mean 9.26 years). 47% female	*Sample*: Registries of five local governments and five hospitals in the province of Rizal, Philippines. *Data*: Semistructured interview and projected test pictures.	Sudden and anticipated from chronic condition.	One year from start of data collection.	Projective test administered on day 1, interview recorded verbatim on day 2.	School grades dropped significantly after the sibling's death. Children's response reflected three stages: shock, disbelief, and denial; guilt, protest, sadness, and acceptance and recovery. Stage 1 was significantly associated with a younger age of deceased sibling, more recent death, and lower social class. Projective stories indicated children whose siblings died suddenly as compared with those whose deaths were anticipated had significantly higher loneliness themes.

Balk, D. (1983b). Adolescents' grief reactions and self-concept perceptions following sibling death: A study of 33 teenagers. *Journal of Youth and Adolescence, 12,* 137–161.	$n = 33$ teenaged siblings. 20 females, 13 males Ages 14–19 years	*Sample*: The Society of Compassionate Friends and The Candlelighters Society. *Data*: Audiotaped/ transcribed interviews.	Accidents, terminal illness	4–84 months	The teenage siblings were interviewed regarding their grief reactions and self-concept perceptions following the death of their sibling. The sample also completed the Offer self-image questionnaire for adolescents (OSIQ).	Results of *t* tests on OSIQ standard scores indicated that the participants were as adjusted as same-age, same-sex normal groups. Chi-square analysis and univariate *F* tests of group differences identified emotional responses significantly associated with sex and age characteristics of the participants. Statistically significant results emerged regarding effects on grades and study habits, perceptions of personal maturity, and importance of religious beliefs. Discriminant analysis indicated that specific emotional responses were influenced by perceptions of family closeness and by perceptions of personal communication with family members.
Birenbaum, L. K., Robinson, M. A., Phillips, D. S., Stewart, B. J., & McCown, D. E. (1990). The response of children to the dying and death of a sibling. *Omega, 20,* 213–228.	$n = 61$ siblings	*Sample*: Three major medical centers in two western states and from six physicians in private practice. *Data*: Questionnaire.	Cancer	Data collected before death during the terminal phase, and two weeks, four months, and one year after the death.	The parent form and the teacher form of the child behavior checklist (CBCL) were used to measure siblings' positive responses and behavior problems.	*T*-test comparisons indicated that the bereaved siblings demonstrated significantly higher levels of behavior problems and significantly lower social competence in comparison with normal children.

(*continued*)

AUTHOR, TITLE, & REFERENCE SOURCE	CHARACTERISTICS OF SAMPLE	SOURCE OF SAMPLE/ DATA	CAUSE OF DEATH	TIME ELAPSED SINCE DEATH	METHODS	FINDINGS
Brent, D. A., Perper, J. A., Moritz, G., Liotos, L., Schweers, J., Roth, C., Balach, L., & Allman, C. (1993). Psychiatric impact of the loss of an adolescent sibling to suicide. *Journal of Affective Disorders, 28*, 249–256.	$n = 25$ adolescent siblings (of 20 adolescent suicide victims). 13 females, 12 males $n = 25$ adolescent controls. 13 females, 12 males	*Sample*: Consecutive survey of adolescent suicide victims in Western Pennsylvania. Unexposed control group demographically matched to the sample group. *Data*: Interviews.	Suicide	6 months	Both groups were assessed as to past, current, and new-onset psychopathology. PTSD symptoms were assessed by use of the Post-Traumatic Stress Disorder Reaction Index (Pynoos et al., 1987). Both parents and subjects were interviewed. Results of the two interviews were combined using a "best-estimate" procedure.	Siblings were much more likely to show a new-onset major depression subsequent to exposure to suicide. New-onset depression was associated with previous psychiatric disorder, family history of any psychiatric disorder, and family history of major depression. Mothers of suicide victims compared with the mothers of controls were also more likely to be depressed six months after the suicide of their child.
Cain, A., Fast, I., & Erickson, M. (1964). Children's disturbed reactions to the death of a sibling. *American Journal of Orthopsychiatry, 34*, 741–745.	$n = 58$. Ages 2 1/2–14 years	*Sample*: Children's outpatient and inpatient psychiatric settings. *Data*: Therapy records, outpatient evaluations (referral materials, developmental histories, psychological tests, psychiatric interview).	Illness, trauma, and homicide.	Not stated	Retrospective chart review. Lists varied forms of illustrated reactions to a sibling's death: guilt; sense of responsibility for the death; distorted concepts of health & illness; distorted attitudes to doctors, hospitals, religion; changes in family structure; impact of parental mourning; identification with deceased child.	Includes comprehensive list of determinants of children's response to death of a sibling. Indicates that dynamics and structure of family are influential in siblings' responses.
Davies, B. (1988a). Shared life space and sibling bereavement responses. *Cancer Nursing, 11*, 339–347.	Two studies: $n_1 = 34$ (21 females, 13 males); $n_2 = 55$ (34 females, 21 males). Ages 6–16 years	*Sample*: Pediatric hematology–oncology clinics, Pediatric oncologist, and Candlelighters. *Data*: Some interviews with mothers, some fathers and siblings.	Cancer	2–36 months	Behavior measured by CBCL. Closeness index developed from interviews with families.	Closeness in age was not related to behavior responses during bereavement. There was, however, a trend for scores on closeness index to predict internalizing behavior.

Davies, B. (1988b). The family environment in bereaved families and its relationship to surviving sibling behavior. *Children's Health Care, 17*, 22–31.	$n = 34$ families 21 females, 13 males Ages $n = 14$, 6–11 years $n = 20$, 12–16 years	*Sample*: From Western U.S. and Canada: Pediatric hematology–oncology clinics, Pediatric oncologist, Candlelighters. *Data*: Semistructured interviews with parents and siblings, standardized questionnaires completed by mothers.	Cancer	2–36 months	Scores on the family environment scale (FES) (Moos & Moos, 1981) and the CBCL (Achenbach & Edelbrock, 1981) were calculated and compared by *t* tests with standardized norms. Pearson correlations were calculated for the FES and CBCL scores and between the FES scores and other selected variables. Content analysis of interview data supplemented quantitative findings.	Bereaved families are more like normal than distressed families. The bereaved families scored significantly higher on two subscales: cohesion and moral/religious emphasis, while they scored significantly lower on achievement orientation. These results indicate that bereaved families are more like normal than like distressed families. Findings from this study suggest that support gained by having a family emphasis on social involvement is associated with the children's behavior scores.
Davies, B. (1991). Long-term outcomes of adolescent sibling bereavement. *Journal of Adolescent Research, 6*, 83–96.	$n = 12$ 9 females, 3 males Ages 11–15 at time of death	*Sample*: General community by means of notices posted on bulletin boards of university campus facilities, community centers, and churches. *Data*: Semistructured interviews with subjects.	Accidents, illness, and suicide.	11–28 years	Grounded theory analysis.	Long-term outcomes included psychological growth, a sense of feeling different, and social withdrawal. The study presents a theoretic scheme relating these outcomes.
Demi, A. S., & Gilbert, C. M. (1987). Relationship of parental grief to sibling grief. *Archives of Psychiatric Nursing, 1*, 385–391.	$n = 22$ parent–sibling pairs (14 parents, 18 siblings) from 9 families. Siblings' age 10–21 years. 11 females, 7 males	*Sample*: Vital statistics record and professional contacts. *Data*: Structured interviews.	Accidents (5), chronic disease (3), suicide (1).	4–24 months	Demographic and experiential data were collected from parents and siblings through structured interviews. The parents completed the Hopkins symptom checklist (HSCL), the CBCL, the impact event scale (IES), and the parental role scale (PRS). The siblings completed the child depression inventory (CDI) and the IES. The pairs were formed by matching each parent with the sibling(s) that he/she evaluated on the CBCL.	Two of the four hypotheses were supported: parent's emotional distress was correlated with sibling's emotional distress, and parental role dysfunction was correlated with sibling's behavior problems; however, parents' grief patterns were not correlated with sibling's grief patterns, nor was parental role dysfunction correlated with sibling's emotional distress. The findings support grief theorists' assertions that children's unexpressed grief may be manifested as behavior problems.

(*continued*)

AUTHOR, TITLE, & REFERENCE SOURCE	CHARACTERISTICS OF SAMPLE	SOURCE OF SAMPLE/ DATA	CAUSE OF DEATH	TIME ELAPSED SINCE DEATH	METHODS	FINDINGS
Dowden, S. (1995). Young children's experiences of sibling death. *Journal of Pediatric Nursing, 10*, 72–79.	$n = 8$ bereaved children. 5 females, 3 males Ages 3–7 years	*Sample*: Prior project with author. *Data*: Interviews (sibs and parents separately), drawings, and storytelling.	Not specifically stated: sudden	6 months–8 years	Qualitative survey and naturalistic inquiry methods were used (Lincoln & Guba, 1985). Semistructured taped interviews were conducted to determine the parents' perception of their child's understanding of death and to see if the child's religious beliefs reflected or differed from their parents. Siblings' interviews were based on a children's book, with discussion of the main themes. The children were then asked to draw a picture of their family and discuss themes with the researcher.	Results from the children's interviews were sorted into seven major categories. It was concluded from this study that children who have experienced a bereavement in their family, especially of a sibling, have a greater and more mature understanding of death and its finality for their developmental age.
Fanos, J. H., & Nickerson, B. G. (1991). Long-term effects of sibling death during adolescence. *Journal of Adolescent Research, 6*, 70–82.	$n = 25$ 12 females, 13 males Age at time of death: 9–18 years	*Sample*: Case records from children who died between 1963 and 1982 and who had been treated at the Cystic Fibrosis Clinics in three children's hospitals (Boston, Oakland, San Francisco). *Data*: Audiotaped and transcribed interviews with siblings.	Cystic fibrosis	2–21 years	Quantitative analysis. HSCL was used to measure anxiety and depression. A 3-point scale (none, moderate, high) was developed to measure guilt. Questions were asked to elicit information in these areas: (a) general sense of being guilty; (b) ruminations over what should have been done or not done in relation to the dead sibling; (c) readiness to accept blame when things happen to self or others; (d) current difficulty in separating from parents.	Subjects were divided into three groups according to age at time of death: 9–12 (latency or preadolescent), 13–17 (adolescent), and 18 (late adolescent). Adolescents had statistically significant higher mean scores on anxiety, depression, and guilt than either of the other two groups.

Finke, L. M., Birenbaum, L. K., & Chand, N. (1994). Two weeks post-death report by parents of siblings' grieving experience. *Journal of Child & Adolescent Psychiatric Nursing, 7*, 17–25.	$n = 43$ siblings from 31 families Age at time of death: birth–19 years	*Sample*: Three major medical centers and six private practice physicians. Families selected from a previous study by Birenbaum (1989). Children all known to be in the terminal phase of cancer. *Data*: Questionnaires and interviews.	Cancer	Data were collected prior to death and two weeks after death	A trained nurse research assistant made home visits to collect data. The instruments included the sibling background interview schedule (SBIS) and the sibling experience with death interview schedule (SEDIS).	The grieving behaviors of children were found to be similar to the grieving behaviors of adults—crying, denial, avoidance, shock, and guilt. The siblings maintained age-appropriate interaction with the dying child. Most parents maintained open communication with the siblings prior to and after the death; however seven siblings were told nothing about the death.
Graham-Pole, J., Wass, H., Eyberg, S., Chu, L., & Olejnik, S. (1989). Communicating with dying children and their siblings: A retrospective analysis. *Death Studies, 13*, 465–483.	$n = 77$ mothers of children over the age of 4 who died following illness	*Sample*: Compassionate Friends National (U.S.) mailout of 540 returned questionnaires. *Data*: Responses of mothers to mailed questionnaires.	Sudden death from fatal illness.	Not stated	Developed Likert scales to quantitatively assess mothers' responses about the helpfulness of discussions about death and dying and correlated the helpfulness of discussions with other variables.	Mothers who talked more freely with dying children also did so with the siblings, and communication was more open with older children. Discussion was more beneficial for both the dying child and their siblings if the ill child was at home immediately before death, if there was extensive and specific discussion about death, when a parent was the major discussant, and if the family's religious faith was also a significant source of support. Following such discussions, the emotional state of the ill child and their sibling differed, with siblings showing significantly more sadness, anger, denial, and fear.

(*continued*)

AUTHOR, TITLE, & REFERENCE SOURCE	CHARACTERISTICS OF SAMPLE	SOURCE OF SAMPLE/ DATA	CAUSE OF DEATH	TIME ELAPSED SINCE DEATH	METHODS	FINDINGS
Hogan, N. S. (1988a). The effects of time on adolescent sibling bereavement. *Pediatric Nursing, 14*, 333–335.	$n = 40$ bereaved siblings. 25 females, 15 males Ages 13–18 years	*Sample*: Compassionate Friends. *Data*: Self-report survey.	Not stated	3–36 months	The Hogan sibling inventory of bereavement (HSIB), which is a 109 item self-report survey instrument, was constructed to measure the sibling bereavement process. These items provided a framework for understanding the way siblings grieve during two phases of bereavement. Items on the HSIB were correlated with length of time since death: 3–18 months and 18–36 months.	The results indicated that 16 HSIB items were significantly correlated to the 3–18-month length of time variable, while only five items were significantly correlated to the 18–36-month length of time variable. There is a shift in assignment of blame from themselves to God during the two time periods. Mothers became the principal person within the family who the bereaved adolescent can talk to about their grief. Data support the old cliché that time tends to heal for these adolescents.
Hogan, N. S., & Balk, D. (1990). Adolescent reactions to sibling death: Perceptions of mothers, fathers, and teenagers. *Nursing Research, 39*, 103–106.	$n = 14$ families. 14 mothers & fathers. 7 females, 7 males Ages 13–18 years	*Sample*: Compassionate Friends. *Data*: Interviews.	Accidents (42.9%), illness (42.9%), and other causes (14.2%).	7–36 months	The HSIB (Hogan, 1987, 1990) was used to collect data.	Mothers held a much more favorable view of their teenagers' self-concept than the fathers or the teenagers themselves. The teenagers and their fathers shared similar self-concept perceptions. The results indicated that the mothers considered grief reactions to be more enduring than did the fathers or the teens.

Hogan, N. S., & DeSantis, L. (1992). Adolescent sibling bereavement: An ongoing attachment. *Qualitative Health Research 2*, 159–177.	$n = 141$ adolescents 91 females, 50 males Ages 11–18 years	*Sample*: Compassionate Friends. *Data*: Written responses by adolescents to mailed questionnaires.	Accident ($n = 83$), illness ($n = 35$), suicide ($n = 12$), homicide ($n = 10$), unknown ($n = 1$)	3 months–5 years	Content analysis of responses to a focused, open-ended question: "If you could ask or tell your dead sibling something, what would it be?"	Six categories were identified: regretting, endeavoring to understand, catching up, reaffirming, influencing, and reuniting. The theme of "ongoing attachment" (the emotional and social bond) remains continuous throughout the bereavement process.
Hogan, N. S., & DeSantis, L. (1994). Things that help and hinder adolescent sibling bereavement. *Western Journal of Nursing Research, 16*, 132–153.	$n = 140$ adolescents. 90 females, 50 males Ages 13–18 years	*Sample*: Compassionate Friends. *Data*: Written responses by bereaved adolescents to mailed questionnaire.	Accidents ($n = 83$), illness ($n = 34$), suicide ($n = 12$), homicide ($n = 10$)	3 months–5 years	Content analysis of responses to two open-ended questions: "What helped you cope with your sibling's death?" and "What made it harder to cope with your sibling's death?"	Five categories were identified as things that helped coping: self, family, friends, social system, and time. Of these categories, self, family, and social system also included descriptions of things that hindered coping. Two themes that emerged from the data were resourcefulness (in the helped categories) and helplessness (in the hindered category)—creating a sense of vulnerability.
Hogan, N. S., & Greenfield, D. B. (1991). Adolescent sibling bereavement: Symptomatology in a large community sample. *Journal of Adolescent Research, 6*, 97–112.	$n = 127$ 89 females, 39 males Ages 13–18 years	*Sample*: Compassionate Friends. *Data*: Mailed questionnaire to bereaved adolescents.	Not specific; 73% sudden, 27% anticipated	3–84 months	Scores on the HSIB were compared for adolescents whose sibling had died within 18 months and those assessed more than 18 months after their sibling's death. The OSIQ was used to examine relationships between bereavement adjustment and self-concept.	Adolescents assessed within 18 months of their sibling's death showed consistently high levels of grief symptomatology. Adolescents assessed at more than 18 months after the death had lower levels, but a significant group continued to have higher levels of grief reactions. These adolescents had dysfunctional patterns of self-concept.

(*continued*)

AUTHOR, TITLE, & REFERENCE SOURCE	CHARACTERISTICS OF SAMPLE	SOURCE OF SAMPLE/ DATA	CAUSE OF DEATH	TIME ELAPSED SINCE DEATH	METHODS	FINDINGS
Hutton, C. J., & Bradley, B. S. (1994). Effects of sudden infant death on bereaved siblings: A comparative study. *Journal of Child Psychology and Psychiatry, 35*, 723–732.	$n = 78$ total: Bereaved group $n = 38$ children 19 females, 19 males average age 6 years. Comparison group $n = 40$ children 20 females, 20 males average age 5.3 years	*Sample*: Bereaved group: Sudden Infant Death Research Foundation in Melbourne, Australia. Comparison group: Infant Welfare Centers. *Data*: Questionnaire and semistructured interviews.	SIDS	3–27 months	The study was designed to incorporate three important features: First, behavior problems and competencies were coded using the CBCL (Achenbach & Edelbrock, 1993). Second, the study was designed with a bereaved group of children whose younger sibling had died of SIDS and a comparison group of nonbereaved children matched with the bereaved group in demographic terms. Finally, the design incorporated a time lag to assess the persistence of behavioral difficulties beyond immediate mourning.	Bereaved siblings were reported to have a prolonged and significantly elevated rate of nonspecific behavioral problems. Bereaved children between 4–11 years showed significantly more behavioral problems, as reported by their mothers, than the comparison group.
Lauer, M. E., Mulhern, R. K., Bohne, J. B., & Camitta, B. M. (1985). Children's perceptions of their sibling's death at home or in hospital: The precursors of differential adjustment. *Cancer Nursing, 8*, 21–27.	$n = 36$ 19 siblings of children who participated in a home care program, 17 siblings of children who died in the hospital	*Sample*: Home care program: Midwest Children's Cancer Center. Hospital: Chemotherapy unit at Milwaukee Children's Hospital. *Data*: In-home interview.	Cancer	1 year	Exploratory/descriptive study.	The majority of siblings of the children involved in the home care program felt more prepared, involved, and were present at the death. However, the hospital group described their experience quite differently. They expressed feelings of isolation from their sibling and parents, not being adequately prepared for the death, and unable to use their parents for support or information.

Leder, S. (1992). Life events, social support, and children's competence after parent and sibling death. *Journal of Pediatric Nursing, 7*, 110–119.	$n = 37$ children. 20 females, 17 males Ages 7–15 years	*Sample*: Medical records department in a southeastern city, a chapter of Compassionate Friends, and attendees at a conference on family bereavement. *Data*: collected from parents through 4 questionnaires. Coddington's Social Readjustment Rating Questionnaire, Family Peer Relationship Questionnaire, Child Support Questionnaire, and Perceived Competence Scale.	Accidents ($n = 14$), illness ($n = 20$), homicide ($n = 2$), suicide ($n = 2$)	1–4 years since death of parent or sibling	A descriptive correlational design.	Stressful life events were related differentially to the four dimensions of children's competence. Statistically significant correlations were positive between life events and cognitive competence, and negative between life events and physical competence.
Mahon, M. M., & Page, M. L. (1995). Childhood bereavement after the death of a sibling. *Holistic Nursing Practice, 9*, 15–26.	$n = 35$ 18 siblings, 11 mothers, and 6 fathers Sibling age: 4–23 years 10 females, 8 males	*Sample*: Families known to the investigators. *Data*: Interviews.	Cancer ($n = 8$), heart disease ($n = 2$), neurodegenerative disease ($n = 1$), stillbirth ($n = 1$) & complications of prematurity ($n = 1$)	3–58 months	This qualitative study was designed to explore the processes of sibling bereavement and to compare children's impressions with those of their parents. The Institute of Medicine model was used as a sensitizing framework for the study. Constant comparative techniques were used to analyze the data.	Sadness was the most common reaction after sibling death. Mothers were most often cited as being helpful; friends and fathers were also helpful. People who were not actively supportive were not helpful. Many children described feeling protective of their parents, and several children described personal growth.
Mandell, F., McAnulty, E., & Carlson, A. (1983). Unexpected death of an infant sibling. *Pediatrics, 72*, 652–657.	$n = 26$ families; 35 siblings (18 females, 17 males). At time of death, siblings ranged in age from 16 months to 6 years	*Sample*: Families who lived in authors' geographic area and could be located by phone. *Data*: Telephone interviews with mothers (30–60 minutes)	SIDS	1–2 1/2 years	Structured interviews that focused on surviving siblings' changes in patterns of sleep, toilet training, feeding habits, peer relationships, and parent–child interaction.	The majority of siblings demonstrated changes in sleep patterns, social interaction and parent–child interaction. However, regression in toilet training and feeding habits were infrequent and not areas of concern for parents.

(*continued*)

AUTHOR, TITLE, & REFERENCE SOURCE	CHARACTERISTICS OF SAMPLE	SOURCE OF SAMPLE/ DATA	CAUSE OF DEATH	TIME ELAPSED SINCE DEATH	METHODS	FINDINGS
Martinson, I., Davies, B., & McClowry, S. (1987). The long-term effects of sibling death on self-concept. *Journal of Pediatric Nursing, 2,* 227–235.	$n = 29$ 10 females, 19 males Ages 9–18 years	*Sample*: 58 midwestern families who participated in a home care program for the dying child (Martinson, 1980). *Data*: Home interviews with parents and subjects.	Cancer	7–9 years	Descriptive study using Piers–Harris self-concept scale for children.	*T*-test comparisons showed that bereaved siblings scored statistically higher on the Piers–Harris Self-Concept Scale for children than the normative group of children. Content analysis of interview transcripts suggested reasons for the higher scores.
Martinson, I. M., & Campos, R. G. (1991). Adolescent bereavement: Long-term responses to a sibling's death from cancer. *Journal of Adolescent Research,* 6, 54–69.	$n = 31$ 13 females, 12 males Ages 17–28 years	*Sample*: From a larger study of home care of 58 Midwestern families. *Data*: Semistructured questionnaire and audiotaped interviews.	Cancer	7–9 years	The subjects completed a questionnaire and were then interviewed. The interviews were transcribed and coded using Ethnograph (a computer program for qualitative data analysis). The questions asked about alterations in life patterns during the last year of the sibling's illness, changes in family relations postdeath, and the overall impact of the death experience. Two rates independently scored the responses and were then combined as a summary measure of the legacy of the death experience.	The majority of adolescent siblings viewed the experience as fostering personal or family growth. However, about one in six regarded the experience as continuing to have a negative impact on their lives. Factors associated with a more positive outlook were good communication in the family, ability to share the death experience with others, expression of pleasure in sibling's company, and reliance on the family for emotional support. Factors associated with a more negative outlook were withdrawal from family interaction, inability to use the family as a source of support, and difficulty in discussing one's experience with death.

McCown, D. (1984). Funeral attendance, cremation, and young siblings. *Death Education, 8*, 349–363.	$n = 65$ 33 females, 32 males. Ages 4–16 years	*Sample*: Medical records of 44 children who died; referrals from doctors, nurses, ministers, social workers, death support groups, and funeral directors. *Data*: home interviews with parents.	Congenital, acquired, or accidental conditions; largest percentage ($n = 14$) died of cancer	2–12 months	Measured sibling problems in first year using standardized child behavior checklist (Achenbach & Edelbrock, 1993).	*T*-test analysis indicated children (especially young children and families) who had attended funerals or memorial services displayed more behavior problems than children who did not attend.
McCown, D. E., & Davies, B. (1995). Patterns of grief in young children following the death of a sibling. *Death Studies, 19*, 41–53.	$n = 90$ 48 females, 42 males Ages 4–16 years	*Sample*: From Arizona, Washington, Oregon, and Alberta. *Data*: Questionnaire answered by parents of the sample.	Cancer (47.5%), cardiac disease (8%), accidents (6.5%), murder or suicide (6.5%), infections (6.5%), metabolic disorder (5%), and aplastic anemia (1.6%)	2–24 months	Observed behaviors were identified using the standardized CBCL (Achenbach & Edelbrock, 1981).	Findings identified behavior problems in 50% or more of the sample. The most common behaviors observed were in the Aggression subscale of the CBCL. This suggested that children use aggressive behaviors to seek attention from parents, rather than an expression of hostility and anger. According to age, the highest incidence of behavioral problems appeared in preschool and school-age children. The three most frequent/consistent behaviors from all age groups were "argues a lot," "stubborn, sullen, or irritable," and "self-conscious or easily embarrassed."

(*continued*)

AUTHOR, TITLE, & REFERENCE SOURCE	CHARACTERISTICS OF SAMPLE	SOURCE OF SAMPLE/ DATA	CAUSE OF DEATH	TIME ELAPSED SINCE DEATH	METHODS	FINDINGS
McCown, D. E., & Pratt, C. (1985). Impact of sibling death on children's behavior. *Death Studies, 9*, 323–335.	$n = 65$ 32 females, 33 males Ages 4–16 years	*Sample*: Referrals from pediatric inpatient units, death support groups, funeral directors, social workers, ministers and schools, urban and rural communities in Oregon and Washington. *Data*: Home interviews with parents (all mothers and 17 fathers).	Cancer (most common 32%), SIDS, cardiac problems, cystic fibrosis, accidents, suicide, Reyes' disease, aspiration, failure to thrive, diabetes, and meningitis	2–13 months	*T*-test comparisons of CBCL scores for bereaved siblings and standardized CBCL norms, *t*-test comparisons of selected variables.	Bereaved children displayed significantly more behavior problems in comparison with standardized norms. Variables of age, place of death, family size, ill child's diagnosis, sex and age of deceased child, and funeral attendance were related to behavior problems in the surviving children.
Pettle Michael, S. A., & Lansdown, R. G. (1986). Adjustment to the death of a sibling. *Archives of Disease in Childhood, 61*, 278–283.	$n = 28$ siblings (from 14 families) Ages 5–21 years	*Sample*: Hospital records. *Data*: Questionnaires completed by parents, teachers, and children. Semistructured interviews with parents.	Cancer	18–30 months	Scores on the Lipsitt self-concept scale, Rutter child behavior scales, and measures of parental emotional disturbance and of family adjustment described the sample.	A high percentage of children were found to be exhibiting emotional or behavioral difficulties, or both, and the results indicated that low self-esteem was common. Parental and child adjustment were not found to be related, nor did they seem to relate to the child's self-esteem. Many children who did not manifest overt difficulties perceived themselves unfavorably in comparison with either their ideal or their dead sibling.
Powell, M. (1991). The psychosocial impact of sudden death syndrome on siblings. *The Irish Journal of Psychology, 12*, 235–247.	$n = 78$ bereaved siblings (from 28 families)	*Sample*: Hospital casualty departments where post-mortem examinations on the SIDS victims were carried out. *Data*: Questionnaires and interviews.	SIDS	1–3 years	The parents were interviewed in their home by the author. The psychosocial impact of SIDS on siblings was based on an analysis of parents' perceptions of their children's reactions to the death and how they coped with their surviving children's response to the loss.	This retrospective assessment showed a peak representation of behavioral upset during the first 3 months of bereavement in the majority (82%) of families. A combination of symptoms, such as seeking parental affection or attention, separation anxiety and fear of being alone, as well as incessant curiosity about the death, remained unresolved for half of these families at a mean interim of 2.9 years after the loss.

Rosen, H. (1984–85). Prohibitions against mourning in childhood sibling loss. *Omega, 15*, 307–316.	*n* = 159 individuals who lost a sibling before the age of 20. 84% female, 16% male Age at time of study: 15–74 years	*Sample*: Word of mouth, press release in local and national newspapers. *Data*: Primarily mailed out questionnaires and some personal interviews.	Illness—primarily cancer (40%), motor vehicle accidents (21%), others accidents (14%), congenital conditions (8%), suicides (7%), war (5%), died at birth or cause unknown (5%)	Not stated	Questionnaires were mailed out and interviews were done with 34 respondents. Analysis of responses focused on three areas: individual reactions to the loss of a sibling, family reactions to the loss of a child and to the surviving sibling(s), and societal responses toward the surviving siblings following the loss of their brother or sister.	Findings suggest that when a child suffers the death of a sibling he or she will most likely experience one or more prohibitions acknowledging and working through the loss. At the family system level, prohibitions may be perceived by the surviving sibling due to the lack of communication within the family about the death. At the social system level, direct injunctions to "be strong" about the loss may contribute to denial of feelings associated with the loss. Surviving siblings may experience prohibitions at one, two, or all three levels.
Williams, M. L. (1981). Sibling reaction to cot death. *The Medical Journal of Australia, 2*, 227–231.	*n* = 49 children from 23 families 31 = <6 years, 8 = 6–9 years, 10 = 10 years +	*Sample*: Melbourne, Australia. *Data*: Interviews.	SIDS	9 months	Interviews with parents and siblings and direct observation of children (through play, drawing, and conversation).	The death of a sibling from SIDS had a major impact on the surviving children. More than 50% had difficulties in coping with the death. Feelings of guilt, anger, anxiety, and sadness frequently led to behavioral and physical symptoms; however, some siblings without major symptoms were felt to have significant psychological and emotional difficulties as well.

REFERENCES

Abramovitch, R., Corter, C., & Lando, B. (1979). Sibling interaction in the home. *Child Development, 50,* 997–1003.

Abramovitch, R., Corter, C., Pepler, D. J., & Stanhope, L. (1986). Sibling and peer interaction: A final follow-up and a comparison. *Child Development, 57,* 217–229.

Abramovitch, R., Pepler, D., & Corter, C. (1982). Patterns of interaction among preschool-age children. In M. E. Lamb & B. Sutton-Smith (Eds.), *Sibling relationships: Their nature and significance across the life span* (pp. 61–86). Hillsdale, NJ: Erlbaum.

Achenbach, T. M., & Edelbrock, C. S. (1981). Behavioral problems and competencies reported by parents of normal and disturbed children aged four through sixteen. *Monographs of the Society for Research in Child Development, 46*(1, Serial No. 188), 1–65.

Achenbach, T. M., & Edelbrock, C. (1993). *Manual for the Child Behavior Checklist and Revised Behavior Profile.* Burlington, VT: University of Vermont, Department of Psychiatry.

Adams, D. W., & Deveau, E. J. (1987). When a brother or sister is dying of cancer: The vulnerability of the adolescent sibling. *Death Studies, 11,* 279–295.

Adams-Greenly, M. (1984). Helping children communicate about serious illness and death. *Journal of Psychosocial Oncology, 2,* 61–72.

The American Heritage Electronic Dictionary. (1992) (3rd ed.). Boston: Houghton-Mifflin.

American Psychiatric Association. (1994). *Diagnostic and statistical manual of mental disorders* (4th ed.). Washington, DC, American Psychiatric Association.

Anthony, S. (1940). *The child's discovery of death.* New York: Harcourt.

Anthony, S. (1972). *The discovery of death in childhood and after.* New York: Basic Books.

Anthony, S. A. (1939). A study of the development of the concept of death. *British Journal of Educational Psychology, 9* (Abstr), 276–277.

Applebaum, D. R., & Burns, G. L. (1991). Unexpected childhood death: Post-traumatic stress disorder in surviving siblings and parents. *Journal of Clinical Child Psychology, 20,* 114–120.

Attig, T. W. (1987). Grief, love and separation. In C. Corr & R. A. Pacholski (Eds.), *Death: Completion and discovery* (pp. 139–148). Lakewood, OH: Association for Death Education and Counseling.

Attig, T. W. (1995). Respecting bereaved children and adolescents. In D. W. Adams & E. J. Deveau (Eds.), *Beyond the innocence of childhood: Helping children and adolescents cope with death and bereavement* (Vol. 3, pp. 43–60). Amityville, NY: Baywood.

Attig, T. W. (1996). *How we grieve: Relearning the world.* New York: Oxford University Press.

Atuel, T. M., Williams, P. D., & Camar, M. T. (1988). Determinants of Filipino children's responses to the death of a sibling. *Maternal Child Nursing Journal, 17,* 115–134.

Aylward, G. P. (1985). Understanding and treatment of childhood depression. *Journal of Pediatrics, 107,* 1–9.

Bain, H. (1974). Chronic vague abdominal pain in children. *Pediatric Clinics of North America, 21,* 991–1000.

Baker, J. E., Sedney, M. A., & Gross, E. (1992). Psychological tasks for bereaved children. *American Journal of Orthopsychiatry, 62,* 105–116.

Balk, D. (1983a). Effects of sibling death on teenagers. *Journal of School Health, 53*(1), 14–18.

Balk, D. (1983b). Adolescents' grief reactions and self-concept perceptions following sibling death: A study of 33 teenagers. *Journal of Youth and Adolescence, 12,* 137–161.

Balk, D. E. (1981). Sibling death during adolescence: Self concept and bereavement reactions. Unpublished doctoral dissertation, University of Illinois at Urbana-Champaign.

Balk, D. E. (1990). The self-concepts of bereaved adolescents: Sibling death and its aftermath. *Journal of Adolescent Research, 5,* 112–131.

Balk, D. E. (1991). Death and adolescent bereavement: Current research and future directions. *Journal of Adolescent Research, 6,* 7–27.

Ball, J. (1976–1977). Widow's grief: The impact of age and mode of death. *Omega, 7,* 307–333.

Bandura, A. (1969). *Principles of behavior modification.* New York: Holt, Rinehart & Winston.

Bandura, A. (1977). *A social learning theory.* Englewood Cliffs, NJ: Prentice–Hall.

Bandura, A., & Walters, R. H. (1969). *Adolescent aggression: A study of the influence of child training practices and family interrelationships.* New York: Ronald Press.

Bank, S., & Kahn, M. D. (1975). Sisterhood-brotherhood is powerful: Sibling subsystems and family therapy. *Family Process, 14,* 311–337.

Bank, S., & Kahn, M. D. (1982). *The sibling bond.* New York: Basic Books.

Bank, S. P., & Kahn, M. D. (1980). Freudian siblings. *Psychoanalytic Review, 67,* 493–504.

Barnhill, L. (1979). Healthy family systems. *Family Coordinator, 28,* 94–100.

Beardsall, L. (1986). *Conflict between siblings in middle childhood.* Unpublished doctoral dissertation. University of Cambridge, Cambridge, England.

Benoliel, J. Q. (1994). Death and dying as a field of inquiry. In I. B. Corless, B. B. Germino, & M. Pittman (Eds.), *Dying, death and bereavement: Theoretical perspectives and other ways of knowing* (pp. 3–13). Boston: Jones & Bartlett.

Betz, C. (1985, June 2). Children's bereavement reactions to death of a family member. Paper presented at the Children and Death Conference, King's College, London, Ontario.

Betz, C. L. (1987). Death, dying and bereavement. A review of literature, 1970–1985. In T. Krulkik, B. Holady, & I. M. Martinson (Eds.), *The child and family facing life-threatening illness* (pp. 32–49). Philadelphia: Lippincott.

Billings, A. G., & Moos, R. H. (1982). Family environment and adaptation: A clinically applicable typology. *American Journal of Family Therapy, 10,* 26–38.

Binger, C., Ablin, A., Feuerstein, R., Kushner, J., Zoger, S., & Mikkelsen, C. (1969). Childhood leukemia: Emotional impact on patient and family. *New England Journal of Medicine, 2804,* 414–418.

Binger, C. M. (1973). Childhood leukemia—Emotional impact on siblings. In J. E. Anthony & C. Koupirnik (Eds.), *The child and his family: The impact of disease and death* (pp. 195–209), New York: Wiley.

Birenbaum, L. (1989). The relationship between parent-sibling communication and coping of siblings with death experience. *Journal of Pediatric Oncology Nursing, 6,* 86–91.

Birenbaum, L. K., Robinson, M. A., Phillips, D. S., Stewart, B. J., & McCown, D. E. (1990). The response of children to the dying and death of a sibling. *Omega, 20,* 213–228.

Blinder, B. J. (1972). Sibling death in childhood. *Child Psychiatry and Human Development, 2,* 169–175.

Bluebond-Langner, M. (1977). Meanings of death to children. In H. Feifel (Ed.), *New meanings of death* (pp. 47–66). New York: McGraw–Hill.

Bluebond-Langner, M. (1978). *The private worlds of dying children.* Princeton, NJ: Princeton University Press.

Bluebond-Langner, M. (1996). *In the shadow of illness: Parents and siblings of the chronically ill child*. Princeton, NJ: Princeton University Press.

Boer, F., & Dunn, J. (Eds.). (1992). *Children's sibling relationships: Developmental and clinical issues*. Hillsdale, NJ: Erlbaum.

Bowlby, J. (1963). Pathological mourning and childhood mourning. *Journal of the American Psychoanalytic Association, 11*, 500–541.

Bowlby, J. (1980). *Attachment and loss, Vol. III: Loss*. New York: Basic Books.

Brent, S. B., & Speece, M. W. (1993). "Adult" conceptualization of irreversibility: Implications for the development of the concept of death. *Death Studies, 17*, 203–224.

Brent, D. A., Perper, J. A., Moritz, G., Liotos, L., Schweers, J., Roth, C., Balach, L., & Allman, C. (1993). Psyciatric impact of the loss of an adolescent sibling to suicide. *Journal of Affective Disorders, 28*, 249–256.

Brett, K. M., & Davies, E. M. B. (1988). "What does it mean?" Sibling and parental appraisals of childhood leukemia. *Cancer Nursing, 11*, 329–338.

Brody, G. H., & Stoneman, Z. (1987). Sibling conflict: Contributions of the siblings themselves, the parent-sibling relationship, and the broader family system. *Journal of Children in Contemporary Society, 19*, 39–53.

Bryant, B. K. (1982). Sibling relationships in middle childhood. In M. E. Lamb & B. Sutton-Smith (Eds.), *Sibling relationships: Their nature and significance across the life span* (pp. 87–122). Hillsdale, NJ: Erlbaum.

Bugen, L. A. (1977). Human grief: A model for prediction and intervention. *American Journal of Orthopsychiatry, 47*, 196–206.

Bullard, I. D., & Dohnal, J. T. (1984). The community deals with the child who has a handicap. *Nursing Clinics of North America, 19*, 309–318.

Cain, A., Fast, I., & Erickson, M. (1964). Children's disturbed reactions to the death of a sibling. *American Journal of Orthopsychiatry, 34*, 741–745.

Cain, L. D., & Staver, N. (1976). Helping children adapt to parental illness. *Social Casework, 57*, 575–580.

Cairns, N. U., Clark, G. M., Smith, S. D., & Lansky, S. B. (1979). Adaptation of siblings to childhood malignancy. *Journal of Pediatrics, 95*, 484–487.

Caplan, G. (1987). Guidance for divorcing parents. *Archives of Diseases of Childhood, 62*, 752–753.

Carey, R. G. (1977). The widowed: A year later. *Journal of Counselling Psychology, 24*, 125–131.

Carey, W. (1972). Clinical application of infant temperament measures. *Journal of Pediatrics, 81*, 823–828.

Castiglia, P. (1988). Death of a sibling. *Journal of Pediatric Health Care, 2*, 211–213.

Chanowitz, B., & Langer, E. (1980). Knowing more (or less) than you can show: Understanding control through the mindlessness-mindfulness distinction. In J. Garber & M. E. P. Seligman (Eds.), *Human helplessness: Theory and applications* (pp. 97–129). New York: Academic Press.

Chess, S., & Thomas, A. (1984). *Origins and evolution of behavior disorders*. New York: Guilford.

Christensen, B. (1977). A family systems treatment program for families of delinquent adolescent boys. Doctoral dissertation, Department of Sociology, Brigham Young University, Provo, Utah: DAI, *37*, 6092a.

Cicirelli, V. G. (1980). Sibling influence in adulthood: A life span perspective. In L. W. Poon (Ed.), *Aging in the 1980's* (pp. 455–462). Washington, DC: American Psychological Association.

Cicirelli, V. G. (1982). Sibling influences throughout the lifespan. In M. E. Lamb & B. Sutton-Smith (Eds.), *Sibling relationships: Their nature and significance across the life span* (pp. 267–284). Hillsdale, NJ: Erlbaum.

Cicirelli, V. G. (1988). Interpersonal relationships among elderly siblings: Implications for clinical practice. In M. Kahn & K. G. Lewis (Eds.), *Siblings in therapy* (pp. 435–456). New York: W. W. Norton.

Cicirelli, V. G. (1993). The longest bond: The sibling life cycle. In L. L'Abate (Ed.), *Handbook of developmental psychology and psychopathology* (2nd ed., pp. 44–59), New York: Wiley.

Cicirelli, V. G. (1995). *Sibling relationships across the life span*. New York: Plenum Press.

Cobb, B. (1956). Psychological impact of long-term illness and death of a child in the family circle. *Journal of Pediatrics, 49*, 746–751.

Cobb, S. (1976). Social support as a moderator of life stress. *Psychosomatic Medicine, 38*, 300–314.

Coffel, D. (1989). The tiger in my life. *Issues in Comprehensive Pediatric Nursing, 12*, 309–310.

Corr, C. A., & Corr, D. M. (1995, August). Answering children's questions about death. Paper presented at the meeting of the International Hospice Institute, Vancouver.

Craft, M. J., Wyatt, N., & Sandell, B. (1985). Behavior and feeling changes in siblings of hospitalized children. *Clinical Pediatrics, 24*, 374–378.

Crosby, J., & Jose, N. (1983). Death: Family adjustment to loss. In H. McCubbin & C. Figley (Eds.), *Stress and the family, Vol. I: Coping with normative transitions* (pp. 76–89). New York: Brunner/Mazel.

Crosby, R. (1982). Self-concept development. *Journal of School Health*, September, *52*, 432–436.

Davids, J. (1993). The reaction of an early latency boy to the sudden death of his baby brother. *Psychoanalytic Study of the Child, 48*.

Davies, E. (1983). *Behavioral response of children to the death of a sibling*. Unpublished doctoral dissertation, University of Washington, Seattle, WA.

Davies, B. (1984). Sibling behaviours during bereavement in relation to selected individual and situational variables. In M. Kravitz & J. Laurin (Eds.), *Nursing Research: A base for practice. Proceedings of the Ninth Nursing Research Conference* (pp. 471–482). Montreal: School of Nursing, McGill University.

Davies, B. (October, 1985). *Behavioral responses of children to the death of a sibling*. Final report submitted to Alberta Foundation for Nursing Research, Edmonton, Alberta.

Davies, B. (1987a). After a sibling dies. In M. A. Morgan (Ed.), *Bereavement: Helping the survivors. Proceedings of the 1987 King's College Conference* (pp. 55–65). London, Ontario: King's College.

Davies B. (1987b). Family reponses to the death of a child: The meaning of memories. *Journal of Palliative Care, 3*, 9–15.

Davies, B. (1988a). Shared life space and sibling bereavement responses. *Cancer Nursing, 11*, 339–347.

Davies, B. (1988b). The family environment in bereaved families and its relationship to surviving sibling behavior. *Children's Health Care, 17*, 22–31.

Davies, B. (1991). Long-term outcomes of adolescent sibling bereavement. *Journal of Adolescent Research, 6*, 83–96.

Davies, B. (1993a). Sibling bereavement: Research-based guidelines for nurses. *Seminars in Oncology Nursing, 9*, 107–113.

Davies, B. (1993b). Sibling responses to the death of a child from SIDS. Unpublished data.

Davies, B. (1995a). Long term outcomes of adolescent sibling bereavement. *Journal of Adolescent Research, 6*, 83–96.

Davies, B. (1995b). Long term effects of sibling death in childhood. In D. Adams & E. Deveau (Eds.), *Beyond the innocence of childhood, Vol. 3: Helping children and adolescents cope with death and bereavement* (pp. 89–98). Amityville, NY: Baywood.

Davies, B. (1995c). Sibling bereavement research: State of the art. In I. B. Corless, B. Germino, & M. Pittman (Eds.), *A challenge for living: Dying, death and bereavement*. Boston, MA: Jones & Bartlett.

Davies, B. (1996). *Long term effects of sibling bereavement*. Unpublished manuscript.

Davies, B. (1997). Commentary on Van Riper's article on sibling bereavement. *Pediatric Nursing, 23*, 594–595.

Davies, B., Chekryn Reimer, J., & Martens, N. (1994). Family functioning and its implications for palliative care. *Journal of Palliative Care, 10*, 29–36.

Davies, B., Chekryn Reimer, J., Brown, P., & Martens, N. (1995). *Fading away: The experience of transition in families with terminal illness.* Amityville, NY: Baywood.

Davies, B., & Eng, B. (1998). Special issues in bereavement and support. In D. Doyle, G. Hanks, & N. MacDonald (Eds.), *Oxford textbook of palliative medicine* (2nd ed., pp. 1077–1084). Oxford: Oxford University Press.

Davies, B., & Kalischuk, R. (1997). *Sibling bereavement responses to death from long-term illness and trauma.* Unpublished manuscript.

Davies, B., & Martinson, I. (1989). Special emphasis on siblings during and after the death of a child. In B. Martin (Ed.), *Pediatric hospice care: What helps* (pp. 186–199). Los Angeles, CA: Children's Hospital of Los Angeles.

Davies, B., Spinetta, J., Martinson, I., McClowry, S., & Kulenkamp, E. (1986). Manifestations of levels of functioning in grieving families. *Journal of Family Issues, 7,* 297–313.

DeFrain, J. D., Taylor, J., & Ernst, L. (1982). *Coping with sudden infant death.* Lexington, MA: Lexington Books, D.C. Heath.

Demi, A. S., & Gilbert, C. M. (1987). Relationship of parental grief to sibling grief. *Archives of Psychiatric Nursing, 1,* 385–391.

DeSpelder, L. A., & Strickland, A. L. (1995). Using life experiences as a way of helping children understand death. In D. W. Adams & E. J. Deveau (Eds.), *Beyond the innocence of childhood: Factors influencing children and adolescents' perceptions and attitudes toward death* (Vol. 1, pp. 45–54). Amityville, NY: Baywood.

Deveau, E. (1995). Perceptions of death through the eyes of children and adolescents. In D. W. Adams & E. J. Deveau (Eds.), *Beyond the innocence of childhood: Factors influencing children and adolescents' perceptions and attitudes toward death* (Vol. 1, pp. 55–92). Amityville, NY: Baywood.

Doherty, W. J. (1988). Sibling issues in cotherapy and coauthoring. In M. D. Kahn & K. G. Lewis (Eds.), *Siblings in therapy: Lifespan and clinical issues* (pp. 399–414). New York: W. W. Norton & Co.

Dominica, F. (1987). Reflections on death in childhood. *British Medical Journal, 294,* 108–110.

Dowden, S. (1995). Young children's experiences of sibling death. *Journal of Pediatric Nursing, 10,* 72–79.

Duff, R. S., & Hollingshead, A. B. (1968). *Sickness and society.* New York: Harper & Row.

Dunn, J. (1985). *Sisters and brothers.* Cambridge, MA: Harvard University Press.

Dunn, J., & Dale, N. (1984). I a daddy: 2-year-old's collaboration in joint pretend play with siblings and with mother. In I. Bretherton (Ed.), *Symbolic play: The development of social understanding* (pp. 131–158). New York: Academic Press.

Dunn, J., & Kendrick, C. (1982a). Siblings and their mothers: Developing relationships within the family. In M. E. Lamb & B. Sutton-Smith (Eds.), *Sibling relationships: Their nature and significance across the life span* (pp. 39–60). Hillsdale, NJ: Erlbaum.

Dunn, J., & Kendrick, C. (1982b). *Siblings: Love, envy, and understanding.* Cambridge, MA: Harvard University Press.

Dunn, J., & Munn, P. (1986). Siblings and the development of prosocial behavior. *International Journal of Behavioral Development, 9,* 265–284.

Easson, E. (1970). *The dying child: The management of the child or adolescent who is dying.* Springfield, IL: Charles C. Thomas.

Ellman, R. (1988). *Oscar Wilde.* New York: Alfred A. Knopf Inc.

Eth, S., & Pynoos, R. S. (Eds.). (1985). *Post traumatic stress disorder in children.* Washington, DC: American Psychiatric Press.

Evans, E., & McCandless, B. (1978). *Children and youth: Psychosocial development.* New York: Holt, Rinehart & Winston.

Faber, A., & Mazlish, E. (1989). *Between brothers and sisters: A celebration of life's most enduring relationship.* New York: Avon Books.

Fanos, J. H., & Nickerson, B. G. (1991). Long-term effects of sibling death during adolescence. *Journal of Adolescent Research, 6,* 70–82.

Faulkner, K. W. (1993). Children's understanding of death. In A. Armstrong-Dailey & S. Z. Goltzer (Eds.), *Hospice care for children* (pp. 9–21). New York: Oxford University Press.

Faux, S. (1993). Siblings of children with chronic physical and cognitive disabilities. *Journal of Pediatric Nursing, 8,* 305–317.

Finke, L. M., Birenbaum, L. K., & Chand, N. (1994). Two weeks post-death report by parents of siblings' grieving experience. *Journal of Child & Adolescent Psychiatric Nursing, 7,* 17–25.

Fitzgerald, H. (1992). *The grieving child: A parent's guide.* New York: Simon & Schuster.

Forrest, D. W. (1974). *Francis Galton: The life and work of a Victorian genius.* London: Paul Elek.

Fortier, J. C., Carson, V. B., Will, S., & Shubkagel, B. L. (1991). Adjustment to a newborn: Sibling preparation makes a difference. *Journal of Obstetric, Gynecological, and Neonatal Nursing, 20,* 73–79.

Fowler, P. (1980). Family development and early behavioral development: A structural analysis of dependencies. *Psychological Reports, 47,* 611–617.

Fox, S. (1985). *Good grief: Helping groups of children when a friend dies.* Boston: New England Association for the Education of Young Children.

Freud, S. (1957). Mourning and melancholia. In J. Strachey (Ed. and Trans.), *The standard edition of the complete psychological works of Sigmund Freud* (Vol. XIV, pp. 243–258). London: Hogarth Press. (Originally published in 1915)

Fulton, R. (1977). *Death, grief and bereavement: A bibliography 1845–1975.* New York: Arna Press.

Fulton, R., & Fulton, J. (1971). A psychosocial aspect of terminal care: Anticipatory grief. *Omega, 2,* 91–100.

Furman, E. (1974). *A child's parent dies: Studies in childhood bereavement.* New Haven, CT: Yale University Press.

Futterman, F. H., & Hoffman, I. (1973). Crisis and adaptation in the families of fatally ill children. In E. F. Anthony & C. Koupernick (Eds.), *The child and his family: The impact of disease and death* (Vol. 2). New York: Wiley.

Gedo, M. M. (1980). *Picasso: Art as autobiography.* Chicago: Chicago University Press.

Gesell, A., Ilg, F., & Bates, A. L. (1974). *Infant and child in the culture of today.* New York: Harper & Row.

Gibbons, M. B. (1992). A child dies, a child survives: The impact of sibling loss. *Journal of Pediatric Health Care, 6,* 65–72.

Glaser, B., & Strauss, A. (1965). *Awareness of dying.* Chicago: Aldine.

Glaser, B., & Strauss, A. (1968). *Time for dying.* Chicago: Aldine.

Glick, I. O., Weiss, R. S., & Parkes, C. M. (1974). *The first year of bereavement.* New York: Wiley Interscience.

Gogan, J., Koocher, G. P., Foster, D., & O'Malley, J. (1977). Impact of childhood cancer on siblings. *Health and Social Work, 2,* 41–57.

Gordon, A. K., & Klass, D. (1979). *They need to know: How to teach children about death.* Englewood Cliffs, NJ: Prentice–Hall.

Gorer, G. (1965). *Death, grief and mourning in contemporary Britain.* London: Cresset.

Gottfried, A. W., & Gottfried, A. E. (1983). Home environments and mental development in young children of middle-class families. In A. W. Gottfried (Ed.), *Home environment and mental development: Longitudinal research* (pp. 309–315). New York: Academic.

Gottlieb, L. N., & Mendelson, M. J. (1990). Parental support and firstborn girls' adaptation to the birth of a sibling. *Journal of Applied Developmental Psychology, 11,* 29–48.

Graham-Pole, J., Wass, H., Eyberg, S., Chu, L., & Olejnik, S. (1989). Communicating with dying children and their siblings: A retrospective analysis. *Death Studies, 13,* 465–483.

Grogan, L. B. (1990). Grief of an adoldescent when a sibling dies. *Maternal Child Nursing, 15,* 21–24.

Grollman, E. (Ed.). (1967). *Explaining death to children.* Boston: Beacon Press.

Grollman, E. A. (1990). *Talking about death: A dialogue between parent and child.* Boston: Beacon Press.

Grollman, E. A. (Ed.). (1995). *Bereaved children and teens.* Boston: Beacon Press.

Gross, R. T., & Dornbusch, S. M. (1983). Enuresis. In A. Levine, *Developmental-behavioral pediatrics* (pp. 573–586). Philadelphia: W. B. Saunders.

Hamovitch, M. D. (1964). *The parent and the fatally ill child.* Los Angeles: Delmar Publishing.

Harding, R. K., & Looney, J. G. (1977). Problems of southeast Asian children in a refugee camp. *American Journal of Psychiatry, 134,* 407–411.

Heiney, S. P. (1991). Sibling grief: A case report. *Archives of Psychiatric Nursing, V,* 121–127.

Heiney, S. P., Hasan, L., & Price, K. (1993). Developing and implementing a bereavement program for a children's hospital. *Journal of Pediatric Nursing, 8,* 385–391.

Heiney, S. P., Wells, L. M., & Gunn, J. (1993). The effects of group therapy on bereaved extended family of children with cancer. *Journal of Pediatric Oncology Nursing, 10,* 99–104.

Hetherington, E. M., & Parke, R. D. (1993). *Child psychology: A contemporary viewpoint* (4th ed.). New York: McGraw–Hill.

Higgins, G. (1977). Grief reactions. *The Practitioner, 218,* 689–695.

Hilgard, J. R. (1969). Depressive and psychotic states as anniversaries to sibling death in childhood. *International Psychiatry Clinics, 6,* 197–207.

Hogan, N. S. (1987). An investigation of the adolescent sibling bereavement process and adaptation (Doctoral dissertation, Loyola University of Chicago, 1987). *Dissertation Abstracts International,* 4024A.

Hogan, N. S. (1988a). The effects of time on adolescent sibling bereavement. *Pediatric Nursing, 14,* 333–335.

Hogan, N. S. (1988b). Understanding sibling bereavement. *The Forum Newsletter: Association for Death Education and Counselling, 12,* 4–5.

Hogan, N. S. (1990). Hogan sibling inventory of bereavement. In J. Touliatos, B. Perlmutter, & M. Straus (Eds.), *Handbook of family measurement techniques* (p. 524). Newbury Park, CA: Sage.

Hogan, N. S., & Balk, D. (1990). Adolescent reactions to sibling death: Perceptions of mothers, fathers, and teenagers. *Nursing Research, 39,* 103–106.

Hogan, N. S., & DeSantis, L. (1992). Adolescent sibling bereavement: An ongoing attachment. *Qualitative Health Research, 2,* 159–177.

Hogan, N. S., & DeSantis, L. (1994). Things that help and hinder adolescent sibling bereavement. *Western Journal of Nursing Research, 16,* 132–153.

Hogan, N. S., & Greenfield, D. B. (1991). Adolescent sibling bereavement: Symptomatology in a large community sample. *Journal of Adolescent Research, 6,* 97–112.

Holahan, C. J., & Moos, R. H. (1983). The quality of social support: Measures of family and work relationships. *British Journal of Clinical Psychology, 22,* 157–162.

Huffington, A. S. (1988). *Picasso: Creator and destroyer.* London: Weidenfeld and Nicholson.

Hutton, C. J., & Bradley, B. S. (1994). Effects of sudden infant death on bereaved siblings: A comparative study. *Journal of Child Psychology and Psychiatry, 35,* 723–732.

International Work Group on Death, Dying and Bereavement. (In press). Children, adolescents and death: Myths, realities and challenges. *Death Studies.*

Jackson, E. (1982). The pastoral counselor and the child encountering death. In H. Wass & C. A. Corr (Eds.), *Helping children cope with death: Guidelines and resources* (pp. 33–47). Washington, DC: Hemisphere.

Jacobson, D. S. (1978). The impact of marital separation/divorce on children: III. Parent-child communication and child adjustment, and regression analysis of findings from overall study. *Journal of Divorce, 2,* 175–194.

Jenkins, J. M. (1992). Sibling relationships in disharmonious homes: Potential difficulties and protective effects. In F. Boer & J. Dunn (Eds.), *Children's sibling relationships: Developmental and clinical issues* (pp. 125–138). Hillsdale, NJ: Erlbaum.

Jonah, B. A. (1986). Accident risk and risk-taking behaviour among young drivers. *Accident Analysis and Prevention, 18,* 255–261.

Jones, H. E. (1933). Order of birth in relation to the development of the child. In C. Murchison (Ed.), *A handbook of child psychology*. Worcester, MA: Clark University Press.

Kahn, M. D. (1983). Sibling relationships in later life. *Medical aspects of human sexuality, 17,* 94–103.

Kahn, M. D. (1988). Intense sibling relationships: A self-psychological view. In M. D. Kahn & K. G. Lewis (Eds.), *Siblings in therapy: Life span and clinical issues* (pp. 3–24). New York: W. W. Norton & Co.

Kahn, M. D., & Lewis, K. G. (1988). *Siblings in therapy: Life span and clinical issues*. New York: W. W. Norton & Co.

Kantor, D., & Lehr, W. (1975). *Inside the family: Toward a theory of family process*. San Francisco: Jossey-Bass.

Kaplan, D. M., Grobstein, R., & Smith, A. (1976). Predicting the impact of severe illness in families. *Health and Social Work, 1,* 72–82.

Kayiatos, R., Adams, J., & Gilman, B. (1984). The arrival of a rival: Maternal perceptions of toddlers' regressive behaviors after the birth of a sibling. *Journal of Nurse Midwifery, 29,* 205–213.

Keefe, R. (1979). *Charlotte Bronte's world of death*. Austin, TX: University of Texas Press.

Kerner, J., Harvey, B., & Lewiston, N. (1979). The impact of grief: A retrospective study of family function following loss of a child with cystic fibrosis. *Journal of Chronic Disease, 32,* 221–225.

Kiritz, S., & Moos, R. H. (1974). Physiological effects of social environments. *Psychosomatic Medicine, 36,* 96–114.

Klass, D. (1988). *Parental grief: Solace and resolution*. New York: Springer.

Kliman, G. W. (1968). *Psychological emergencies of childhood*. New York: Grune and Stratton.

Knafl, K. A. (1982). Parent's views of the responses of siblings to a pediatric hospitalization. *Research in Nursing and Health, 5,* 13–20.

Knafl, K. A., & Dixon, D. M. (1983). The role of siblings during pediatric hospitalization. *Issues in Comprehensive Pediatric Nursing, 6,* 13–22.

Knudson, G. G., & Natterson, J. M. (1960). Participation of parents in the hospital care of fatally ill children. *Pediatrics, 26,* 482.

Koocher, G. P. (1973). Childhood, death and cognitive development. *Developmental Psychology, 9,* 369–375.

Koocher, G. P. (1974). Talking with children about death. *American Journal of Orthopsychiatry, 44,* 404–411.

Kramer, R. F. (1981). Living with childhood cancer: Healthy siblings' perspective. *Issues in Comprehensive Pediatric Nursing, 5,* 155–165.

Krell, R., & Rabkin, L. (1979). The effects of sibling death on the surviving child: A family perspective. *Family Process, 18,* 471–477.

Krulik, T., Holaday, B., & Martinson, I. M. (Eds.). (1987). *The child and family facing life-threatening illness: A tribute to Eugenia Waechter*. Philadelphia: Lippincott.

Kubler-Ross, E. (1969). *On death and dying*. New York: Macmillan.

Lamb, M. E. (1978). Interactions between eighteen-month-olds and their preschool-aged siblings. *Child Development, 49,* 51–59.

Lamb, M. E., & Sutton-Smith, B. (1982). *Sibling relationships: Their nature and significance across the life span*. Hillsdale, NJ: Erlbaum.

Lascari, A. D. (1978). The dying child and the family. *The Journal of Family Practice, 6,* 1279–1286.

Lascari, A. D., & Stehbens, J. A. (1973). The reactions of families to childhood leukemia: An evaluation of a program of emotional management. *Clinical Pediatrics, 12,* 210–214.

Lattanzi, M. E. (1989). Bereavement care for siblings. *Journal of the Association of Pediatric Oncology Nurses, 6,* 32.

Lauer, M. E., Mulhern, R. K., Bohne, J. B., & Camitta, B. M. (1985). Children's perceptions of their sibling's death at home or in hospital: The precursors of differential adjustment. *Cancer Nursing, 8,* 21–27.

Lauer, M. E., Mulhern, R. K., Hoffman, R. G., Schell, M. J., & Camitta, B. M. (1989). Long-term follow-up for parental adjustment following a child's death at home or hospital. *Cancer, 63,* 988–994.

Lavigne, C. U., & Ryan, M. (1979). Psychological adjustment of siblings of children with chronic illness. *Pediatrics, 63,* 616–627.

Lazar, A., & Torney-Purta, J. (1991). The development of the subconcepts of death in young children: A short-term longitudinal study. *Child Development, 62,* 1321–1333.

Lazarus, R. S. (1966). *Psychological stress and the coping process.* New York: McGraw–Hill.

Lazarus, R. S., & Folkman, S. (1984). *Stress, appraisal and coping.* New York: Springer.

Leder, S. (1992). Life events, social support, and children's competence after parent and sibling death. *Journal of Pediatric Nursing, 7,* 110–119.

Leebman, W. M. (1978). Recurrent abdominal pain in children. *Clinical Pediatrics, 17,* 149–153.

Legg, C., Sherick, I., & Wadland, W. (1974). Reaction of preschool children to the birth of a sibling. *Child Psychiatry and Human Development, 5,* 3–39.

Levine, M. (1983). *Developmental behavioral pediatrics.* Philadelphia: W. B. Saunders.

Lewin, K. (1950). *Field theory in social science.* New York: Harper & Row.

Lewis, I. C. (1967). Leukemia in childhood: Its effects on the family. *Australian Paediatric Journal, 3,* 244–247.

Lewis, M., & Volkmar, F. (1990). *Clinical aspects of child and adolescent development,* (3rd ed., pp. 63–69). Philadelphia: Lea & Febiger.

Lincoln, Y. S., & Guba, E. G. (1985). *Naturalistic inquiry.* Beverly Hills, CA: Sage.

Lindemann, E. (1944). Symptomatology and management of acute grief. *American Journal of Psychiatry, 101,* 141–148.

Lobato, D., Faust, D., & Spirito, A. (1988). Examining the effects of chronic disease and disability on children's sibling relationships. *Journal of Pediatric Psychology, 13,* 389–407.

Maddison, D., & Walker, W. L. (1967). Factors affecting the outcome of conjugal bereavement. *British Journal of Psychiatry, 113,* 1057–1067.

Mahon, M. M. (1993). Children's concept of death and sibling death from trauma. *Journal of Pediatric Nursing, 8,* 335–344.

Mahon, M. M., & Page, M. L. (1995). Childhood bereavement after the death of a sibling. *Holistic Nursing Practice, 9,* 15–26.

Mandell, F., Dirks-Smith, T., & Smith, M. (1988). The surviving child in the SIDS family. *Pediatrician, 15,* 217–221.

Mandell, F., McAnulty, E. & Carlson, A. (1983). Unexpected death of an infant sibling. *Pediatrics, 72,* 652–657.

Mandell, F., McClain, M., & Reece, R. (1987). Sudden and unexpected death: The pediatrician's response. *American Journal of Diseases of Children, 141,* 748–750.

Marris, P. (1958). *Widows and their families.* London: Routledge & Kegan Paul.

Martinson, I., Davies, B., & McClowry, S. (1987). The long-term effects of sibling death on self-concept. *Journal of Pediatric Nursing, 2,* 227–235.

Martinson, I., Davies, B., & McClowry, S. (1991). Parental depression following the death of a child. *Death Studies, 15,* 259–267.

Martinson, I. M. (1980, June). *Home care for the child with cancer.* Final report (National Cancer Institute grant CA19490). Minneapolis, MN: University of Minnesota.

Martinson, I. M., Armstrong, G. D., Geis, D. P., Anglim, M. A., Gronseth, E. C., MacInnis, H., Nesbit, M. E., & Kersey, J. H. (1978). Home care for children dying of cancer. *Pediatrics, 62,* 106–113.

Martinson, I. M., & Campos, R. G. (1991). Adolescent bereavement: Long-term responses to a sibling's death from cancer. *Journal of Adolescent Research, 6,* 54–69.

Martinson, I., McClowry, S., Davies, B., & Kulenkamp, E. (1994). Changes over time: A study of family bereavement following childhood cancer. *Journal of Palliative Care, 10,* 29–36.

Maslow, A. H. (1968). *Toward a psychology of being.* Princeton, NJ: Van Nostrand.

McClowry, S., Davies, B., May, K., Kulenkamp, E., & Martinson, I. (1987). The empty space phenomenon: The process of grief in the bereaved family. *Death Studies, 11,* 361–374.

McClowry, S. G. (1992). Temperament theory and research. *Image: Journal of Nursing Scholarship, 24,* 319–325.

McClowry, S. G. (1995). The influence of temperment on development during middle childhood. *Journal of Pediatric Nursing, 10,* 160–165.

McConville, B. (1985). *Sisters: Love and conflict within the lifelong bond.* London: Pan Books Ltd.

McCown, D. (1982). *Selected factors related to children's adjustment following sibling death.* Unpublished doctoral dissertation, Oregon State University, Corvallis.

McCown, D. (1984). Funeral attendance, cremation and young siblings. *Death Education, 8,* 349–363.

McCown, D. (1987). Factors related to bereaved children's behavioral adjustment. In C. Barnes (Ed.), *Recent advances in nursing series: Caring for sick children* (pp. 85–93). England: Churchill-Livingstone.

McCown, D. E., & Davies, B. (1995). Patterns of grief in young children following the death of a sibling. *Death Studies, 19,* 41–53.

McCown, D. E., & Pratt, C. (1985). Impact of sibling death on children's behavior. *Death Studies, 9,* 323–335.

McCubbin, H., & Figley, C. (1983). Bridging normative and catastrophic family stress. In H. McCubbin & C. Figley (Eds.), *Stress and the family: Vol. l: Coping with normative transitions* (pp. 218–228). New York: Brunner/Mazel.

McGoldrick, M., & Walsh, F. (1983). A systemic view of family history and loss. In L. R. Wolberg & M. L. Aronson (Eds.), *Group and family therapy* (pp. 252–270). New York: Brunner/Mazel.

Mechanic, D. (1974). Social structure and personal adaptation: Some neglected dimensions. In G. Coelho, D. A. Hamburg, & J. E. Adams, *Coping and adaptation* (pp. 32–44) New York: Basic Books.

Melear, J. D. (1973). Children's conceptions of death. *Journal of Genetic Psychology, 123,* 359–360.

Melvin, N. (1995). Children's temperament: Intervention for parents. *Journal of Pediatric Nursing: Nursing Care of Children and Families, 10,* 152–159.

Miller, S. M., & Grant, R. P. (1978). Predictability and human stress: Evidence, theory and conceptual clarification. Unpublished manuscript, University of Pennsylvania, Philadelphia.

Minuchin, S. (1974). *Families and family therapy.* Cambridge, MA: Harvard University Press.

Moos, R. H., & Moos, B. S. (1981). *Family environment scale manual.* Palo Alto, CA: Consulting Psychologists Press.

Morrissey, J. (1963a). A note on interviews with children facing imminent death. *Social Casework, 44,* 343–345.

Morrissey, J. (1963b). Children's adaptations to fatal illness. *Social Work, 8,* 81–88.

Morrissey, J. (1965). Death anxiety in children with a fatal illness. In H. J. Parad (Ed.), *Crisis Intervention* (pp. 324–338). New York: Family Service Association of America.

Mufson, T. (1985). Issues surrounding sibling death during adolescence. *Child and Adolescent Social Work Journal, 2,* 204–218.

Mulhern, R. K., Lauer, M. E., & Hoffman, C. B. (1983). Death of a child at home or in the hospital: Subsequent psychological adjustment of the family. *Pediatrics, 71,* 743–747.

Murphy, L. (1974). Coping, vulnerability, and resilience in childhood. In G. Coelho, D. Hamburg, & J. Adams (Eds.), *Coping and adaptation* (pp. 69–100). New York: Basic Books.

Murphy, L. B., & Moriarty, A. E. (1976). *Vulnerability, coping and growth*. New Haven, CT: Yale University Press.

Murphy, L. B., Murphy, G., & Newcomb, T. (1937). *Experimental social psychology* (pp. 348–363). New York: Harper.

Murphy, S. O. (1993). Siblings and the new baby: Changing perspectives. *Journal of Pediatric Nursing, 8*, 277–288.

Nadelman, L., & Begun, A. (1982). The effect of the newborn on the older sibling: Mothers' questionnaires. In M. E. Lamb & B. Sutton-Smith (Eds.), *Sibling relationships: Their nature and significance across the life span* (pp. 39–60). Hillsdale, NJ: Erlbaum.

Nagy, M. (1948). The child's theories concerning death. *Journal of Genetic Psychology, 73*, 3–27.

Nagy, M. (1959). The child's view of death. In H. Feifel (Ed.), *The meaning of death* (pp. 79–98). New York: McGraw–Hill.

Natterson, J. M, & Knudson, A. G. (1960). Observations concerning fear of death in fatally ill children and their mothers. *Psychosomatic Medicine, 22*, 456–465.

Neubauer, P. B. (1982). Rivalry, envy, and jealousy. *The Psychoanalytic Study of the Child, 37*, 121–142.

Nihira, K., Mink, I., & Meyers, C. (1981). Relationship between home environment and school adjustment of TMR children. *American Journal of Mental Deficiency, 86*, 8–15.

Nixon, J., & Pearn, J. (1977). Emotional sequelae of parents and siblings following the drowning or near-drowning of a child. *Australian and New Zealand Journal of Psychiatry, 11*, 265–268.

Normand, C. L., Silverman, P. R., & Nickman, S. L. (1996). Bereaved children's changing relationship with the deceased. In D. Klass, P. R. Silverman, & S. L. Nickman (Eds.), *Continuing bonds* (pp. 87–110). Washington, DC: Taylor & Francis.

Nuckolls, K. B., Cassel, J., & Kaplan, B. H. (1972). Psychosocial assets, life crisis and the prognosis of pregnancy. *American Journal of Epidemiology, 95*, 431–441.

Olson, D., Sprenkle, D., & Russell, C. (1979, March). Circumplex model of marital and family systems: I. Cohesion and adaptability dimensions, family types, and clinical applications. *Family Process, 18*, 3–28.

Opie, N. D. (1992). Childhood and adolescent bereavement. *Annual Review of Nursing Research, 10*, 127–141.

Osterweis, M., Solomon, F., & Green, M. (Eds.). (1984). *Bereavement: Reactions, consequences, and care*. Washington, DC: National Academy Press.

Oxford English dictionary (1971). (Vol. II). Oxford: Oxford University Press.

Parker, L., & Whitehead, W. (1982). Treatment of urinary and fecal incontinence in children. In D. C. Russo & J. W. Varni (Eds.), *Behavioral pediatrics: Research and practice* (pp. 143–174). New York: Plenum Press.

Parkes, C. M. (1971). Psycho-social transitions: A field for study. *Social Science and Medicine, 5*, 101–115.

Parkes, C. M. (1972). *Bereavement: Studies of grief in adult life*. New York: International Universities Press.

Parkes, C. M. (1975). Determinants of outcome following bereavement. *Omega, 6*, 303–323.

Parkes, C. M. (1986). *Bereavement: Studies of grief in adult life* (2nd ed.). London: Tavistock.

Parkes, C. M., & Brown, R. J. (1972). Health after bereavement: A controlled study of young Boston widows and widowers. *Psychosomatic Medicine, 34*, 449–461.

Parkman, S. E. (1992). Helping families say good-bye. *American Journal of Maternal Child Nursing, 7*, 14–17.

Payne, J. S., Goff, J. R., & Paulson, M. A. (1980). Psychosocial adjustment of families following the death of a child. In J. L. Schulman & M. J. Kupst (Eds.), *The child with cancer: Clinical approaches to psychosocial care—research in psychosocial aspects* (pp. 183–193). Springfield, IL: Charles C. Thomas.

Peck, R. (1966). The development of the concept of death in selected male children (Doctoral dissertation, New York University, 1966). *Dissertation Abstracts International 27,* 1294B. (University Microfilms No. 66-9468)

Peretz, D. (1970). Development, object-relationships, and loss. In B. Schoenberg, A. Carr, D. Peretz, & A. Kutscher (Eds.), *Loss and grief: Psychological management in medical practice* (pp. 3–19). New York: Columbia University Press.

Pettle Michael, S. A., & Lansdown, R. G. (1986). Adjustment to the death of a sibling. *Archives of Disease in Childhood, 61,* 278–283.

Piaget, J. (1932). *The moral judgment of the child.* London: Routledge & Kegan Paul.

Piaget, J. (1959). *The language and thought of the child* (M. Gabain, Trans.). London: Routledge & Kegan Paul.

Pierce, P. J. (1994). *The ultimate Elvis: Elvis Presley day by day.* New York: Simon & Schuster.

Piers, E. (1976). *The Piers-Harris self-concept scale.* (Research Monograph No. 1). Nashville, TN: Counselor Recordings and Tests.

Piers, E., & Harris, D. (1969). *The manual for the Piers-Harris children's self-concept scale.* Nashville, TN: Counselor Recordings and Tests.

Pollock, G. (1962). Childhood parent and sibling loss in adult patients. *Archives of General Psychiatry, 7,* 295–305.

Pollock, G. (1978). On siblings, childhood sibling loss and creativity. *Annual of Psychoanalysis, 6,* 443–481.

Pollock, G. H. (1986). Childhood sibling loss: A family tragedy. *Pediatric Annals, 15,* 851–855.

Powell, M. (1991). The psychosocial impact of sudden death syndrome on siblings. *The Irish Journal of Psychology, 12,* 235–247.

Poznanski, E. O. (1972). The "replacement child": A saga of unresolved parental grief. *Behavioral Pediatrics, 81,* 1190–1193.

Prugh, D. (1985). *The psycho-social aspects of pediatrics.* Philadelphia: Lea & Febiger.

Pynoos, R., Frederick, C., Nader, K., Arroyo, W., Eth, S. Nunez, W., Steinberg, A. & Fairbanks, L. (1987). Life threat and posttraumatic stress in school age children. *Archives of General Psychiatry, 44,* 1057–1063.

Pynoos, R. S., & Nader, K. (1987). *The Childhood Post-Traumatic Stress Disorder—Parents Questionnaire.* (Available from R. S. Pynoos, Neuropsychiatric Institute and Hospital, University of California–Los Angeles, Los Angeles, CA 90024.)

Raimbault, G. (1981). Children talk about death. *Acta Pediatrica Scandinavia, 70,* 179–182.

Rando, T. A. (1991). *How to go on living when someone you love dies.* New York: Bantam.

Raphael, B. (1977). Preventive intervention with the recently bereaved. *Archives of General Psychiatry, 34,* 1450–1454.

Raphael, B. (1983). *The anatomy of bereavement.* New York: Basic Books.

Richmond, J. B., & Waisman, H. A. (1955). Psychological aspects of management of children with malignant diseases. *American Journal of Diseases of Childhood, 89,* 42–47.

Romond, J. L. (1990). "It's sad and you hurt a lot": Letters from bereaved brothers and sisters. *Journal of Christian Nursing, Fall,* 4–8.

Rosen, E. J. (1996). The family as healing resource. In C. A. Corr & D. M. Corr (Eds.), *Handbook of childhood death and bereavement* (pp. 223–243). New York: Springer Publishing.

Rosen, H. (1984–85). Prohibitions against mourning in childhood sibling loss. *Omega, 15,* 307–316.

Rosen, H. (1986). *Unspoken grief: Coping with childhood sibling loss.* Lexington, MA: Lexington Books, D.C. Heath.

Rosenblatt, B. (1969). A young boy's reaction to the death of his sister. *Journal of the American Academy of Child Psychiatry, 8,* 321–335.

Rosenzweig, S. (1943). Sibling death as a psychological experience with reference to schizophrenia. *Psychoanalytic Review, 30*, 177–186.

Rubin, S. S. (1985). The resolution of bereavement: A clinical focus on the relationship to the deceased. *Psychotherapy: Theory, Research, Training and Practice, 22*, 131–135.

Rudestam, K. E. (1977). Physical and psychological response to suicide in the family. *Journal of Consulting and Clinical Psychology, 45*, 167–170.

Russell, M. T., & Russell, M. A. (1989). Temperament and accident occurrence in children: A pilot study. *Australian Journal of Advanced Nursing, 7*, 43–46.

Salemson, J. (1976). *The unspeakable confessions of Salvador Dali* (as told to Andres Parenaud). New York: William Morrow.

Samuels, H. R. (1980). The effect of an older sibling on infant locomotor exploration of a new environment. *Child Development, 51*, 607–609.

Sandmaier, M. (1994). *Original kin: The search for connection among adult sisters and brothers*. New York: Dutton.

Schacter, S. (1959). *The psychology of affiliation*. Stanford, CA: Stanford University Press.

Schilder, P., & Wechsler, D. (1934). The attitude of children towards death. *Journal of Genetic Psychology, 45*, 406–451.

Schoenberg, B., Carr, A. C., Peretz, D., Kutscher, A. H., & Cherico, D. J. (1975). Advice of the bereaved for the bereaved. In B. Schoenberg, A. C. Carr, D. Peretz, A. H. Kutscher, & D. J. Cherico (Eds.), *Bereavement: Its psychosocial aspects* (pp. 362–367). New York: Columbia University Press.

Schor, D. P. (1985). Temperament and the initial school experience. *Child Health Care, 13*, 129–134.

Schorsch, A. (1979). *Images of childhood: An illustrated social history*. New York: Mayflower Books.

Schucter, S. R. (1986). *Dimensions of grief: Adjusting to the death of a spouse*. San Francisco, CA: Jossey-Bass.

Schwab, J. J., Chalmers, J. M., Conroy, S. J., Ferris, P. B., & Markush, R. E. (1965). Studies in grief: A preliminary report. In B. Schoenberg, L. Gerber, A. Wiener, A. H. Kutscher, D. Peretz, & A. Carr (Eds.), *Bereavement: Its psychosocial aspects*. New York: Columbia University Press.

Shrier, D. (1980). The dying child and surviving family members. *Developmental and Behavioral Pediatrics, 1*, 152–157.

Silverman, P. R., & Nickman, S. L. (1996). Children's construction of their dead parents. In D. Klass, P. R. Silverman, & S. L. Nickman (Eds.), *Continuing bonds: New understandings of grief* (pp. 73–86). Washington, DC: Taylor & Francis.

Simon, K. (1993). Perceived stress of non-hospitalized children during the hospitalization of a sibling. *Journal of Pediatric Nursing, 8*, 298–304.

Speece, M. (1995). The search for the mature concept of death: Progress on its specification and definition. *The Forum Newsletter, 6*, 20–22.

Speece, M. W. (1986). Children's understanding of death: Three components. In J. D. Morgan (Ed.), *Children and death* (pp. 71–79). Proceedings of the 1985 King's College Conference, London, Ontario: King's College.

Speece, M. W., & Brent, S. B. (1984). Children's understanding of death: Three components of a death concept. *Child Development, 55*, 1671–1685.

Speece, M. W., & Brent, S. B. (1991). The "adult" concept of irreversibility. In J. D. Morgan (Ed.), *Young people and death*. Philadelphia: The Charles Press.

Speece, M. W., & Brent, S. B. (1992). The acquisition of a mature understanding of three components of the concept of death. *Death Studies, 16*, 211–229.

Spinetta, J. (1977). Adjustment in children with cancer. *Journal of Pediatric Psychology, 2*, 49–51.

Spinetta, J. (1981). The sibling of the child with cancer. In J. Spinetta & P. Deasy-Spinetta (Eds.), *Living with childhood cancer* (pp. 133–142). St. Louis: Mosby.

Spinetta, J. J. (1972). Death anxiety in leukemic children. (Doctoral dissertation, University of Southern California, 1972). *Dissertation Abstracts International 33,* 1807–1808.

Spinetta, J. J., Rigler, D., & Karon, M. (1973). Anxiety in the dying child. *Pediatrics, 52,* 841–845.

Spinetta, J. J., Rigler, D., & Karon, M. (1974). Personal space as a measure of the dying child's sense of isolation. *Journal of Consulting and Clinical Psychology, 42,* 751–756.

Spinetta, J., Swarner, J., & Sheposh, J. (1981). Effective parental coping following the death of a child from cancer. *Journal of Pediatric Psychology, 6,* 251–263.

Stehbens, J. A., & Lascari, A. D. (1974). Psychological follow-up of families with childhood leukemia. *Journal of Clinical Psychology, 30,* 394–397.

Stein, A., Forrest, G., Woolley, H., & Baum, J. (1989). Life threatening illness and hospice care. *Archives of Diseases in Childhood, 64,* 687–702.

Steiner, G. L. (1965). *Children's concepts of life and death: A developmental study* (Doctoral dissertation, Columbia University). *Dissertation Abstracts Internal 26,* 1164. (University Microfilms No. 65-8864)

Stephenson, J. (1986). Grief of siblings. In T. A. Rando (Ed.), *Parental loss of a child* (pp. 321–338). Champaign, IL: Research Press.

Stewart, L. (1962). Social and emotional adjustment during adolescence as related to development of psychosomatic illness in adulthood. *Psychological Monographs, 65,* 175–215.

Stewart, R. B. (1983). Sibling attachment relationships: Child-infant interaction in the strange situation. *Developmental Psychology, 19,* 192–199.

Stewart, R. B. (1990). *The second child: Family transition and adjustment.* Newbury Park, CA: Sage.

Stillion, J. M. (1985). *Death and the sexes: An examination of differential longevity, attitudes, behaviors and coping skills.* New York: Hemisphere/McGraw–Hill.

Stillion, J. M. (1995). Gender differences in children's understanding of death. In D. W. Adams & E. J. Deaveau (Eds.), *Beyond the innocence of childhood: Factors influencing children and adolescents' perceptions and attitudes toward death* (Vol. 1, pp. 29–44). Amityville, NY: Baywood.

Stoneman, Z., & Berman, P. W. (Eds.). (1993). *The effects of mental retardation, disability, and illness on sibling relationships: Research issues and challenges.* Baltimore, MD: Brookes.

Strauss, A., & Corbin, J. (1990). *Basics of qualitative research: Grounded theory procedures and techniques.* Newbury Park, CA: Sage.

Sullivan, H. (1953). *Conceptions of modern psychiatry.* New York: Norton.

Suomi, S. J. (1982). Sibling relationships in non-human primates. In M. E. Lamb & B. Sutton-Smith (Eds.), *Sibling relationships: Their nature and significance across the life span* (pp. 329–356). Hillsdale, NJ: Erlbaum.

Sutton-Smith, B. (1982). Birth order and sibling status effects. In M. E. Lamb & B. Sutton-Smith (Eds.), *Sibling relationships: Their nature and significance across the life span* (pp. 153–166). Hillsdale, NJ: Erlbaum.

Sutton-Smith, B., & Rosenberg, B. G. (1970). *The sibling.* New York: Holt, Rinehart & Winston.

Taylor, C. (1982). *Mereness' essentials of psychiatric nursing.* St. Louis: Mosby.

Thomas, A., & Chess, S. (1977). *Temperament and development.* New York: Brunner/Mazel.

Thomas, A., & Chess, S. (1980). *Dynamics of psychological development.* New York: Brunner/Mazel.

Thomas, A., Chess, S., & Birch, H. (1968). *Temperament and behavior disorders in children.* New York: New York University Press.

Thomas, R. M. (1979). *Comparing theories of child development.* Belmont, CA: Wadsworth.

Tietz, W., McSherry, L., & Britt, B. (1977). Family sequelae after a child dies due to cancer. *American Journal of Psychotherapy, 31,* 417–425.

Tooley, K. (1973). The choice of a surviving sibling as "scapegoat" in some cases of maternal bereavement—A case report. *Journal of Child Psychology and Psychiatry, 16,* 331–339.

Townes, B., & Wold, D. (1977). Childhood leukemia. In E. Pattison (Ed.), *The experience of dying* (pp. 138–143). Englewood Cliffs, NJ: Prentice–Hall.

United Nations. (1995). *Compendium of Human Settlements Statistics*, 5th issue. New York: Author.

Vachon, M. (1976). Stress reactions to bereavement. *Essence, 1*, 23.

Vandereycken, W., & Van Vreckem, E. (1992). Siblings as co-patients and co-therapists in eating disorders. In F. Boer & J. Dunn (Eds.), *Children's sibling relationships: Developmental and clinical issues* (pp. 109–123). Hillsdale, NJ: Erlbaum.

Van Eerdewegh, M., Clayton, P., & Van Eerdewegh, P. (1985). The bereaved child: Variables influencing early psychopathology. *British Journal of Psychiatry, 147*, 188–194.

Van Riper, M. (1997). Death of a sibling: Five sisters, five stories. *Pediatric Nursing, 23*, 587–593.

Versano, I., Zeidel, A., & Matoth, Y. (1977). Recurrent abdominal pain in children. *Pediatrician, 6*, 90–99.

Vess, J., Moreland, J., & Schwebel, A. I. (1985). Understanding family role allocation following a death: A theoretical framework. *Omega, 16*, 115–128.

Viney, L. L., & Clarke, A. M. (1974). Children coping with crisis: An analogue study. *British Journal of Social and Clinical Psychology, 13*, 305–313.

Waechter, E. H. (1964, 1987). Death, dying and bereavement: A review of the literature. In T. Krulik, B. Holaday, & I. M. Martinson (Eds.), *The child and family facing life-threatening illness* (pp. 3–31). Philadelphia: Lippincott.

Waechter, E. H. (1968). Death anxiety in children with fatal illness (Doctoral dissertation, Stanford University, 1968). University Microfilms, Ann Arbor, Michigan, No. 69-310.

Waechter, E. H. (1971). Children's awareness of fatal illness. *American Journal of Nursing, 71*, 1168–1172.

Walker, C. (1988). Stress and coping in siblings of childhood cancer patients. *Nursing Research, 37*, 206–212.

Walker, C. L. (1993). Sibling bereavement and grief responses. *Journal of Pediatric Nursing, 8*, 325–334.

Waskow, H., & Waskow, A. (1993). *Becoming brothers*. New York: The Free Press.

Wass, H., & Corr, C. A. (Eds.). (1984). *Helping children cope with death: Guidelines and resources* (2nd ed.). Washington, DC: Hemisphere Publishing Corporation.

Watanabe-Hammond, S. (1988). Blueprints from the past: A character work perspective on siblings and personality formation. In M. D. Kahn & K. G. Lewis (Eds.), *Siblings in therapy: Life span and clinical issues* (pp. 356–378). New York: W. W. Norton & Co.

Webb, N. B. (1993). Assessment of the bereaved child. In N. B. Webb (Ed.), *Helping bereaved children: A handbook for practitioners* (pp. 19–42). New York: The Guilford Press.

Weisman, A. D., & Worden, J. W. (1976). The existential plight in cancer: Significance of the first 100 days. *International Journal of Psychiatric Medicine, 7*, 1–15.

Weisner, T. S. (1982). Sibling interdependence and child caretaking: A cross-cultural view. In M. E. Lamb & B. Sutton-Smith (Eds.), *Sibling relationships: Their nature and significance across the lifespan* (pp. 305–328). Hillsdale, NJ: Erlbaum.

Weisner, T. S. (1989). Comparing sibling relationships across cultures. In P. G. Zukow (Ed.), *Sibling interaction across cultures* (pp. 11–25). New York: Springer-Verlag.

Weitzman, L. J. (1982). Sex-role specialization. In J. Muff (Ed.), *Socialization, sexism and stereotyping* (pp. 21–47). Toronto: Mosby.

Weston, D. L., & Irwin, R. C. (1963). Preschool child's response to death of infant sibling. *American Journal of Diseases of Children, 106*, 564–567.

Whiting, B. B., & Whiting, J. W. M. (1975). *Children of six cultures: A psychocultural analysis*. Cambridge: Harvard University Press.

Wideman, J. E. (1984). *Brothers and keepers*. New York: Penguin Books.

Wieczorek, R., & Natadoff, J. (1981). *A conceptual approach to the nursing of children*. Philadelphia: Lippincott.

Wiener, J. M. (1970). Reaction of the family to the fatal illness of a child. In B. Schoenberg, A. C. Carr, D. Peretz, & A. H. Kutscher (Eds.), *Loss and grief: Psychological management in medical practice* (pp. 87–101). New York: Columbia University Press.

Williams, M. L. (1981). Sibling reaction to cot death. *The Medical Journal of Australia, 2,* 227–231.

Wishart, J. G. (1986). Siblings as models in early infant learning. *Child Development, 57,* 1232–1240.

Wolfelt, A. (1983). *Helping children cope with grief.* Muncie, IN: Accelerated Development.

Wolfelt, A. D. (1996). *Healing the bereaved child.* Ft. Collins, CO: Companion.

Zelauskas, B. (1981). Siblings: The forgotten grievers. *Issues in Comprehensive Pediatric Nursing, 5,* 45–52.

Zukow, P. G. (Ed.). (1989). *Sibling interaction across cultures: Theoretical and methodological issues.* New York: Springer-Verlag.

INDEX